SECOND
EDITION

The
# MATH
We Need to
# KNOW
# DO
and DO in
Grades **PreK–5**

SECOND EDITION

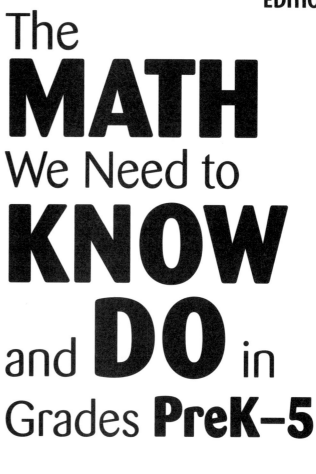

# The MATH We Need to KNOW and DO in Grades PreK–5

## CONCEPTS, SKILLS, STANDARDS, AND ASSESSMENTS

### PEARL GOLD SOLOMON

**CORWIN PRESS**
A SAGE Publications Company
Thousand Oaks, California

*For information:*

Corwin Press, Inc.
2455 Teller Road
Thousand Oaks, California 91320
www.corwinpress.com

Sage Publications Ltd.
1 Oliver's Yard
55 City Road
London EC1Y 1SP
United Kingdom

Sage Publications India Pvt. Ltd.
B-42, Panchsheel Enclave
Post Box 4109
New Delhi 110 017  India

Printed in the United States of America.

**Library of Congress Cataloging-in-Publication Data**

Solomon, Pearl G. (Pearl Gold), 1929-
The math we need to know and do in grades preK-5 : concepts, skills, standards, and assessments / Pearl G. Solomon.— 2nd ed.
   p. cm.
Rev. ed. of: The math we need to "know" and "do." c2001.
Includes bibliographical references and index.
ISBN 1-4129-1719-0 (cloth : acid-free paper) — ISBN 1-4129-1720-4 (pbk. : acid-free paper)
   1. Mathematics—Study and teaching (Elementary)—United States. 2. Mathematics—Study and teaching (Middle school)—United States. I. Solomon, Pearl G. (Pearl Gold), 1929- Math we need to "know" and "do." II. Title.
QA135.6.S6255 2006
372.7—dc22
                                2005037828

This book is printed on acid-free paper.

06  07  08  09  10  10  9  8  7  6  5  4  3  2  1

| | |
|---|---|
| *Acquiring Editor:* | Faye Zucker |
| *Editorial Assistant:* | Gem Rabanera |
| *Project Editor:* | Astrid Virding |
| *Copyeditor:* | Kristin Bergstad |
| *Typesetter:* | C&M Digitals (P) Ltd. |
| *Cover Designer:* | Rose Storey |
| *Graphic Designer:* | Scott Van Atta |

# Contents

Guide to Figures in Chapter 3     vii

Preface     xiii

Acknowledgments     xix

About the Author     xxi

1. **Designing a Standards-Based Math Curriculum**     1

   Knowledge     1
   Organization and Design of Curricula     2
   The Mathematics Content Standards: Key Ideas     4
   Mathematics Content Standards: Processes and Dispositions     5
   Mathematics Content Standards: The Knowledge Content Set     5
   How Teachers Can Use the Following Chapters     11

2. **The Designed-Down Content Branches: Embedded Concepts and Performance Indicators**     15

   A Guide to Chapter 2     15

3. **Scaffolds for Teachers and Problems for Students**     61

   A Guide to Chapter 3     61

**Resource A: Assessing the Content Standards**     195

   Using Rubrics     195
   Informal and Formal Written Assessments     196
   Assessment Analysis     197

**References**     199

**Additional Reading**     203

**Index**     205

# Guide to Figures
# in Chapter 3

| Topic | Page | Figure |
|---|---|---|
| Number System | | |
| counting | 63 | 1, 2 |
| conservation of number | 64 | 3 |
| sorting/seriation | 65, 67 | 4, 5, 7 |
| comparing groups | 66 | 6 |
| teen numbers | 67 | 8 |
| subitizing | 68 | 9 |
| count by ten | 68 | 10 |
| Beginning Multiplication | | |
| skip counting | 69 | 11 |
| grouping | 70 | 12 |
| doubling | 70 | 13 |
| Ordinal Numbers | 71 | 14 |
| Place Value | | |
| additive | 72 | 15 |
| trading/regrouping | 72, 73, 74 | 16, 17, 18 |
| multiplying by ten | 75, 76 | 19, 20 |
| dividing by ten | 76, 77 | 21, 22 |
| Rounding | 78, 79 | 23, 24 |
| Addition | | |
| counting on | 80 | 25 |
| counting back | 80 | 25 |
| commutativity | 81 | 26 |

| Topic | Page | Figure |
|---|---|---|
| combinations of ten | 82, 83 | 27, 28 |
| part-part, whole | 84 | 29, 30 |
| more than two parts | 85 | 31 |
| trading/regrouping/algorithm | 86, 87 | 32, 33, 34 |
| number sequences | 88 | 35 |
| Subtraction | | |
| as finding the difference | 89 | 36, 37 |
| two places | 90 | 38 |
| missing addend | 91 | 39 |
| negative values/number line | 92 | 40 |
| problem solving | 93 | 41 |
| trading/regrouping/algorithm | 93, 94 | 41, 42 |
| Multiplication | | |
| repeated addition | 95 | 43 |
| doubling | 96 | 44 |
| patterns | 97 | 45 |
| commutation | 98 | 46 |
| fact tables | 97, 99, 100 | 45, 47, 48 |
| commutation table | 99 | 47 |
| multi-digit/algorithm | 100, 102, 103 | 48, 49, 50 |
| Cartesian/combinations | 104 | 51 |
| Division | | |
| quotition/measurement | 106 | 52 |
| partition | 108 | 53 |
| related to fractions/partition | 108 | 53 |
| algorithm | 109 | 54 |
| multi-digit estimation | 110 | 55 |
| division by zero | 110 | 56 |
| Fractions | | |
| part and size of whole | 111, 112 | 57, 58 |
| as parts of sets | 113, 115 | 59, 60, 61 |

| Topic | Page | Figure |
|---|---|---|
| as part of one whole and set | 115 | 62 |
| as comparative size | 116 | 63 |
| more than one whole | 117 | 64 |
| equivalents | 117, 118, 119 | 65, 66, 67 |
| patterns/algorithm | 120 | 68 |
| as ratios | 121 | 69 |
| comparing ratios | 123 | 70 |
| scale | 123 | 71 |
| complex problem | 124 | 72 |
| addition of | 124 | 76 |
| subtraction of | 131 | 77 |
| multiplication of/fractions of | 133, 135, 137 | 78, 79, 80 |
| Multiplicative Relationships | | |
| common multiples | 125 | 73 |
| factors | 126 | 74, 75 |
| Decimals | | |
| money equivalents | 138 | 81 |
| place value | 138, 139 | 82, 83 |
| parts of whole size | 141 | 84 |
| percentage/fractions/estimation | 143 | 85 |
| percentage change | 144 | 86 |
| Measurement | | |
| units of measure | 149 | 87 |
| length | 151 | 88 |
| area | 152, 153 | 89, 90 |
| weight | 154 | 91 |
| capacity | 155 | 92 |
| area/volume | 154 | 93, 94 |
| money equivalents | 159, 160 | 95, 96, 97, 98 |
| money in decimal form | 160 | 98 |
| giving change | 161 | 99 |

| Topic | Page | Figure |
|---|---|---|
| time | 163 | 100 |
| time zones | 163 | 101 |
| elapsed time | 164 | 102 |
| calendar | 165 | 103, 104 |
| temperature | 167 | 105 |
| Geometry | | |
| shapes | 167 | 106 |
| articulating shapes | 168 | 107 |
| comparing perimeter and area | 169 | 108 |
| surface/solid figure | 170 | 109 |
| hidden forms | 171 | 110 |
| symmetry | 171 | 111 |
| congruent triangles, transformations | 172, 173 | 112, 113 |
| square/triangular numbers | 173 | 114 |
| horizontal/vertical lines | 174 | 115 |
| lines, rays, segments | 175 | 116 |
| planes | 176 | 117 |
| comparing shapes | 176 | 118 |
| angles | 177 | 119 |
| circles | 178, 179 | 120, 121 |
| cylinders/surface area | 180 | 122 |
| Multiple Representation/Data Collection | | |
| data tables | 181, 182 | 123, 124 |
| data graph (pictograph) | 183 | 126 |
| bar graph | 184 | 125, 127 |
| pie graph | 185 | 128 |
| table/graph | 185 | 129 |
| maps and grids | 186 | 130, 131 |
| line plot | 187 | 132 |
| stem-and-leaf plot | 189 | 133 |
| scatter plot | 188 | 134 |

| Topic | Page | Figure |
|---|---|---|
| Probability/Possibility | | |
| probability | 190 | 135 |
| combinations/tree diagrams | 191, 193 | 136, 137 |
| Distributions | | |
| mean, mode | 194 | 138 |

# Preface

## WHAT THIS BOOK IS ABOUT ■

Since the publication of the first edition of this text, accountability for the achievement of high standards by educational systems was federally legislated in the form of required state-produced high-stakes assessments and improvement mandates by the No Child Left Behind (NCLB) legislation (U.S. Department of Education, 2001; Linn, Baker, & Betebenner, 2002). The legislation was initially responsive to heightened public attention and criticism of the problems of our educational systems. Not the least of that criticism was directed at the performance of our students in mathematics, especially when it was compared to that of students from other countries on international tests such as the Trends in International Mathematics and Science Study (TIMSS; National Center for Education Statistics, 2005). The NCLB legislation called for mandated assessments in literacy and mathematics from Grades 3–8 and identified specific sanctions for schools failing to show improvement in terms of adequate yearly progress. Although the tests are developed on a state level, the sanctions are powered by the withholding of federal funds.

A mixture of criticism and support continues to confront the assessments and their connected mandates. Most of the negative response is related to the sanctions imposed on poorly performing schools and the resulting stress on teachers and students. A recent report by the National Conference of State Legislatures (Dillon, 2005) says the law sets unrealistic expectations and defies commonsense notions of how to rate schools. State lawmakers also cite the conflict of NCLB with other legislation that protects the disabled. There has actually been some backtracking on previously instituted state-generated actions and a push for more state control over NCLB criteria and sanctions. Unfortunately, despite evidence that the assessments have begun to improve student performance in some places, unresolved deficiencies or gaps in the overall achievement of specifically identified groups of students continue the calls for improvement (University of the State of New York, 2005).

Despite the varying opinions on the value of high-stakes assessments in the context of the stress and limitations they place on teachers and students and their possible misuse, it is my firm belief that assessment has a vital role in the educative process. It is most productive, however, when used as a tool through which the teacher manages instruction. When intensive professional development has accompanied careful curriculum construction and attention is paid to teacher ownership, assessments matched to that curriculum have contributed to improved student performance. I will address this issue further in Chapter 1 (for in-depth analyses, see Solomon, 1995, 2002, 2003).

Although there are still a number of possible, unproven reasons for the less-than-desired overall performance of U.S. students and the persistent gaps for certain groups of students, the first possibility that our educational community responded to was that our curriculum may have been an affecting factor. Comparisons of math curriculum in our country to that in countries more successful on the international assessments revealed that ours covered too many topics repetitively and lacked intensity and focus. The initial response to this possible reason for failure, therefore, was to develop standards that outlined the necessary curriculum. Standards, initially published by the National Council of Teachers of Mathematics (NCTM, 1989, 2000), were then individually adapted by states to create state standards documents.

The state standards documents have helped to remedy some of the deficiencies in the curriculum, but some early versions of the state standards have been recently criticized for lack of clarity and specificity (Klein et al., 2005). This book may provide some of what is missing. The first edition of *The Math We Need to Know and Do* was actually cited by the New York State Education Department as a key resource for its newly issued and much more explicit standards document.

My own observations of teachers in various states and socially different schools reveal that despite published curriculum documents, most of what is taught in schools today is still governed by published texts and workbooks. There is much that is worthwhile in today's textbooks for young learners; they provide drill and practice for operations and some good and varied application activities. New-generation technology like graphing calculators and computer software that allows for exploration and spatial problem solving, as well as access to data sets on the Internet, is even more hopeful if used properly. The deficiency in the technology and some texts lies in the fact that they do not clearly delineate for the teachers or the students what exactly one needs to know to be an effective quantitative problem solver. Nor do they help teachers understand and build upon what research has taught us about how learning happens. Frequently, our students learn how to do the procedures in the books without constructing mathematical concepts that may be generalized to novel or real-life problems. Curriculum documents published by State Education Departments try to define the skills and expectations but usually neglect to clarify the underlying or embedded mathematical concepts—and frequently are too general to override the day-to-day teacher-friendly comforts of text programs.

Pedagogical texts for teachers do this, but often they, too, neglect the concepts. Strangely, very old mathematics textbooks stated very clearly and simply what the necessary concepts were. *New Practical Arithmetic*, which was written by Benjamin Greenleaf (1872), brings the learner from the very elementary notations of single digit numbers all the way to cube roots and the applications of stocks, bonds, taxes, principal, and interest within 322 small (4″ by 6″) pages.

On these pocketbook-sized pages are 465 paragraph sections that include precise definitions and succinct statements of the concepts as well as limited exercises. What Greenleaf did establish, for his time, was a clear mathematical knowledge base.

Although the world has gained much new knowledge since 1872, and topics like probability, statistics, and mathematical modeling have to be added to help prepare our students for the technology-based modern world, the basic known content or knowledge base of elementary mathematics is not that different. The modern world, however, may not offer children the same kind of learning experiences. Hands-on real-life experiences are replaced by computer games, and automatized facts, drill, and practice by calculator computations. Nevertheless, our pedagogical knowledge base, especially our knowledge about how children learn, is much expanded. We use many new and better approaches to learning and teaching. Preoccupation with this new pedagogical knowledge has perhaps distracted us from the mathematics knowledge itself. For example, knowing that estimation skills and the ability to factor algebraic expressions with understanding and facility depend upon quick mental retrieval of multiplication facts can lead us to value the automatization of facts. Knowing that automatization may be easier at earlier developmental stages might encourage us to allocate that expectation to an early grade.

This book accepts the current climate of accountability by assessment and focuses on both the identification of the specific embedded concepts—*what we need to know*—and the matching skill expectations—*what we need to be able to do*—in order to apply and demonstrate what we know. Using current national and state standards as a guide, it covers these elements of mathematics content for Grades K–5, relates it to the current expanded pedagogical knowledge, and offers suggestions for instructional approaches and sequencing.

It is designed as a resource for teachers to use as they

- Plan curriculum for a school, particular grade level, or specific lesson
- Assess their students' knowledge, both formally and informally
- Respond to individual conceptual or procedural problems among their students
- Review their own mathematical concepts

Like Greenleaf, I have tried to be parsimonious with words. For in-depth discussions of the background research, readers can refer to the literature cited in the References. This is also not a mathematics textbook, although it will provide some illustrative activities for students. Instead, it will compensate for the missing components of recent texts and curriculum guides—statements of the very specific concepts and procedures embedded in mathematical knowledge. These are phrased succinctly and precisely in Chapter 2 as the *embedded concepts (What students need to know)* and articulated *skill or performance indicators (What students need to be able to do)*. These tell us more precisely exactly what students need in order to solve the problems in their texts, the real world, and the state assessments. They tell us some of what students need to know in order to have life-long comfort and ease with new mathematical problems and to compete with others in a technological future. They will help teachers analyze whether their students have achieved the specifics of that knowledge and guide them in the correction of unsound or incomplete constructions of knowledge.

This book is a resource meant to be used by teachers in conjunction with other materials: texts, workbooks, manipulatives, and technology. It can also serve as an adjunct textbook for teachers-in-training—one that focuses more intensely on the content as it applies rather than generalizes the pedagogy. In order to accomplish our purpose of clarity in the presentation of the concepts, the embedded concepts and their matching skills and performance indicators are presented in numbered-table form in Chapter 2. Chapter 3 then provides correspondingly numbered suggestions for the matching instructional dialogue, manipulatives, and sample problems that can be used by the teacher to help develop the concept or skill. The problems are designed to develop the embedded concepts, but are also forms of *"proximal"* assessment. Proximal assessment is the informal form of assessment that teachers, who are close to those they assess, need to do in the classroom as they teach. With minor additions, however, the problems can be adapted for more formal forms of assessment.

There are clear purposes for this separation. Chapter 2 can be used to plan school curriculum from a multi-grade or single-grade perspective. Teachers can use it as a daily assessment check and lesson planning guide, and as an easy reference for a look back at the grounding concepts from previous grades. If further clarification is needed, or the teacher needs suggestions for how to scaffold the concept with dialogue and problems to solve, there is a simple cross-check to the more comprehensive Chapter 3. However, no single activity or set of activities is guaranteed to assure the new knowledge for all students. Just doing a prescribed activity is not enough: The embedded concept has to be constructed by the student and assessed by the teacher.

Although there are suggestions offered for the vocabulary and substance of the teacher-directed dialogues and peer interactive discourses that can help students construct new knowledge, this is far from a script. It is different from many curriculum guides produced by teachers in that it shows the sequential and specific development of concepts over the grades, rather than at a specific grade. The reason for this is so that teachers may check for prior knowledge and know where a particular concept can lead. It is hoped that this will make their curriculum more responsive to the individual differences among their students.

The concepts or content standards included are a composite from many sources. Many were identified over time by careful personal and shared collegial observation of students' thinking: from pre-kindergarten through graduate classes in math teaching methods. They reflect mathematics educators' most current research on how children learn mathematics as reported in the literature, but also pull from resources as disparate and remote as Piaget, Greenleaf, and a comprehensive curriculum guide published by the Baltimore schools in 1952 (Baltimore Public Schools, 1952). They are functionally based on the ideas and organization of the year 2000 versions of the standards for mathematics developed by the National Council of Teachers of Mathematics (2000) and other state and local agencies. These may be more comprehensive in terms of the pedagogy rationale and should be consulted in tandem with this book. Most of these documents are, however, less specific and organized about the content knowledge, particularly the embedded concepts and definitions. This leaves much for the teacher to provide. For example, the standards statements are often framed in terms of understanding, such as: "Students will understand the relationship between multiplication and division." Chapter 2 and certainly Chapter 3 are more explicit about what it is that the students need to understand. Concept statements and scaffolds for building understanding would include ideas such as,

> In multiplication we know the size of each group and the number of the groups we add repeatedly, but not the size of the whole. We multiply to find the whole. In division we know the whole and either the number of groups or the size of the group, but not both. We divide to find the size of each group or the number of groups.

This book will fill some of the gaps, but certainly not every possible construction of knowledge. Others may be identified or newly constructed by teachers as they begin to teach in a different way—with a clearly identified concept or construct in mind. If they provide opportunities for their students to reason and solve problems creatively, new concepts for both teacher and student may be intersubjectively (Lerman, 1996) constructed.

The book is presented in three chapters, which should be considered in sequence. Chapter 1 provides a rationale for the suggested learning approach and explains the organization and sequence of the following chapters. Chapter 2 provides the actual content standards in numbered table form, showing median grade-level expectations for concepts and skills or performance indicators and suggestions for mathematics language vocabulary and usage. The content standards are organized to agree with the organization of the NCTM standards with some exceptions that are explained in Chapter 1. Chapter 3 provides articulated illustrative activities and problems that can be used with students, either for concept development or assessment purposes. It also contains suggestions for using tools other than text materials: manipulatives, calculators, educational software and graphics programs (commercial and shareware), and Web sites.

# Acknowledgments

For their inspiration and contributions to the additions and revisions of this second edition of *The Math We Need to Know and Do,* I would like to offer my gratitude to the teachers and administrators of the East Ramapo Central School District in Spring Valley, New York. I have worked with the dedicated faculty of this district as a consultant for the past ten years. Although the intent of our relationship was for them to learn from me, they need to know that I learned so much from them. It was this new knowledge that motivated me to update and revise what I had previously written. I would particularly like to mention David Fried, Assistant Superintendent, and Rhoda Fischer, Director of Curriculum, for their faith in me and their concern for the children of the district they serve. However, there is also a whole team of classroom teachers with whom I shared the task of writing curriculum and assessments for the K-12 program in mathematics. I do not think I would have continued my interest and endeavors in math education without their inspiration and knowledge.

The structure of this manuscript is very complex, but copy editor, Kristin Bergstad and senior project editor, Astrid Virding were always patiently and expertly at my side as we strove for the best possible outcome. I am most grateful for their efforts and expertise. As I have in the past, I would also like to thank my colleagues at St. Thomas Aquinas College, and my husband, Mel, and grandchildren Joseph and Edward for their patience and support. Edward was particularly helpful as I bounced possible activities and scaffolds off his middle school student eyes, ears, and prior knowledge.

Corwin Press thanks the following reviewers for their contributions to this book:

Carol Amos, Elementary School Teacher, Twinfield Union School, Plainfield, VT

Joseph DiGarbo, Elementary School Teacher, Mohegan Elementary School, Uncasville, CT

Melissa Miller, Middle School Teacher, Randall G. Lynch Middle School, Farmington, AR

# About the Author

 **Pearl Gold Solomon** is Professor Emeritus of Teacher Education at St. Thomas Aquinas College in Sparkill, New York. She received a doctorate in educational administration from Teachers College, Columbia University. She has served as a public school teacher and administrator, director, and officer for professional organizations and as a consultant to many school districts, the New York State Education Department, and the U.S. Department of Education. She is the recipient of a number of special awards from the state and community for her work in science, math, health, and career education.

As director of the St. Thomas Aquinas Marie Curie Mathematics Science Center, her activities included authorship and management of Eisenhower, National Science Foundation, and Goals 2000 grants. As a private consultant, she has acted as a mathematics and science curriculum and assessment specialist and presenter for a number of school districts, including the cities of New York and Chicago. Present endeavors include contracts as consultant and evaluator of math and science funded programs for Columbia University and New York University, and an SBIR for the National Institutes of Health (NIH). She has also continued graduate-level teaching assignments on a part-time basis for both preservice and inservice teachers.

Dr. Solomon is a frequent speaker at professional conferences and the author of several books published by Corwin Press, including *No Small Feat: Taking Time for Change* (1995); *The Curriculum Bridge: From Standards to Actual Classroom Practice* (1998; 2nd ed., 2003), which was selected as an outstanding academic book for 1999 by the American Library Association's Choice Magazine; *The Math We Need to "Know" and "Do": Content Standards for Elementary and Middle Grades* (2001), which was selected as a finalist for Outstanding Writing Award from the American Association of Colleges of Teacher Education; and *The Assessment Bridge: Positive Ways to Link Tests to Learning, Standards, and Curriculum Improvement* (2002).

# 1

# Designing a Standards-Based Math Curriculum

## KNOWLEDGE ■

Education is preparation for life. Derived from the Latin, it also means *to lead forth*—perhaps to knowledge. But what is the knowledge to which we educators must lead our students? Knowledge is defined as an acquaintance with a fact, a perception, or an idea. A suggested classification of knowledge divides it into procedural and conceptual components. The two categories are distinguishable and yet intersecting. They are not hierarchical; one does not necessarily come before the other. They differ in that procedural knowledge is more rigid and limited in its adaptability, but highly efficient, especially when it is applied with meaning. Conceptual knowledge is more flexible—it reorganizes and stretches itself as it tries to connect new perceptions and previous generalizations. Conceptual knowledge may then reform itself as a new generalization. Reasoning requires conceptual knowledge (for an in-depth discussion of conceptual and procedural knowledge, see Hiebert & Wearne, 1986).

A chef following an often-used recipe is efficiently carrying out his procedural knowledge. He knows that it must be done in a certain order and with specific ingredients and quantities. Suppose one of his ingredients is unavailable. He has a problem. When he tries to innovate with a substitute ingredient, he calls upon his conceptual knowledge, reorganizes it; connects it to other concepts and perhaps to a new generalization; and then with practice connects it to a new procedure. The best procedures are those built with conceptual knowledge, those learned with meaning. Conceptual knowledge may, however, also come from procedural knowledge. An infant puts blocks one on top of the other, perhaps in a self-initiated procedure or perhaps copying an adult. Eventually a concept is formed: The larger blocks need to be at the bottom. *The conceptual and procedural knowledge components that we expect our students to have, and that therefore we must lead them to, form our content standards.* Our expectations are based on our own knowledge, our experience, and our predictions about what our students will need. Content standards describe what we value and what we want our students to know or be able to do.

The reason for the discussion above is that in the past mathematics has often been taught as a set of specific procedures, sometimes disconnected from the real problems that will confront us in life, and frequently without clarification of the mathematical concepts that are embedded within the procedures. Doing mathematics requires a set of clarified concepts and procedures that develop over time. Experiences with objects and verbalization—both monologic and interactive—help that development. The concepts enlarge our capability to solve problems; the procedures make us more efficient. An understanding of this dual nature of knowledge also provides a rationale for the organization of standards-based curriculum.

## ■ ORGANIZATION AND DESIGN OF CURRICULA

Although concepts and procedures develop individually for each student over time, it is useful for the teacher to know what the necessary ones are—the ones that can help the student do mathematics and solve mathematical problems. The common procedures we use and some of the concepts we share are in what has been called *"the consensual domain"* (Cobb, 1990). This shared knowledge is the content of our curriculum. The framework for this curriculum content includes normed expectations for achievement or **content standards.** The multiplication facts are shared knowledge in the consensual domain. That we expect third and fourth graders to know their multiplication facts is a normed expectation or standard based on history, teachers' experience, and the average achievements of children in these grades. In the present societal context, the standards are also formally set and monitored by state and federal guidelines and legislation.

**Content standards** organize and describe the curriculum. They serve as guides for instruction that are planned to help students achieve the knowledge of the consensual domain. They tell us what students should know or be able to do. Many state-developed documents label their content standards as **performance indicators** that emphasize what students should be able to do. Performance indicators that focus primarily on procedural knowledge are then used as a basis for matching measurement guidelines or **test expectations,** which are translated into the mandated high-stakes assessments that are used to hold schools accountable for the performance of their students (Solomon, 2002, 2003). **Embedded concept** knowledge, which describes what students should know, is assumed necessary for the measured performance of procedural knowledge, but the concepts are rarely stated explicitly. Clearly stated mathematical concepts within curriculum documents may prove to be helpful in achieving consensus and guiding instruction. Moreover, it is important not to neglect separate measures of the embedded concepts. Test items that ask for explanations specifically seek concept knowledge and can be used as a diagnostic that determines why a procedure is not understood.

**Design
Direction**

**Delivery
Direction**

**Figure 1.1**
Curriculum Planning

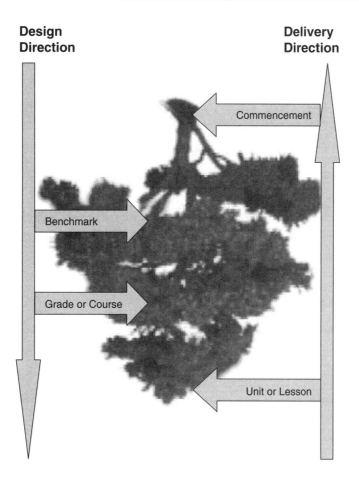

When constructed, classroom activities and assessments should be reflections of the concepts and procedures of the standards. An analogy that might help is to compare them to the two sides of your hand. The back of your hand, like the standard, defines its form and its potential, but the palm is the implement and measure of what your hand does. Content standards define the framework for the actions of instruction and the assessments we need to help guide us and our students while providing accountability to our publics.

Standards can be very general statements of expectations at a terminal or commencement point or more specific and assigned to a particular stage in development or grade level. The upside-down tree in Figure 1.1 illustrates a design process for standards-based curricula (Solomon, 2003). Like the trunk of a tree, general standards lead to a widely reaching set of more specific branches, twigs, and leaves. Curriculum is *designed down* from more general *commencement* levels to the more specific *benchmarks* and then to the even more specific levels of the course, grade, and unit. But it must work both ways. Just as the leaves of a tree must manufacture food and nurture the trunk, the more specific "designed-down" content standards of every lesson must feed the general ones—they make the general ones happen. Curriculum is *delivered up*—up toward the general or commencement standards. None of this works if the connections of internal flow are impeded. The junctures where twigs meet branches and branches meet trunks are particularly important. The outcome of each lesson of the leaves is fed through a twig to the branch that is the unit and then into a larger one that is the grade level. Several grade levels may feed into a larger branch at a benchmark juncture and this, in turn, finally meets the main trunk. The tree is shown upside down because the design is the beginning and we think of the processes as "design down" and "deliver up." At the same time, there must be horizontal articulation. As the leaves turn toward the sun, the carbon dioxide must enter them. There must be a balance between the concepts and the procedures.

The preplanned design is only the first step. The settings and activities of well-planned classroom activities must have a reasonable probability of helping *all* students to be successful in these measures. They should encompass a wider scope of the variables of the classroom experience: the teachers' knowledge and carefully reviewed previous experience, the discourse, the materials, the allocation of time and space, the cultural and social contexts of peers and adults.

## ■ THE MATHEMATICS CONTENT STANDARDS: KEY IDEAS[1]

What kind of mathematical knowledge do we expect of all students when they enter the technological world of the third millennium? What are the steps for getting them there? Consider the upside-down tree for mathematics curricula. Beginning at the trunk, at the commencement level, we should expect that *all* students can do the processes of mathematics, such as reasoning, communicating, and problem solving. Nevertheless, the processes of mathematics are not performed in a vacuum. They depend upon and produce a content set of conceptual and procedural knowledge about mathematics. However, before we address the specifics of the processes and content knowledge standards, there are some key ideas that should be considered.

- In its traditional sense, mathematical **reasoning** includes both quantitative and spatial concepts, but it also has embedded *verbal constructs and a special language.* In addition, effective reasoning may also involve *metacognitive processes.* Thinking about what you are doing and purposely comparing problems and solutions may increase the power of reasoning (Kramarski & Mevarech, 2003).

- The special language of mathematical **communication** involves a system of **numbers and other symbols**. The symbols represent values and orders or something that changes the value. Not only do we need to use this language to communicate with others, the symbols may be necessary for our own internal concept formation. There is also a special language for sharing proof.

- A logical search for truth or **proof** requires reasoning and is a special power of mathematics (Herbst, 2002). Proof to oneself also strengthens the constructions of knowledge.

- As we observe, reason, connect, and communicate, we can develop and use an intuitive **number and spatial sense** that allows us to estimate values, judge relative size, visualize hidden parts of forms, decide on appropriate strategies for problem solving, predict the result of operations and transformations, and evaluate the reasonableness of our problem solutions.

## MATHEMATICS CONTENT STANDARDS: ■ PROCESSES AND DISPOSITIONS

Our expectations of students' ability to do the processes of mathematics reflect the way research has shown us that all learning happens; like all learning, doing mathematics involves connecting prior knowledge and new perceptions. Doing mathematics requires and builds both conceptual and procedural knowledge. Doing the processes of mathematics means that students can do the following:

- *Perceive* and make observations of the world from a mathematical perspective, sensitive to similarities, differences, patterns and change in size, value, time, and form.

- *Connect* these observations to each other and to other concurrent observations and prior knowledge (e.g., the form of a sphere and a rolling ball).

- *Represent* forms and number systems in multiple ways and models to help them visualize, communicate ideas, organize data, and construct concepts.

- *Communicate* what they perceive to others using multiple forms of representation and the special language of mathematics.

- *Analyze and solve problems* using mathematical *reasoning,* which is based on conceptual knowledge, and do this efficiently with meaningful procedures.

- *Justify* and *defend* their solutions with logical *proofs.*

Conceptual knowledge can also be knowledge about oneself; it can be an attitude, a value, or a goal (Anderson & Douglass, 2001). Attitudes, values, and goals control the learning process. Doing mathematics also requires that students:

- Have *confidence* in their ability to do mathematics.

- *Appreciate* the beauty and power of mathematics.

## MATHEMATICS CONTENT STANDARDS: ■ THE KNOWLEDGE CONTENT SET

For the purpose of description, we can organize the knowledge content set into six major branches. It is important to realize, however, that these branches are overlapping—both in their interdependence and in their function as we enact mathematical processes. For example, our operations are dependent on our number system, and our number system determines the form of our operations. We need knowledge of our number system, measurement, and data representation as we communicate to others what we have perceived. The content standards described in Chapter 2 include designed-down concepts and procedures from the following major commencement level branches:

- **Number system:** The language of our common *number system* (which is based on our genetically and experientially determined sense of space and quantity and the number of finger or toe digits) allows us to perceive and communicate quantities in words and symbols. By making the left-to-right position of the symbols have different values we are able to express all quantities with only ten symbols including the placeholder zero. There are other number systems.

- **Operations on numbers:** We can perform *operations on numbers.* Operations are systems that help us solve problems that involve change or comparisons. They allow us to determine values not directly counted or measured. Reasoning with our conceptual knowledge and using our number sense can help us predict the result of operations. The language of real-world problems needs to be translated into the language of mathematics so that we can solve the problems efficiently by performing operations.

- **Geometric forms and properties:** Defined two-dimensional surface areas and three-dimensional objects that take up space have different *geometric forms and properties.* Knowledge of the dimensions and properties of these forms, and the relationships among them, helps us solve problems and make use of the systematic relationship between the types of forms and their practical functions (e.g., the rolling sphere, the Roman arch, the sturdy triangle).

- **Measurement and data collection:** We use our number system to *measure* the dimensions and characteristics of objects and areas as they exist, or change in time and space. We also measure time itself and other values and phenomena such as money, light, wind, energy, votes, and the popularity of TV shows. Collections of *measurements* are called *data.*

- **Algebra: Patterns, expressions, relationships, and functions:** Within the systems of numbers, forms, and data there are recognizable *patterns* and *relationships*. Patterns help us reason, organize, and *automatize* concepts (see ahead) into more efficient procedures. We use *symbols* to express the patterns and relationships. The symbols can represent either variable or constant values. When patterns express specific relationships between constant and variable values, they are called *mathematical functions* (each input has a specific output or rule that guides it). Conceptual and procedural knowledge of functions is very useful in complex problems solving and prediction.

- **Data analysis, statistics, and probability:** Data can be collected and analyzed to show patterns and trends that can help us make predictions. Statistics are systems used to organize data and analyze it in many different ways. Some events are clearly predictable, but others are *uncertain. Probability* systems help us deal with uncertainty by giving us a way to have reasonable expectations about the possibility of the occurrence of an event.

Figure 1.2 represents an organization of the intersecting sets of process and content branches of mathematics as well as the dispositions or attitudes that affect all of them. They are placed between the inclusive and articulated

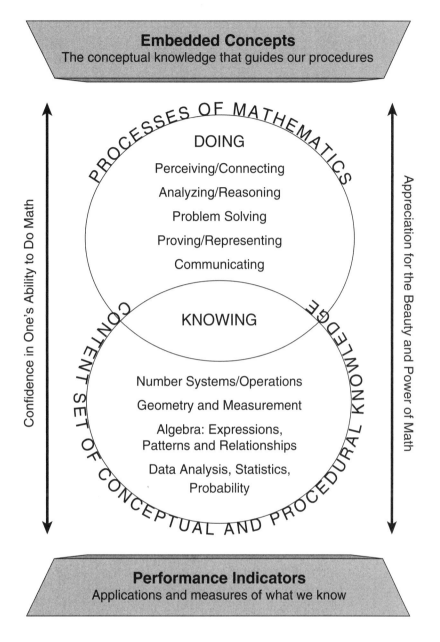

**Figure 1.2**
The Content Standards:
What Students Should Know
and Be Able to Do

anchors of Embedded Concepts and Performance Indicators. Our distinction between these two anchors is that the embedded concepts focus clearly on the underlying ideas of mathematics that we wish our students to know, while the performance indicators focus on the demonstrations, applications, and measures of that knowledge.

The presentation of the very specific designed-down content standards in Chapters 2 and 3 incorporates several critical premises about what students need, how learning happens, and how teachers use curriculum. The content and organization of these chapters responds to these premises in the specific manner described below.

*Premise 1: Inclusivity.* Although Chapters 2 and 3 represent most of the general topics typically included in math standards for Grades K–5, they do not pretend to be all-inclusive, neither of the general topics nor of the embedded concepts and procedures within them. They may, however, be a substantive starting place for designing and implementing curriculum and assessments. Teachers and their students may discover needed additions and make some corrections. The important thing is to recognize the ideas for oneself, communicate them to others, and then reach a useful consensus about what is critical for us all to learn.

*Premise 2: Timing.* For some concepts and for some students learning happens all at once. For many others it is an iterative process that takes place over time as students develop meaning in a very individualized way. Sometimes this meaning is "buggy" or incorrect and is corrected by new perceptions. The grade-level expectations in Chapter 2 are therefore presented in three phases: exploration, concept mastery, and procedural or algorithmic mastery. In some cases, this sequence may all happen in one grade—even in one lesson; in others the span may be longer than three grades. The expectations listed are suggested medians based on observations of students and references to varied texts and assessments. Teachers should adjust these on a local basis. The idea behind the three phases is that as students engage in the mathematical processes they begin with explorations: perceiving, observing, trying to find solutions. At first, they may find solutions without crystallizing a concept that is permanently implanted as a schema in memory. They may need help from teachers and/or peers in the form of interactive dialogue to do this.

*Premise 3: Algorithms.* Once the concept is formed, further experience may *automatize* its retrieval from memory, and learners can incorporate it into strategies or procedures that can be efficiently employed. The common algorithms are an example of procedural strategies. The algorithms were invented over time as efficient procedures for solving common mathematics problems. Students should be able to use the algorithms in the consensual domain but be encouraged to invent and prove their own strategies as well. A good rule of thumb for the use of traditional algorithms by students is to evaluate the potential usefulness of the algorithm—as a tool for solving real problems in the current technological world; as a written record that might help organize concepts; and as a procedure, learned in its application to simple, easily understood problems, that can then be extrapolated to more complex applications. In the past, much time has been spent by students in the process of developing skill, speed, and accuracy in using these algorithms—perhaps detracting from a focus on the more powerful ideas of mathematics and distracting students from interpretations of problems that would allow for quick mental solutions. These algorithms were most often learned without attention to understanding how and why they worked. Analysis of problems hinged on *key words* that told you which algorithm to use; the selected procedure was applied without conceptual understanding or recognition that sometimes the problem could be easily solved mentally.

Students should be encouraged to use their concept-based number or spatial sense to interpret a problem and estimate its answer before applying a procedure. They may, however, need the teacher's help and some practice to reach the third procedural mastery phase. In some cases, when the child's struggle with the construction of a concept is discouraging, it may even be necessary to move over the concept to a rotely learned procedure, but attempts to recursively revive the concept should continue. In general, moving to a procedure first should be avoided because there is some evidence that learning a procedure rotely—without the underlying concepts—may encumber concept development and handicap further development of mathematical processes (Morrow, 1998; Usikin, 1998).

*Premise 4: Automaticity.* In order to be able to estimate and use reasoning to solve problems, students need a repertoire of easily retrieved bits of conceptual and procedural knowledge. That repertoire includes related addition and subtraction facts for combinations up to 20 and multiplication and division tables to 12 as well as the standard unit equivalents for measurement. The need for automaticity may have been somewhat subsumed by the prevalent use of calculators, but a missing bank of automatized facts may be detrimental to the development of mathematical knowledge. My own experiences with children and with other cognitive research has also demonstrated that the earlier the requirement or motivation for automatization, the easier it is to embed facts in long-term memory—and retain them there. As it does for the learning of a second language, the brain may have optimum development times for automatization of number facts.

We use the term "automatize" as an outcome descriptor to differentiate from the traditional term *memorize* in order to emphasize that the process of imprinting the facts should be a meaningful one, utilizing reasoning and pattern recognition. Automaticity implies fast retrieval from memory, but strengthened by reasoning and the conceptual knowledge of patterns it also allows for fast reconstruction should a fact be temporarily lost (Cumming & Elkins, 1999; Phillips, 2003).

*Premise 5: Verbalization and Language.* Although I have tried to use clear and simplified language, the words of the content standards are adult terms that express the consensual domain. It is not necessary for the children to use the exact words, as long as the teacher is convinced that the meaning has been correctly constructed. In some cases, students will be able to demonstrate the concept only by doing things with objects or giving examples, but verbalization of the concept in different ways should be encouraged and listened to. Verbalization of a concept helps place the concept in long-term memory. In order to verbalize, children need a shared language. The special language of mathematics, in both symbolic and word form, should be specifically attended to (Ginsburg, 1983, 1989).

*Premise 6: Embedded Assessment.* The performance indicators and assessment expectations can be used for formal assessments, but they are also designed to be embedded in the informal assessments of everyday activities, in the dialogues, the questions, and the cues that teachers toss to students to help them construct new knowledge or correct pre-existing concepts (Chatterji, 2003; Solomon, 2005).

*Premise 7: Representative Materials.* Pictures and concrete materials, including real and representative manipulatives, increase the possibilities of mathematical perceptions. They provide useful, often indispensable, problem-solving strategies as they lead to concept formation. Manipulatives respond to individual differences in learning styles and forms of intelligence, increasing the feelings of self-efficacy for those who are more kinesthetic or tactile in their learning approach. They are particularly helpful at the early levels when children are still at concrete operational stages, and sometimes even necessary for adults whose concepts need to be redeveloped. We need, however, to remember that representative manipulatives are in essence analogies for the real thing, and conscious connections have to be made. Further transitions have to be carefully constructed as children move from the concrete materials to the symbolic forms. The words of everyday language count as well. There needs to be interactive dialogue connecting the words that explain the concept, the manipulatives, and the written symbols of the language of mathematics (Fuson & Briars, 1990).

Learners vary in their need for manipulatives and sometimes reject them once the concept or efficient procedure has been developed. They can become cumbersome when dealing with large numbers, and teachers need to use their best judgment about whether they are of value once the embedded concept is developed. A good rule of thumb is to use the materials to introduce concepts and abandon them for most students when they have made a conceptual shift to the symbolic form or operation. For some students, teachers will have to return to the concrete materials in remedial or small group sessions.

*Premise 8: Problem-Solving Strategies.* In addition to the use of representative materials, there are other problem-solving strategies that teachers may help students develop. In general, connections to real-life situations work as they provide motivation and help students retrieve their prior knowledge (Riley, Greeno, & Heller, 1983). Other strategies include:

- Acting out the problem with physical movements (e.g., touching each item for one-to-one correspondence)
- Making a picture, concept map, or Venn diagram
- Individual and shared analysis of problems to identify given information and desired objective
- Organizing given data on a table
- Generation, comparison, and evaluation of validity of different solution methods

- Purposeful analysis of problems based on their underlying specific concepts may also be considered a general strategy, but one that is dependent on the concepts themselves. I will make specific suggestions for these concept-based strategies in Chapter 3, but they are also embedded in the content standards.

*Premise 9: Technology.* Calculators and computers are not substitutes for the conceptual and procedural knowledge needed for automaticity in retrieval of basic facts, number and spatial sense, and process skills. Nor should they take away from the teacher-managed and peer-interactive discourse of doing mathematics. But they can help students build knowledge. They are, in a way, our modern algorithms—short-cut procedures for complex computations—just as the wristwatch is a technological substitute for telling the time by looking at the position of the sun. They should be considered as necessary and effective tools in learning and living, used like books, worksheets, manipulatives, balances, compasses, protractors are now, and like slide rules were in the past.

For some students, the motivation and immediate feedback of computer managed drill and practice activities will be helpful if used in conjunction with other activities. Graphing calculators that allow for quick connections between equations and graphs, and graphic drawing programs that provide easy depiction, manipulations, and transformations of figures are particularly useful. Real databanks retrieved from the Internet offer a fine supplement to the data collected by students themselves. Because of the almost universal existence of technology, it is no longer necessary for students to spend time building speed in completing multi-digit addition, subtraction, multiplication, and division algorithms. As soon as the student provides evidence of automaticity in fact retrieval, an understanding of the algorithm strategy, and reasonable accuracy, multi-digit problems should be estimated first and then done with a calculator. Some recursive practice with the algorithms can be done from time to time, but we cannot overlook the fact that being able to use technological tools is an important content standard in itself—necessary for survival in the third millennium (Solomon, 2003; University of the State of New York, 1989; Usikin, 1998).

## HOW TEACHERS CAN USE ■ THE FOLLOWING CHAPTERS

### A Guide for Writing Grade-Level Curriculum

As previously explained, the process standards are not separately presented in Chapters 2 and 3, but continuously embodied in the performance indicators and in the challenges of the exemplars in Chapter 3. The two listed disposition or attitude standards are similarly implied in the real-life applications of Chapter 3 and fostered by the careful attention to conceptual development in

Chapter 2. The six major branches of the content set are presented in an order that generally corresponds to the traditional level of concentration on that branch as students progress through the grades. As a consequence, the sequence of the branches also reflects an increasing degree of mathematical complexity. For example, counting is presented first and the multiple representations of data at the end. However, each major branch has preparatory concepts at every grade level so teachers will find concepts that are appropriate for early grades in the final two branches. Within the major overlapping branches, each specific minor branch is presented in the order of a presumed developmental sequence.

When preparing grade-level curriculum, teachers should go through Chapter 2 and check off all standards appropriate for their own grade level, using the median expectations listed. There may be additional standards that are required by state documents or assessments that need to be considered, and some adjustments required by the particular group of students. The order in which the major branches are presented is optional. One branch can be presented at a time, or the teacher may choose to alternate between them. For example, the standards on the rotary clock might be a good introduction to fractions. Another alternative is to follow the order of a textbook, using all sections of this book as a side-by-side accompaniment and day-to-day reference as described below.

## A Day-to-Day Reference Guide for Instruction and Informal Assessment

Once the curriculum sequence has been decided upon, teachers may use Chapter 2 as a daily reminder of what students need to know (for an in-depth discussion on assessment, see Solomon, 2002). Having the desired concept clearly in mind will help teachers construct planned and unplanned dialogues and activities that meet the needs of each student. The concept-matching and correspondingly numbered suggestions for scaffolds or instructional-mapping dialogue in Chapter 3 will help guide them in this process, but individual student's prior knowledge, motivating goals, and the teacher's own experience with successful activities should be considered. The matching exemplars can be used as they are presented and can also serve as models for the selection or creation of other similar experiences that will help the student develop a concept or automatize a procedure. The topical index for Chapters 2 and 3 will provide easy access to these for a particular lesson or unit.

The performance indicators and assessment expectations will clearly delineate the forms and measures of the informal assessments that need to be an integral part of every day's activity because they provide the feedback necessary for reflective practice. Based on the responses to these informal assessments, teachers can make day-to-day and moment-to-moment adjustments in their instructional decisions.

## Formal Assessments

Formal assessments for the purpose of program evaluation at critical grade benchmarks or at the end of a particular unit of study can be constructed directly from the performance indicators and assessment expectations in Chapter 2 and from the exemplars in Chapter 3. Formal assessments can be prepared for analysis and individualized for students as outlined below (examples of the analytical tools and reports may be found in the Resource section following Chapter 3).

• Each item on the assessment (written test or other alternative form) should be articulated with a particular standard by number.

• If possible, items should be prepared in multiple forms that reflect the mastery levels. For example, students might be able to solve a problem conceptually with concrete materials or diagrams, but be unable to translate the problem to algorithm form and solve it without materials. Clearly stated rubrics are needed for open-ended questions (see examples in the Resource section following Chapter 3).

• The expected level for each standard needs to be established. Is the expectation at the exploration level or should the concept mastery or procedural mastery level be reached? Where is each student in reference to this expectation?

• An optional, above standard mastery level, which is not listed in Chapter 2, could be added. This might assume, for example, that the student has reached a level of the particular concept where, in addition to solving problems presented by others, the student could create new problems that require that concept or apply the concept to other contexts or interdisciplinary connections.

• Comprehensive written assessment instruments should be constructed with a balance of short and extended response, mental math, and multiple-choice items. The instrument should also consider the sequence and number of items in terms of their cognitive demand or difficulty.

• When reporting to the students themselves and their parents, the standards should be shared. A report would list the number of the standard and a rubric that corresponds to the three or four developmental levels. The achievement level reached by the student for each standard would be noted, and there would be an indication whether or not that level equaled or exceeded expectation.

• Individual student analyses and standard-by-standard analyses of class means can then provide knowledgeable direction for instruction. There are several computer-based management programs that can facilitate each of these analyses and reports. Examples of assessment items matched to standards will be found in Chapter 3. An example of a report to students or parents and a computer-based class analysis will be found in the Resource section following Chapter 3.

• An ultimate technology-based strategy that responds to assessment data would then provide teachers with interventions or instructional strategies designed to meet specifically diagnosed needs. For example, the technology would match a specifically diagnosed unfulfilled expectation or missing concept from Chapter 2 to a scaffolding dialogue or problem experience from Chapter 3. A data-based matching intervention (DBMI) system would place into the age of technology the best teaching strategies of individualized instruction—and perhaps finally make such instruction truly feasible in a classroom environment.

## ■ NOTE

1. The standards of the National Council of Teachers of Mathematics (2000) are the basis for the standards presented in this text, but the presentation differs in that it relates the standards to the forms of knowledge and its acquisition, presents the processes first, adds perception and attitude standards, and includes succinct definitions of embedded terms. For greater elaboration and examples see the standards themselves.

# 2

# The Designed-Down Content Branches

## *Embedded Concepts and Performance Indicators*

### A GUIDE TO CHAPTER 2 ∎

Chapter 2 takes the major branches of the mathematical *content standards* that are listed in Chapter 1 and designs them down to minor branches and some very specific things that students should know and be able to do. In response, however, to the integrated nature of process and content knowledge, there are no separate sections for the mathematical processes. Instead, they are embedded in the indicators and expectations of each content branch within the actions prescribed by such words as *solve, prove, analyze, describe, compare, connect, interpret, predict, construct, justify,* and *explain.* Illustrative teacher actions that are designed to engage students in the processes and help students develop the concepts are described in Chapter 3, in the form of scaffolding dialogues with probing questions and prompts, exploratory problems, and constructivist activities with manipulatives (also see Premises 5, 7, and 8, below, for initial generalizations).

The *content branches* are designed down to answer questions such as: What concepts and procedures in the division operations branch do you need to know before you can solve problems that require the operation? What do you look for when you *analyze* a problem? What facts and patterns should you quickly recall to make solutions more obvious? How do you do the procedures of the division algorithm? Why do they make sense? How can you divide by a decimal? How is division *connected* to fractions? How can you *prove* the relationship between division and multiplication? There is some sequence organization of the content branches based on developmental expectations and traditional concentrations. For example, number and numeration are first and probability last. Nevertheless, the suggested grade level range for attainment of the concepts and indicators within each branch demonstrates the gradual over-time development of conceptual and procedural knowledge. The three levels represent the following stages of development: A, Exploration; B, Concept Mastery; and C, Algorithmic or Procedural Mastery. In addition, because of the inter-related nature of mathematical knowledge, the branches themselves need to be addressed as overlapping segments.

The specifics of the content branches are stated in two sections. The *embedded concepts* are specific statements of the underlying mathematical constructs of conceptual knowledge that students need in order to understand mathematics and its procedures. Students should be encouraged to express or *verbalize* the concepts as they apply to the procedures and their observations. The designed-down *performance indicators* and *assessment expectations* tell the teacher what mathematical procedures the students must be able to do and how they must prove that they have constructed the concepts and achieved the content standards. If the indicator states that students should be able to *communicate* in their *analysis* with words and appropriate representations that they are able to distinguish whether a particular problem requires them to divide a whole group into a given number of parts and find out how large each part is, or whether it asks them how many parts of a given size will be in the whole, a matched assessment item should measure the ability to make this distinction (see the Resource section following Chapter 3 for further suggestions for assessment).

Each section of concepts and expectations is also preceded by some basic vocabulary and language suggestions, but as teachers prepare to address the concepts and expectations listed they should also refer to the explications of necessary transitions, suggested scaffolding dialogue, and activities that are presented in Chapter 3. The numbers of each specific branch with its embedded concepts and expectations correspond to the numbers in Chapter 3.

## Number System/Counting Patterns/Algebra

*Language check: number names, before, after, more, less, larger than, smaller than, total, property, equal to, odd/even*

| | Content Branches | Suggested Grade-Level Timing* | | | Embedded Concepts | Performance Indicators/ Assessment Expectations |
|---|---|---|---|---|---|---|
| | Major/minor | A | B | C | | |
| 1. | One-to-one correspondence | K–1 | 1 | | Each item touched in sequence corresponds to the next number on the mental number line. | Touching and naming item and identifying position on number line |
| 2. | Cardinal principle | K | 1 | | The last number counted is the group total. | Repeating the last number counted after short interval |
| 3. | Size conservation/number | K–1 | 1 | 1 | Order of counting or arrangement does not affect total number. Spacing of same number of objects does not affect quantity. | Repeating the total in a rearranged set Repeating an equal total quantity when group is expanded |
| 4. | Size seriation | K | 1 | 2 | Objects can be arranged in size order (increasing and decreasing). | Correct arrangement of objects in size order |
| 5. | Sorting/classifying | K | 1 | 2–4 | Objects can be grouped according to like properties. They can also be put in order according to properties other than size (e.g., lightest to darkest, fastest to slowest). | Identifying property used for correct grouping and class inclusion. Logical arrangement of objects based on identified property |
| 6. | Counting; naming, reading, and writing numerals: by (1) up to 20; by (1) to 100 | K | K | 1 | There are patterns: recognition of the "teens" as additions to ten. Each time you count up to nine you go on to the next decade. | Correct item counting. Touching and naming position on a number line. Identification of ten and ___ more for each number to twenty; ability to read and write number symbols |
| 7. | Subitizing: Recognition of small groups of numbers | K | 1 | 2 | You can recognize the totals of small groups of items by looking at them (e.g., three has one in the middle and one on each side; five is made of two and three). | Ability to quickly identify (subitize) totals of small groups (recognize group size on sight) |

*NOTE: A = Exploration, B = Concept Mastery, C = Algorithmic or Procedural Mastery

*(Continued)*

(Continued)

**18**

*NOTE: A = Exploration, B = Concept Mastery, C = Algorithmic or Procedural Mastery

## Number System/Counting Patterns/Algebra
*Language check: number names, before, after, more, less, larger than, smaller than, total, property, equal to, odd/even*

| | Content Branches | Suggested Grade-Level Timing* | | | Embedded Concepts | Performance Indicators/ Assessment Expectations |
|---|---|---|---|---|---|---|
| | Major/minor | A | B | C | | |
| 8. | Counting: by (10) up to 100 | K | 1 | 2 | There are patterns in the decades (e.g., the names of the decades (groups of ten) sound like the numbers and *ty*). All numbers that name the decade end in zero. | Touching and naming decade position on number line; increasing automaticity (fast retrieval from memory) |
| 9. | Counting: by (5) up to 50; by two up to 20. Odd and even numbers: by (3) up to 36 by (4), (6), (8) by (7), (9) | 1<br>1<br><br>2<br>3<br>3 | 1<br>2<br><br>2<br>3<br>4 | 2<br>2<br><br>2<br>3<br>4 | *Skip counting* overlooks a given quantity of numerals in the mental number line. There are patterns in skip counting: by five all numbers end in 5 or zero. Counting by two, all numbers are even numbers; the ones in between are odd numbers. Then come the doubling patterns. Counting by four skips one of the counts by two: (6) twos are twice as much as (3) twos (see Chapter 3). | Correct *skip count* explanation. Recognition of patterns; odd and even numbers<br><br>Increasing automaticity in counting, matching counted items with symbol, *connecting patterns* to each other |
| 10. | Ordinality: first to tenth; to twentieth | K<br>1 | 1<br>2 | 2<br>3 | Ordinal numbers tell us the position of an item in a group and are order dependent. Shifting the order of a group changes the position number, but not the total. | Correct identification of order position of given item in a group |
| 11. | Place value: 1 → 100 1 → 1000 1 → 10,000 1 → 100,000 1 → 1,000,000 | 1<br>2<br>3<br>4<br>5 | 1<br>2<br>4<br>5<br>6 | 2<br>3<br>4<br>5<br>6 | Our number system is based on ten. There are only ten symbols for each place 0–9. For higher values we use the next place to the left. A symbol (1) in the tens place has a value of ten, but (1) in the ones place has a value of one. *Zero is a place holder.* | Correct reading and writing of numbers and regrouping of a value as separate components of system units (dissembling) (e.g., 107 ones are equal to (1) one hundred, (0) tens and (7) ones) |

## Number System/Counting Patterns/Algebra

*Language check: number names, before, after, more, less, larger than, smaller than, total, property, equal to, odd/even*

| Content Branches | Suggested Grade-Level Timing* | | | Embedded Concepts | Performance Indicators/ Assessment Expectations |
|---|---|---|---|---|---|
| Major/minor | A | B | C | | |
| 12. Systematic equalities: | | | | Ten of any units in a place is equal to one in the next higher place: | Correct regrouping with concrete materials; explaining the system generalization |
| to 99 (100) | 1 | 1 | 2 | (10) ones are equal to (1) ten | Renames and/or represents numbers as equal value symbolic alternatives including other multiples of ten (e.g., 6,000 = 60 hundreds or 600 tens). Makes connections to money |
| to 999 (1000) | 1 | 2 | 3 | (10) tens are equal to (1) hundred | |
| to 10,000 | 3 | 4 | 5 | (10) hundreds = 1000; | |
| to 1,000,000 | 4 | 5 | 6 | 10,000 = (10) thousands, but it also equals (100) hundreds, etc. | |
| 13. Place value: Left and right shift for multiplication and division; | | | | Each digit in a place is ten times greater than the same digit on its right. Each digit in a place is ten times smaller than the same digit on its left. You make values ten times bigger by shifting one place to the left and ten times smaller by shifting one place to the right. | Ability to explain and demonstrate *generalization* by multiplying or dividing any value by 10 and multiples of 10 using right or left shift (at appropriate grade level) |
| by 10, 100; | 2 | 3 | 4 | | |
| by 1000 | 3 | 4 | 5 | | |
| 14. Place value: Decimals (see #109): to hundredths | 4 | 5 | 5 | As above, but values less than one are decimals, and we separate the symbols for wholes and decimals with a period or decimal point and the word "and" when reading. 25.23 is read "*twenty-five and twenty-three one hundredths*" (avoid reading "point"). We need zeros for missing digits above the lowest decimal place. | Ability to read combinations of whole numbers and decimals |
| to thousandths | 5 | 6 | 6 | | Ability to dissemble (regroup value into separate components) for each place (23.23 = 2 tens, 3 ones, 2 tenths, and 3 one hundredths) |
| 15. Estimation: Front-end estimation | 2 | 3 | 4 | It is helpful to estimate numbers to make them easier to communicate and use. Estimates check our calculators. Sometimes we just look at the largest place value (the front end) and use zero place holders for the lower ones. | Ability to explain the need for estimation and make some judgments on whether front end or rounding is appropriate; use of estimation in conjunction with calculator computations |

*NOTE: A = Exploration, B = Concept Mastery, C = Algorithmic or Procedural Mastery

*(Continued)*

(Continued)

| Content Branches | Suggested Grade-Level Timing* | | | Embedded Concepts | Performance Indicators/ Assessment Expectations |
|---|---|---|---|---|---|
| Major/minor | A | B | C | | |

## Number System/Counting Patterns/Algebra
*Language check: number names, before, after, more, less, larger than, smaller than, total, property, equal to, odd/even*

| | A | B | C | Embedded Concepts | Performance Indicators/ Assessment Expectations |
|---|---|---|---|---|---|
| 16. Rounding numbers one place | 1 | 2 | 3 | When rounding numbers, we think about whether or not the digit in the next lower place is more or less than halfway to the place we want to round to. For rounding to the nearest ten, we know that 5 ones are halfway to one ten, so 5 or more ones are regrouped for one more ten (round up), and we use zero as a place holder for the ones. If there are less than 5 ones, we just drop them (round down) and use a zero to hold their place. | Ability to explain the *generalization* for rounding. Correct rounding to next place and use of rounding in estimation |
| 17. Rounding numbers more than one place | 4 | 5 | 6 | Numbers can be rounded to the nearest hundred or thousand, etc. To the nearest hundred, for any value less than 50 or half the hundred, we round down and use zero place holders; for 50 or more than half the hundred, we round up to the next hundred. To the nearest thousand, we round down for any value less than 500 or half the thousand, and up for 500 or more than 500. | Correct rounding to given value (up to values as expected in #12). Use of rounding in estimation. Ability to explain generalization |

## Operations/Patterns/Algebraic Expressions: Addition, Subtraction Facts
*Language check: add, subtract, more, less, part, whole, combine, separate, symbol, compare, difference between, regroup*

| | A | B | C | Embedded Concepts | Performance Indicators/ Assessment Expectations |
|---|---|---|---|---|---|
| 18. Add and subtract to 10 on a number line, counting all | K | 1 | 2 | Addition is an increase on the number line; subtraction is a decrease on the number line. When you add there is more and the numbers get higher. When you subtract there is less and the numbers get lower. The operations can be represented by number sentences with numbers and symbols that stand for the real things. The symbols for the operations are: adding or combining (+) and subtraction or separating (−). | Correct new number by *counting all (CA)*, up or down when solving change-/result-unknown problems of given item (see Chapter 3 for sample problems); ability to explain generalization |
| 19. Add/subtract to 10 on number line, counting on from the first number | K | 1 | 1 | It is easier to *count on* (or down) from the first number (COF) that tells where you have already counted on the number line (cardinal principle must be in place) than to *count all* the numbers. | Correct new number by counting on from first (COF) or counting down from first, in change-/result-unknown problems (see Chapter 3) |

*NOTE: A = Exploration, B = Concept Mastery, C = Algorithmic or Procedural Mastery

**Operations/Patterns/Algebraic Expressions: Addition, Subtraction Facts**

*Language check: add, subtract, more, less, part, whole, combine, separate, symbol, compare, difference between, regroup*

| Content Branches | Suggested Grade-Level Timing* | | | Embedded Concepts | Performance Indicators/ Assessment Expectations |
|---|---|---|---|---|---|
| Major/minor | A | B | C | | |
| 20. Add to 10 on a number line, counting from the larger number. Use choice for subtraction | 1 | 1 | 2 | It is easier to count on from the larger number. For example, in addition if the problem is 2 + 7, start with the 7. In subtraction it is sometimes easier to count up: e.g., for 9 – 7 count up from the 7. For 9 – 2, count down. Addends are commutative: 2 + 3 = 3 + 2. | Correct new number for addition by counting from larger number (COL); use of either counting down or counting up—whichever is easier (choice)—in change-unknown, result-unknown, and start-unknown problems |
| 21. Addition: part/whole recognition | K | 1 | 2 | Addition is a combination of parts to form a whole. | Ability to analyze problems and identify parts and whole |
| 22. Addition/subtraction as inverse operations: related facts to 18 | 1 | 2 | 3 | Whole quantities can be separated into parts. Subtraction is a separation of the parts from the whole. When you add the parts together, you re-form the whole. | Ability to analyze problems as requiring addition or subtraction (see Chapter 3 for examples); identify parts and whole and the operation; automatization of related facts to 18 |
| 23. Equalities of sets; use of = for same as; add to five add to ten | K 1 | 1 2 | 2 2 | Different combinations of parts can be the same whole: 2 + 3 = 5, 4 + 1 = 5 7 + 3 = 10, 8 + 2 = 10 | Recognition of different combinations that are the same whole in equalizing word problems; proof with manipulatives and balances; automatization to ten |
| 24. Addition: three single-digit numbers to total of 10; associative principle | 1 | 1 | 2 | More than two parts can be combined to form a whole. They can be combined in any order, and the total will be the same. | Proof of associative principle with manipulatives or balance. Ability to alternate sub-totals when adding three numbers from a story problem |
| 25. Equalities of regrouped sets to total of 10; to 11–22 | 1 1 | 1 2 | 2 2 | Regrouping values to form ten can make adding easier (8 + 5 can be regrouped as 8 + 2 + 3). We can describe equal combinations in symbol form. | Regrouping to make use of automatization of sums to ten; application to symbolic form |
| 26. Algebra (missing addend) | 1 | 2 | 3 | We can find a missing addend (part) if we know the whole and the other addend (part): 2 + [ ] = 5. | Correct missing addend; translation of word problem to symbolic form |

*NOTE: A = Exploration, B = Concept Mastery, C = Algorithmic or Procedural Mastery

(Continued)

(Continued)

| Content Branches | A | B | C | Embedded Concepts | Performance Indicators/ Assessment Expectations |
|---|---|---|---|---|---|
| | Suggested Grade-Level Timing* | | | | |

**Operations/Patterns/Algebraic Expressions: Addition, Subtraction Facts**
*Language check: add, subtract, more, less, part, whole, combine, separate, symbol, compare, difference between, regroup*

| # Content Branches | A | B | C | Embedded Concepts | Performance Indicators/ Assessment Expectations |
|---|---|---|---|---|---|
| 27. Estimation to precision: addition of two-digit numbers to 99—no regrouping | 1 | 2 | 3 | When adding two-digit numbers, we combine like place value parts (ones to ones, tens to tens). We use symbols in an algorithm to keep track of what we are doing. We can estimate by just adding the tens, but for exact measurement start with ones. | Correct choice of concrete material and correct placement of two-digit numbers from a story problem; correct estimation and addition using algorithm |
| 28. Addition: three single-digit numbers | 1 | 2 | 3 | It is efficient to look for doubles and to form tens when adding the columns. Ten plus six is sixteen. | Increased efficiency; evidence of reasoning in applying procedures |
| 29. Addition: three-digit numbers to 999—no regrouping | 2 | 3 | 4 | Like place value parts are combined. We can estimate by combining the values in the largest place: When adding amounts over 200 and 300, the answer must be at least 500. | Correct choice of concrete materials and correct placement of two-digit addends in algorithms based on story problems; correct estimates and addition using algorithm |
| 30. Addition: two-digit numbers with regrouping; three digits; four digits | 1 / 2 / 3 | 2 / 3 / 4 | 3 / 4 / 5 | Because our number system does not have more than nine units in a place, sums of ten or more can be regrouped as one or more tens and up to nine ones. (10) tens can be regrouped as (1) 100. The addition algorithm helps us keep track of what we are doing. | Correct regrouping and correct use of concrete materials; correct transition to symbolic algorithm; proof with materials |
| 31. Addition series: same addend, increasing addend | 2 / 3 | 3 / 4 | 4 / 5 | We can create number patterns by continuously adding the same number or a number that increases each time. | Ability to recognize addition patterns in series; reasoning with and then without concrete materials |
| 32. Subtraction as separation of a part from the whole. One digit from one digit without regrouping / One digit from two digits | 1 / 1 | 1 / 2 | 2 / 2 | Subtraction finds the value of a part when you know the whole value and the value of another part. In some problems the part you know is separated from the whole. We sometimes call that "take away." The part you don't know or what is left is the difference between the part you know and the whole. To find the difference we count up from the part or down from the whole, whichever is easier. | *Analysis of problems:* Identification of whole, known part, and difference sought from real or story problems (comparison, change-unknown, start-unknown, referent-unknown) using real or manipulative materials; evidence of "choice" of counting up or down for maximum efficiency. Ability to analyze *canonical* and *non-canonical* problems (see #'s 32 and 34 in Chapter 3 for illustrations) |

Major/minor

*NOTE: A = Exploration, B = Concept Mastery, C = Algorithmic or Procedural Mastery

**Operations/Patterns/Algebraic Expressions: Addition, Subtraction Facts**

*Language check: add, subtract, more, less, part, whole, combine, separate, symbol, compare, difference between, regroup*

| | Content Branches | Suggested Grade-Level Timing* | | | Embedded Concepts | Performance Indicators/ Assessment Expectations |
|---|---|---|---|---|---|---|
| | | A | B | C | | |
| | Major/minor | | | | | |
| 33. | Subtraction: comparing wholes | 1 | 1 | 2 | Subtraction finds the difference between two whole values. To find the difference, you can count up from the smaller or down from the larger value, whichever is easier. | Correct use of terms *more, less, same as*; then symbols for these; analysis and solution of compare problems |
| 34. | Algebra: finding a missing addend by subtraction from the sum | 4 | 5 | 6 | We can find the value of a missing addend by subtracting the one we know from the sum. We call the number sentence or expression with a missing value an equation. | *Analysis* of problems: Identification of whole, known part, and difference sought from real or story problems (comparison, change-unknown, start-unknown, referent-unknown) using real or manipulative materials |
| | Introduction of terms *variable* and *constant* | 5 | 6 | 7 | Missing values (values we do not know) in an expression can be represented by letters, which we call variables. Values we know are constants. | Translation of addition problems into equations; identification of variables and constants |
| 35. | Inequalities: Use of symbols and problems: < and > ≠ ≤ and ≥ Unequal unknown numbers that add up to a known whole | 1 3 5 | 1 4 6 | 2 5 7 | Combinations and single amounts can be more or less than each other. Subtraction finds the difference. We can find the value of two unequal numbers we do not know if we know the difference between them and we know their sum. If we subtract the difference between them from the sum, we are left with the sum of two equal values. The value of one of these is the smaller number. | *Interpretation* and use of symbols. *Analysis* and solution of inequality problems; ability to plot an inequality on a number line. Analysis and solution of problems where two parts are unknown, but difference between them and whole is known (see Chapter 3) |
| 36. | Algebra: Negative and positive integers | 5 | 6 | 7 | Sometimes we need to measure and show values that are less than zero, like very cold temperatures or the below-sea-level depth of the ocean. Values that are less than zero are shown with a raised minus (negative) symbol in front of them and values greater than zero with a plus (positive) sign. | Ability to identify and record negative and positive values on a number line |

*NOTE: A = Exploration, B = Concept Mastery, C = Algorithmic or Procedural Mastery

(Continued)

(Continued)

## Operations/Patterns/Algebraic Expressions: Addition, Subtraction Facts

*Language check: add, subtract, more, less, part, whole, combine, separate, symbol, compare, difference between, regroup*

| Content Branches / Major/minor | Suggested Grade-Level Timing* A | B | C | Embedded Concepts | Performance Indicators/ Assessment Expectations |
|---|---|---|---|---|---|
| 37. Subtraction: two digits from two digits—no regrouping | 1 | 2 | 3 | Like place value parts must be subtracted from like place value parts. | Correct estimation, then computation with concrete materials; transition to algorithm (see note below) |
| 38. Subtraction: one digit from two digits with regrouping. Two digits from two digits—regrouping | 1 | 1 | 2 | If we don't have enough of the kind of place value part we need, we can regroup into equal quantities. In the problem (23 − 7), 23 is either two tens and three ones or one ten and thirteen ones. We can subtract 7 from thirteen ones but not from three ones (see Chapter 3 for hints on transition to algorithm). | Correct estimation/correct regrouping (concrete materials → symbolic algorithm) |
| 39. Subtraction: three digits from three digits—regrouping | 2 | 3 | 4–5 | *Regrouping can skip places in our number system.* It is true that (1) one hundred is the same as 100 ones, but for exact answers it is better to move one step at a time and not skip places when subtracting across zeros. First regroup the one hundred into (10) tens, and then one ten into ten ones. The place with a zero can be filled by regrouping larger place value parts into smaller parts that belong in the place held by zero. | Correct estimation/correct regrouping across zero Effective and accurate use of subtraction algorithm with three-digit minuend and subtrahend |
| More than three digits—regrouping | 3 | 4 | 5 | When regrouping across zeros, it is better to move one step at a time. Use calculator checks. | As above with four digits in all types of word problems and using the common algorithm |

*NOTE: A = Exploration, B = Concept Mastery, C = Algorithmic or Procedural Mastery

**Operations/Patterns/Algebraic Expressions: Addition, Subtraction Facts**

*Language check: add, subtract, more, less, part, whole, combine, separate, symbol, compare, difference between, regroup*

| Content Branches | Suggested Grade-Level Timing* A | B | C | Embedded Concepts | Performance Indicators/ Assessment Expectations |
|---|---|---|---|---|---|
| | Major/minor | | | | |
| 40. Multiplication as repeated addition of groups of size 2 to 5 | 2 | 3 | 4 | Every time we skip count we add another equal amount. Multiplication is a process of repeated addition. If we keep track of the number of times we have added an equal amount to get a total, "times" means the number of times a quantity has been repeatedly added: $5 \times 1$ means 5 added one time, $5 \times 2$ means 5 added two times, etc. (use arrays & calculators). | Correct *analysis* of word problems that speak of repeated equal additions; e.g., "Every day of the week Jon got two new pennies that he saved." How many times did he receive pennies? How many pennies in all? Recognition of "groups" and "totals" in arrays |
| 41. Multiplication number sentences in horizontal and vertical forms, finding patterns, multiples of 2, 5, 10 | 2 | 3 | 4 | Repeated addition creates patterns, e.g., twice as many repeats counts up to a double total: $4 \times 5$ is double $2 \times 5$, or 4 fives are double 2 fives, or twice as much as 10, which equals 20. | Correct analysis of word problems Translation into number sentence and vertical forms |
| Equations with multiples | 3 | 4 | 5 | $3 \times [\ ] = 18$ means what number repeated 3 times is equal to 18? | Translation of problems into equation form |
| 42. Multiplication of multiples of 2–10, tables, fact families | 3 | 4 | 5 | We can make a multiplication *table* to show the patterns of repeated additions. Multiplication by zero means that there is no amount to add. Anything multiplied by zero is zero. | Increasing automaticity of multiplication facts Ability to retrieve facts lost from LTM (long-term memory) by using *analysis and reasoning from known facts* |
| 43. Multiplication: Commutativity | 3 | 4 | 5 | The sum of a number of groups repeated a certain number of times is the same as the sum you get when a group the same size as the number of times the first group was repeated is repeated a number of times equal to the size of the first group: $5 \times (3)$* has the same total as $3 \times (5)$, but they represent *different arrays of things*. *See Chapter 3 for clarification of this concept and notation. | Concrete demonstration for *proof of commutativity* Automaticity in retrieval of commutative facts |

*NOTE: A = Exploration, B = Concept Mastery, C = Algorithmic or Procedural Mastery

*(Continued)*

| Content Branches | Suggested Grade-Level Timing* | | | Embedded Concepts | Performance Indicators/ Assessment Expectations |
|---|---|---|---|---|---|
| | A | B | C | | |
| Major/minor | | | | | |

**Operations/Patterns: Multiplication**

*Language check: times, as much, double, product, partial product, multiple*

| Content Branches | A | B | C | Embedded Concepts | Performance Indicators/ Assessment Expectations |
|---|---|---|---|---|---|
| 44. Multiplication as comparison or enlargement (change) in size | 3 | 4 | 5 | Multiplication is also a process that changes the value or size of a single object. One balloon can become twice as large or 3 times bigger, or half times larger/half as big (this prepares for multiplication by fractions). | Correct *analysis of word problems* which address the concept of size change; ability to estimate comparisons in figures |
| 45. Multiplication patterns: tens, hundreds | 4 | 4 | 5–6 | Using left shift or counting we know that ten × ten = one hundred. But 20 × 10 is 2 tens × 1 ten or 200; 20 × 20 is 2 tens × 2 tens = 4 hundreds. Then 2 hundreds is 4 thousands. | *Pattern recognition;* correct estimation and ability to mentally compute even multiples of tens and hundreds |
| 46. Multiplication: Two-digit multiplicands by single-digit multipliers of 2–10 | 2 | 3 | 4 | *Like parts need to be multiplied separately, but the sum of partial products equals the whole product:* e.g., 23 × 3 is the same as 20 × 3 plus 3 × 3 (distributive principle). We can estimate answers by multiplying by the tens. Use concrete materials and then transition to algorithm. | Correct estimation and exact answers; identification of the multiplier and repeated groups (multiplicand) in word problems; *ability to prove that partial products add up to whole product total* |
| 47. Multiplication: algorithm | 3 | 4 | 5 | The multiplication algorithm organizes the problem and partial products. | Correct estimation, placement of sub-totals in algorithm; *proof of algorithm strategy* |
| 48. Multiplication: Single-digit multipliers and two-digit multiplicands with regrouping | 4 | 4 | 5–6 | When we organize partial products, we regroup products of ten or more for the next higher place value so that like parts in our number system are combined. A product of 23 is regrouped as 2 tens and 3 ones. | Correct estimation; correct placement of sub-totals (partial products) and ability to identify these; correct regrouping; *ability to solve and construct problems* |
| 49. Two-digit multipliers and two-digit multiplicands with regrouping, using concrete materials and algorithm | 3 | 4 | 5 | In the algorithm 16 × 25, 25 is repeatedly added, first six times, and then ten times. Use calculator to demonstrate this (following concrete manipulation in which five unit cubes are repeated 16 times and 2 tens blocks are repeated 16 times). | Correct estimation; correct place value of partial products; ability to distribute 16 × 25 as (16 × 20 + 16 × 5) or as (10 × 20 + 10 × 5 + 6 × 20 + 6 × 5) |

*NOTE: A = Exploration, B = Concept Mastery, C = Algorithmic or Procedural Mastery

| Content Branches | Suggested Grade-Level Timing* A | B | C | Embedded Concepts | Performance Indicators/ Assessment Expectations |
|---|---|---|---|---|---|
| Major/minor | | | | | |
| **Operations/Patterns: Multiplication** *Language check: times, as much, double, product, partial product, multiple* | | | | | |
| 50. Multiplication: three-digit multipliers and multiplicands with regrouping, using algorithm | 4 | 5 | 6 | 3 tens × 2 hundreds = 6 thousands, 3 hundreds × 2 hundreds = 6 ten thousands. As above for higher multipliers and multiplicands—that the total product is the sum of the partial products. | Ability to mentally compute even multiples of hundreds, hundreds of times; $400 \times 800 =$ 320,000; correct estimation and computation with three-digit multiplicands and multipliers; correct use of calculator |
| 51. Cartesian multiplication: single chance correspondence | 2 | 3 | 4 | Number patterns can help us compute. If we know the pattern or the relationship, we can compute one number from the other. Diagrams help us to see the patterns. We can also describe the patterns in an equation *(an introduction to functions)*. | Ability to compute a total from the number pattern (e.g., Everyone has two eyes; how many eyes do five children have?) |
| 52. Multiplication series; enlargement by the same multiplier | 5 | 6 | 7 | If we know the multiplication pattern in a series, we can predict the next number or any future number. Finding common factors (see below) for the numbers helps us see the patterns. The patterns can be expressed in symbol form as a function. For example, for the three table, $N = 3 \times (n)$, where (n) stands for the ordinal position of the number in a series and (N) its cardinal value. | *Analysis of series; generalization of function and expression in symbolic form* |
| **Operations/Patterns: Division** *Language check: divided into, divided by, divisor, dividend, quotient, remainder* | | | | | |
| 53. Division as repeated subtraction; backward skip counting | 2 | 3 | 4 | Skip counting backwards from a whole is repeated subtraction of equal quantities or groups. The groups form equal parts of the whole (use calculators to keep track of the number of groups). | Can orally skip count backwards by 2, 5, and 10, and backwards on the calculator while keeping track of number of repetitions |

*NOTE: A = Exploration, B = Concept Mastery, C = Algorithmic or Procedural Mastery

*(Continued)*

(Continued)

| Content Branches | Suggested Grade-Level Timing* | | | Embedded Concepts | Performance Indicators/Assessment Expectations |
|---|---|---|---|---|---|
| | A | B | C | | |
| **Major/minor** | | | | | |
| **Operations/Patterns: Division** *Language check: divided into, divided by, divisor, dividend, quotient, remainder* | | | | | |
| 54. Division as sharing to form equal groups (partition) | 2 | 3 | 4 | Sharing involves forming equal parts or groups from a whole. In sharing division you know the whole and the number of groups or parts, but not the size of the group or part. With a given whole, the size of each part depends on the number of parts or groups. The larger the number of parts, the smaller the size of each group or part and vice versa. The size of each group is the quotient. | Ability to predict change in size of group with increase or decrease in number of parts; automaticity of responses when given partition problems: "Twenty candies can fill five baskets with four candies. How many candies could you put in four baskets?" (First, more or less as a predictor) |
| 55. Division: as inversely related to multiplication (quotion or measurement division) | 2 | 3 | 4 | In multiplication, we know the size of each group and the number of the groups we add repeatedly, but not the size of the whole. We multiply to find the whole. In some division problems, we know the whole and the size of the group, but not the number of groups. We divide to find the number of groups. The answer is the called the quotient. | Analysis of word problems to identify what represents the whole and what represents size of each group, and then compute and label the number of groups; ability to predict and prove changes in number of groups with increase or decrease in size of group |
| 56. Division as shrinkage | 3 | 3 | 4 | Division can also be a process in which a whole shrinks a given number of times, such as: What is three times (less) smaller than twelve? (related to fractions). | Ability to analyze word problems to identify what represents the original size and then compute changed size as a result of shrinkage |
| 57. Division facts, tables; patterns: doubling, halving Division by 2, 3, 4, 5, 6, 10 | 2 | 3 | 4 | Pattern recognition: If $5 \times 6 = 30$ and $6 \times 5 = 30$, then there are 5 sixes or 6 fives in 30: $30 \div 6 = 5$, $30 \div 5 = 6$. If there are 3 fours in 12, then there are 6 fours in 24. If there are 4 fives in 20, then there are only 2 fives in 10. | Increasing automaticity with facts and problems involving quotion (grouping): How many groups of 6 are there in 42, etc.? $42 \div 6 = [\ ]$ and $42 \div [\ ] = 7$. Ability to explain canonical and non-canonical sentences |
| 58. Division facts to 144 | 3 | 4 | 5 | Pattern recognition (in addition to reciprocal of multiplication): the number of parts and the size of the parts are commutative. These quantities are called factors of the product. The same product may have other factors for the same whole or product. | Increasing automaticity in retrieval from long-term memory, use of reasoning when lost from memory |

*NOTE: A = Exploration, B = Concept Mastery, C = Algorithmic or Procedural Mastery

(Continued)

**Operations/Patterns: Division**
*Language check: divided into, divided by, divisor, dividend, quotient, remainder*

| | Content Branches | Suggested Grade-Level Timing* | | | Embedded Concepts | Performance Indicators/ Assessment Expectations |
|---|---|---|---|---|---|---|
| | Major/minor | A | B | C | | |
| 59. | Division as related to fractions (the sharing model) or partition division | 3 | 4 | 5 | In sharing division, each part is a fraction of the whole. Twenty-eight divided into four parts is the same as 1/4 of 28 or 1/4 × 28. In each case you are looking for the size of the part: 28 ÷ 4 = [ ]; 28 ÷ [ ] = 7; 1/4 of 28 = [ ]; 1/4 of [ ] = 7; 1/4 × [ ] = 7 | Correct identification of the whole, the number of parts, and what is sought in canonical and non-canonical problem sentences |
| 60. | Division: short form algorithm; no remainder | 3 | 4 | 5 | Like place parts must be divided separately. The partial quotients are recorded in the right place. We then find the sum for partial quotients. To divide 44 by 2: 4 tens divided by 2 equals 2 (tens) and 4 ones ÷ 2 = 2 ones, and their sum is 22. Whole values cannot always be divided evenly. Sometimes there is a remainder. In the algorithm, we can rename remainders to the next smaller place and add them to what is there. | Ability to estimate quotient to nearest ten, identify partial quotients and parts that have not yet been divided; first in concrete materials, then in the algorithm; correct placement of quotient; explanation of remainders in partial and final quotient |
| | Short form with remainders | 4 | 5 | 6 | | Correct use of algorithm |
| 61. | Division of three-digit numbers by one-digit number: short and long form, remainders across zero | 4 | 5 | 6 | The long form division algorithm helps us keep track of partial products and remainders. Numbers can be renamed and reorganized so that division can be done or made easier. The final quotient is the sum of all the partial quotients. | Ability to estimate quotients and identify partial quotients and parts that have not yet been divided (see Chapter 3) Correct use of algorithm |
| 62 | Division by zero | 4 | 5 | 6 | Zero divided into 4 or any number of parts is still zero, and there are zero fours in zero; therefore 0 ÷ 4 = 0. However, the number of zeros in 4 is an undefined amount, therefore 4 ÷ 0 is undefined. | Proof of generalization using verbal constructs or materials (sets of data with some zero readings are good to explain undefined amount) |
| 63. | Division of three- and four-digit numbers by a two-digit number: long form with remainders across zero | 5 | 6 | 7 | When dividing by a two-digit number you are dividing into groups of 20 or 30 (or 2 tens or 3 tens). It is good to estimate first. Hundreds divided by tens are tens or 6 hundred (600) divided by 2 tens (20) = 3 tens or 30. Thousands divided by tens are hundreds. When doing the algorithm it is useful to round the divisor down to the digit with the largest place value. If you are dividing by 24 or 26, round to 2 tens. Do not round up (see Chapter 3). | Ability to *mentally compute* division of multiples of 10 by divisors of 10, 20, 30, 40 (e.g., 200 ÷ 10; 600 ÷ 20; 1200 ÷ 30; 8000 ÷ 40); ability to compute exact quotients, and identify partial quotients and remainders for word problems involving two-digit divisors and four-digit dividends |

*NOTE: A = Exploration, B = Concept Mastery, C = Algorithmic or Procedural Mastery

## Number System/Patterns/Operations: Fractions/Ratios/Proportions

Language check: numerator, denominator, equivalent, ratio

| Content Branches | Suggested Grade-Level Timing* | | | Embedded Concepts | Performance Indicators/ Assessment Expectations |
|---|---|---|---|---|---|
| Major/minor | A | B | C | | |
| 64. Fractions: equal parts of a whole; unit fraction words and numerals, 1/2, 1/4 | K–1 | 2 | 3 | Whole things can be equally shared. The whole then becomes parts with special names depending on their size. These names are fractions. The size of the part depends upon the size of the whole. | Ability to identify one half of a whole item in a word problem picture; recognition that the same fraction part of different sized whole will be different |
| 65. Fractions as parts of wholes: Naming the denominator as the number of parts: 1/2, 1/3, 1/4, 1/5, 1/8, 1/10 | 1 | 2 | 3 | The more parts made out of a whole, the smaller each part. The bottom number of the fraction (denominator) tells you how many parts were made from the whole. | Ability to predict comparative size of parts of the same whole with a different number of sharers; recognition of number of parts the whole has been divided into from the fraction name |
| 66. Comparing unit fractions (including inequalities) | 2 | 3 | 4 | Unit fractions of the same whole can be ordered according to their size. The higher the denominator, the smaller the size. | Ability to order unit fractions from symbols |
| 67. Fractions: related to division; equal parts of a set; unit fractions | 2 | 3 | 4 | Whole groups of things can also be equally shared and the parts described by fractions. This is like division. The numerator tells the size of the whole set and the denominator the number of parts. The actual size of each part or group depends on the size of the whole. You have to divide the numerator by the denominator to find the size of the equal parts. | Ability to use a fraction to describe a part from a number story; ability to predict comparative size of equal unit fractions of different wholes (1/2 of 20 vs. 1/2 of 40); ability to compute size of part for unit fractions |
| 68. Fractions as parts of wholes: Parts equal to whole 2/2, 4/4, 8/8 More-than-unit fractions Naming the numerator | 2 | 3 | 4 | The total number of parts is equal to the whole. The whole can be expressed as all the parts in one whole or 2/2, 4/4, 8/8. Less than the total number of parts in one whole is less than a whole. More than the number of parts in one whole is more than a whole. The top number (numerator) tells you how many of these parts you are thinking about. | Ability to rename 2/2, 4/4, 8/8 as equalities; ability to describe different unit fractions or fractions with the same denominator as inequalities using symbols < , > ; and prove understanding of relationship between fractions (e.g., 2/2 = 1 whole, 3/2 > 1 whole, 1/2 < 1 whole) |
| 69. Operations on fractions: addition and subtraction of like fractions | 2 | 3 | 4 | Fractions can be combined and separated. If the denominators are the same, the numerators are just added or subtracted. This is because they are like parts. | Ability to analyze and solve simple word problems involving addition or subtraction of fractions with like denominators |

*NOTE: A = Exploration, B = Concept Mastery, C = Algorithmic or Procedural Mastery

**Number System/Patterns/Operations: Fractions/Ratios/Proportions**
*Language check: numerator, denominator, equivalent, ratio*

| | Content Branches | Suggested Grade-Level Timing* | | | Embedded Concepts | Performance Indicators/ Assessment Expectations |
|---|---|---|---|---|---|---|
| | Major/minor | A | B | C | | |
| 70. | Fractions: more-than-unit fractional parts of a set | 4 | 5 | 6 | To find the size of more than one unit fraction of a set, you find the size of one unit by dividing by the denominator, and then you multiply by the number of unit parts, the numerator. | Ability to compute the value of more than unit fractional parts of multiple wholes from story problems |
| 71. | Fractions as shrinkage | 2 | 3 | 4 | Fractions are used to describe how much smaller a size or value is compared to another: e.g., half as many. | Ability to estimate half size shrinkage from diagrams, real objects; use the fraction to describe comparison figures |
| 72. | Fractions as sharing of more than one whole where the number of parts is greater than the number of wholes | 4 | 5 | 6 | If you divide two wholes into three parts, the size of each part is less than one whole or 1/3 of one whole plus 1/3 of the other or 2/3; 2/3 can mean two wholes divided into three parts. A fraction is another way of expressing division. | Ability to form fractions from division number stories; ability to *predict* whether the size of the part is smaller or greater than one whole |
| 73. | Fractions: simple equivalents: Halves, fourths; Thirds, sixths; fifths, tenths | 1 2 4 | 2 3 5 | 3 4 6 | Equal parts of a whole can be combined to form larger equal parts, and the combination of the smaller parts is the same size as a larger equal part of the whole. Smaller equal parts can be formed from larger parts. The smaller the part, the more parts you need to have the same amount of a whole. The higher the denominator, the smaller the part and the more parts you need to have the same amount of the whole (use concrete pieces, fraction bars and fraction number lines). | Ability to identify equivalents and *predict* whether or not numerators or denominators will be higher or lower; e.g., 1/2 = ?/4 (will the numerator be higher or lower than one?) |
| 74. | Comparing equivalent fractions; using patterns to compute equivalents | 5 | 6 | 7 | Equivalent fractions have observable patterns. For example, if the numerator is twice as large, the denominator is twice as large (2/3 = 4/6). | Ability to identify patterns |

*NOTE: A = Exploration, B = Concept Mastery, C = Algorithmic or Procedural Mastery

(Continued)

**Number System/Patterns/Operations: Fractions/Ratios/Proportions**
*Language check: numerator, denominator, equivalent, ratio*

| Content Branches | Suggested Grade-Level Timing* | | | Embedded Concepts | Performance Indicators/ Assessment Expectations |
|---|---|---|---|---|---|
| Major/minor | A | B | C | | |
| 75. Finding equivalent fractions | 4 | 5 | 6 | If we enlarge or reduce the numerator of a fraction by multiplying or dividing it by a value (factor), we can form an equivalent fraction by multiplying or dividing the denominator by the same factor: 3/4 is equal to 6/8 because $2 \times (3) = 6$ and $2 \times (4) = 8$, and two is the multiplier by which both numerator and denominator were enlarged. | Ability to change fractions to equivalents with common denominators<br><br>Explanation of *generalization; proof* that value is not changed (use manipulatives) |
| 76. Renaming fractions that have values greater than one (improper fractions) Representing fractions and whole numbers on a number line | 4 | 5 | 6 | Fractions that have values greater than one are sometimes called improper fractions and can be changed to mixed numbers. Mixed numbers can be changed to improper fractions. They are different representations of the same value. | Ability to interchange the representation of mixed numbers and improper fractions; ability to sequence common fractions (less than one), whole numbers, and mixed numbers on a number line |
| 77. Fractions as ratios of part to whole; equivalent word and symbol expressions of ratio | 4 | 5 | 6 | The values of the numerator and denominator in a fraction can also express a pattern or relationship called a ratio. Ratios represent either a relationship between parts and the whole or a relationship between different parts of the whole. Ratios can also represent the *relationship* of a given number of items in a group to the whole group of items: 2/3 represents two parts (items) out of a whole group of three parts (items). The ratio expressed as 2/3 can also be expressed in word form as 2 out of 3 or 2 : 3. | Ability to *analyze simple word problems* that describe a part/whole ratio and express the ratio in words and as a fraction; ability to apply concept of ratio to simple probability problems and express probability as a ratio in word and fraction form |
| 78. Fractions as ratios of parts to parts | 5 | 6 | 7 | Ratios can also represent the relationship between different parts of groups of things. A ratio of 2/3 can mean that for every two parts of one kind in a whole group there are three parts of another kind. This ratio can also be expressed in word form as: 2 is to 3, or 2 to 3; or symbolically as 2 : 3. If there were no other parts in this group, the size of the whole would be five (or multiples of 5), and one kind of part would be 2/5 of the whole while the other would be 3/5 of the whole. | Ability to distinguish between part/whole and part/part ratios; ability to convert part/part data into part/whole ratios; correct translation of part/part ratio word problem statements into symbolic form |

*NOTE: A = Exploration, B = Concept Mastery, C = Algorithmic or Procedural Mastery

| Content Branches | Suggested Grade-Level Timing* | | | Embedded Concepts | Performance Indicators/Assessment Expectations |
|---|---|---|---|---|---|
| Major/minor | A | B | C | | |

**Number System/Patterns/Operations: Fractions/Ratios/Proportions**
*Language check: numerator, denominator, equivalent, ratio*

| Content Branches | A | B | C | Embedded Concepts | Performance Indicators/Assessment Expectations |
|---|---|---|---|---|---|
| 79. Proportions | 5 | 6 | 7 | Statements of equivalent ratios are called proportions. The patterns of equivalent fractions or proportions can also help us compute unknown parts and wholes. Five out of ten parts is the same as one out of two parts or half the total number of parts. When the size of the denominator increases or decreases, the size of the numerator must change proportionately (by the same factor) in order for the fractions to be equivalent. For any two equivalent fractions, the product of the denominator of one fraction and the numerator of the second is equal to the product of the denominator of the second fraction and the numerator of the first. | Ability to *analyze proportion word problems* and compute unknown quantities using common factors (multiples or divisors) Ability to use product of extremes = product of means = product of extremes algorithm and simple linear equations to solve problems |
| 80. Proportions in scale drawings | 5 | 6 | 7 | Sizes in scale drawings are proportional to the sizes in reality. | Interpretation of scale drawings; construction of scale drawings |
| 81. Inequalities: halves, thirds, fourths: 3/4 > 1/2 1/2 > 1/3 | 4 | 5 | 6 | If fractions are not equivalent, you can use close equivalents to estimate their relative size (e.g., 3/4 is more than 1/2 because 1/2 is equivalent to 2/4). | Ability to order halves, thirds, and fourths, and to solve inequalities: 1/2 < 3/4; 1/2 < 2/3; 2/3 < 3/4; 1/3 < 1/2 |
| Ordering by other comparisons | 5 | 6 | 7 | You can also compare the size of fractions by comparisons to one whole: 7/8 is more than 5/7 because it is only 1/8 less than whole. | Ability to order other fractions without converting to equal denominators(use fraction number lines and concrete materials) |

*NOTE: A = Exploration, B = Concept Mastery, C = Algorithmic or Procedural Mastery

## Multiplicative Functions/Algebra

*Language check: referent, multiple, increment, operator, factor, least common factor and least common multiple*

| | Content Branches | A | B | C | Embedded Concepts | Performance Indicators/Assessment Expectations |
|---|---|---|---|---|---|---|
| | **Major/minor** | | | | | |
| 82. | Preparation for multiple factors; associative principle | 5 | 6 | 7 | The multiplication process is one in which the same value is either added repeatedly or proportionally enlarged in size. The multiplier tells how many repeats there are or the size of the enlargement. If the original value or referent is multiplied in separate steps or increments and each time it is the previous product that is multiplied, the same end result can be obtained by multiplying the original referent by the product of each incremental step. For example, blowing up a balloon to two times the size and then making the new size balloon three times bigger is the same as blowing the original up to six times its size. $3 \times (2 \times N) = 6 \times N$ | Ability to *analyze* word problems and identify the referent and abstract operator (multiplier); ability to provide alternate increments for reaching the same enlargement or repeated addition |
| 83. | Factors | 5 | 6 | 7 | Factors are all the whole number values (referent and abstract operators) that can be combined in the multiplication process to give a particular value of the product. Dividing a multiple by one factor results in another factor with no remainder. | Ability to identify all factors in a given number Given a number and a factor, correct identification of other factors Identification of quotients and dividends as factors |
| 84. | Multiples | 5 | 6 | 7 | Multiples are the products of factors. | Ability to use the term *multiple* in framing a problem |
| 85. | Prime number | 5 | 6 | 7 | A prime number is a whole number with exactly two factors: itself and 1. *The number 1 is not a prime number because it does not have two factors.* | Ability to identify a prime number and *prove* what it is |
| 86. | Composite numbers | 5 | 6 | 7 | A composite number is a whole number that has more than two factors. | Ability to identify a composite number and *prove that it is composite* |

*NOTE: A = Exploration, B = Concept Mastery, C = Algorithmic or Procedural Mastery

**Multiplicative Functions/Algebra**
*Language check: referent, multiple, increment, operator, factor, least common factor and least common multiple*

| | Content Branches | A | B | C | Embedded Concepts | Performance Indicators/Assessment Expectations |
|---|---|---|---|---|---|---|
| | **Major/minor** | | | | | |
| 87. | Common multiples | 5 | 6 | 7 | A common multiple is a computed value that is the same multiple for two different starting numbers. A balloon of size four blown up three whole times will be the same size as a balloon of size three blown up four times. Both balloons will now be size 12. So will a balloon of size 2 blown up six times, etc. Twelve is a common multiple of the different numbers 3, 4, 2, 6, 12, and 1. | Ability to identify the common multiple of two or more numbers and prove that it is the common multiple |
| 88. | Common factors | 5 | 6 | 7 | Common factors are whole number quotients that are the same for different multiples: 3 and 4 are common factors of 12. See Chapter 3 for scaffolds and illustrations. | Ability to explain meaning of common factors; identify common factors of two or more numbers and *prove* them correct |
| 89. | Greatest common factor | 5 | 6 | 7 | The greatest common factor (G.C.F.) is the largest factor that is common (or the same) for two different numbers. | Ability to define, explain, predict, and compute the greatest common factor |
| 90. | Least common multiple | 5 | 6 | 7 | The least common multiple (L.C.M.) is the smallest value that is a multiple of each of two or more different values. If the original values are prime numbers then the L.C.M. is the product of the different values. If both values share common factors, the *least common multiple* will be less than their product. | Ability to predict and compute the least common multiple for different values |
| 91. | Finding equivalent fractions | 5 | 6 | 7 | If we enlarge or reduce the numerator of a fraction by multiplying or dividing it by a value, we can form an equivalent fraction by multiplying or dividing the denominator by the same value: 3/4 is equal to 6/8 because $3 \times (2) = 6$ and $4 \times (2) = 8$, and 2 is the value by which both numerator and denominator were enlarged. The greater the denominator, the smaller the size of each part, and the more parts necessary for an equivalent fraction. Parts that are twice as small require twice as many parts to be equivalent. | Explanation of *generalization* for finding equivalent fractions *Proof that value is not changed* (use manipulatives) Ability to change fractions to equivalents with common denominators |

(Continued)

| Content Branches | Suggested Grade-Level Timing* | | | Embedded Concepts | Performance Indicators/ Assessment Expectations |
|---|---|---|---|---|---|
| | A | B | C | | |

**Multiplicative Functions/Algebra**
*Language check: referent, multiple, increment, operator, factor, least common factor and least common multiple*

| | A | B | C | | |
|---|---|---|---|---|---|
| 92. Least common denominator: changing fractions with unequal denominators to equivalents with equal denominators | 5 | 6 | 7 | In order to perform operations on unlike fractions, we have to change them to equivalents with a common denominator. The least common denominator of a group of fractions is the least common multiple of all the denominators. We can find the least common denominator for groups of fractions by multiplying (or dividing) the numerator and the denominator of a fraction by the same number because this does not change its value. See Chapter 3 for suggestions for calculator use. | Ability to identify common denominators for fractions such as halves, fourths, eighths, thirds, sixths, tenths, and twelfths |
| 93. Addition and subtraction of unlike fractions with horizontal and vertical representation of fraction problems (without regrouping) | 5 | 6 | 7 | Unlike fractions cannot be added or subtracted until they are put into equivalent form with a common denominator. Once they have a common denominator, they can be added or subtracted by combining or finding the difference in the numerators. | Ability to add and subtract unlike fractions (as above) without regrouping |
| 94. Addition and subtraction of unlike fractions with regrouping from whole numbers | 5 | 6 | 7 | Regrouping from whole numbers to equivalent fractions allows us to solve some addition and subtraction fraction problems. | Ability to add and subtract unlike fractions (as above) with regrouping |
| 95. Multiplication of fractions by whole numbers | 4 | 5 | 6 | When a fraction is multiplied by a whole number, the fraction is repeatedly added or changed a whole number of times. The product is a fraction whose numerator is the product of the original (multiplicand) numerator and the whole number multiplier, and the denominator is the same as that of the repeated (multiplicand) fraction. | Ability to *analyze and* solve problems that require multiplication of fractions by whole numbers using conceptually repeated additions |

*NOTE: A = Exploration, B = Concept Mastery, C = Algorithmic or Procedural Mastery

## Multiplicative Functions/Algebra

*Language check: referent, multiple, increment, operator, factor, least common factor and least common multiple*

| | Content Branches | Suggested Grade-Level Timing* | | | Embedded Concepts | Performance Indicators/ Assessment Expectations |
|---|---|---|---|---|---|---|
| | Major/minor | A | B | C | | |
| 96. | Multiplication of whole numbers by unit fractions | 5 | 6 | 7 | When a whole number is multiplied by a fraction, it is the same as finding the fractional part of the whole number or set: 1/2 × 12 is the same as 1/2 of 12 because it means taking the whole only a half of a time. | Ability to *analyze and solve* problems that require the multiplication of whole numbers by unit fractions using conceptually partitioned repeated additions |
| 97. | Multiplication of whole numbers by more-than-unit fractions | 5 | 6 | 7 | 1/3 × 12 is equal to 4, but 2/3 × 12 is two times more than 4 and equal to 8. When you multiply by a more-than-unit fraction, you divide by the denominator and multiply by the numerator. | Ability to *analyze and solve* problems that require the multiplication of whole numbers by more-than-unit fractions; use of algorithm |
| 98. | Predicting products of fractional multiples of fractions | 5 | 6 | 7 | The product of a fraction multiplied by a fraction less than one whole is always less than the value. It is the same as finding the fractional part of the fraction: 1/2 times 1/4 = 1/8, or 1/2 of 1/4 is 1/8. | Ability to *predict* whether the product of a value and a fraction will be more or less than the value; *prove* this with fraction bars |
| 99. | Using number sense to compute fractional multiples of fractions | 5 | 6 | 7 | 1/2 of 2/3 is going to be 1/3;1/3 of 3/4 is 1/4; 1/2 × 1/40 is 1/80; 1/5 × 5/6 is 1/6; 1/2 of 2½ is 1¼. | Ability to mentally compute some obvious fractional multiples of fractions |
| 100. | Unit fractions of unit fractions | 5 | 6 | 7 | Finding a unit fractional part of a unit fraction value (or *multiplying the value by the fraction as above*) has the same effect as dividing the value by the denominator of the unit fractional part. It makes the value that much smaller: 1/4 of 1/5 is going to be four times smaller than 1/5; 1/5 will be divided into four smaller parts and each part will be only 1/20. You can see that the computed value has a denominator that is the product of the two denominators. | Ability to explain why multiplying a unit fraction by a unit fraction results in a product of smaller value; and why the product is a fraction with a denominator that is the product of the two denominators, and the numerator is equal to (1), which is the product of the two numerators of (1) |
| 101. | Unit fractions of more-than-unit fraction<br><br>Multiplication of fractions algorithm | 5 | 6 | 7 | 1/3 of 1/7 would be 1/21, but 1/3 of 2/7 is twice as much or 2/21. You can see that for this problem it was also necessary to multiply the numerators. A shortcut algorithm strategy is just to multiply the numerators and denominators. | Ability to explain algorithm and compute unit fractions of fractions (see Chapter 3) |

*NOTE: A = Exploration, B = Concept Mastery, C = Algorithmic or Procedural Mastery

*(Continued)*

(Continued)

| Content Branches | Suggested Grade-Level Timing* | | | Embedded Concepts | Performance Indicators/Assessment Expectations |
|---|---|---|---|---|---|
| Major/minor | A | B | C | | |

**Multiplicative Functions/Algebra**

*Language check: referent, multiple, increment, operator, factor, least common factor and least common multiple*

| Content Branches | A | B | C | Embedded Concepts | Performance Indicators/Assessment Expectations |
|---|---|---|---|---|---|
| 102. More-than-unit fractions of more-than-unit fractions | 6 | 7 | 8 | To find more than one unit fraction of a unit fraction, you can find the smaller unit fraction value by multiplying the denominators; then because it is more than one unit, multiply the numerators: 2/3 of 1/2 = 2/6 because 1/3 of 1/2 = 1/6 and 2/3 of 1/2 is twice as much as 1/3 of 1/2. For more-than-unit fractions of more-than-unit fractions, the shortcut algorithm is also to multiply numerators and denominators: 2/3 of 3/2 would be three times as much as 2/3 of 1/2 = 2/6. It equals 6/6 or one whole. The shortcut algorithm is to multiply numerators and denominators: 2/3 × 3/2 = 6/6. | Ability to explain and apply the multiplication of fractions algorithm; ability to *analyze fraction of fraction problems* |
| 103. Reducing fractions to lowest terms | 4 | 5 | 6 | In order to make our mathematical language and operations simpler we often change fractions to their equivalents with the smallest denominator. We know that dividing the numerator and denominator by the same value does not change the value, and so we try to find the largest value (factor) by which we can divide both numerator and denominator. | Correct computation of lowest term equivalents. *Note: Do not belabor this if it is not specifically required, but it may be helpful to note differences between invented strategies and algorithms; e.g., it is easy to understand that half of 2/3 is 1/3, but if you use the algorithm for 1/2 × 2/3, it makes sense to change your answer of 2/6 to 1/3* |
| 104. The division meaning of fractions (more conceptual review) | 5 | 6 | 7 | The fraction form also represents the division operation. One half is one whole divided by two, and 4/2 = 4 ÷ 2. We can express any division problem with a fraction or change a fraction into a division problem and get a quotient. Changing a fraction into the quotient it represents may help to make problems easier to solve. | Ability to translate division problems and statements to fraction form and find quotients for fractions; use of calculator to get decimal value of fractions |

*NOTE: A = Exploration, B = Concept Mastery, C = Algorithmic or Procedural Mastery

**Multiplicative Functions/Algebra**

*Language check: referent, multiple, increment, operator, factor, least common factor and least common multiple*

| Content Branches | Suggested Grade-Level Timing* | | | Embedded Concepts | Performance Indicators/ Assessment Expectations |
|---|---|---|---|---|---|
| Major/minor | A | B | C | | |
| 105. Division of whole numbers by unit fractions | 5 | 6 | 7 | Whole numbers can be divided by fractions if we think about how many fractions of the given size are in the given wholes. There will always be more than one common fraction part in even one whole because the fraction is less than the whole. The number of unit fraction parts in one whole is always equal to the denominator, and therefore the number of the unit fraction parts in more than one whole is equal to the denominator times the number of wholes. | Ability to demonstrate the division of a whole number by a unit fraction using fraction bars or other objects; ability to identify divisor and dividend from a division by fraction problem and tell what the quotient represents; ability to mentally compute exemplars of the process |
| 106. Division of whole numbers by more-than-unit fractions | 5 | 6 | 7 | In any whole there will be fewer more-than-unit fractions than there are unit fractions. If the fraction numerator is (2), then there will be half as many or the number of unit fractions divided by (2). To find a more-than-unit fraction of a number, we multiply the number by the denominator (to find the number of unit fractions) and divide the multiple by the numerator. | Ability to demonstrate the division of a fraction by a more-than-unit fraction using fraction bars or other objects; ability to identify divisor and dividend and mentally compute exemplars of the process Ability to use the division by fractions algorithm |

**Number System/Operations/Patterns: Decimals**

*Language check: tenths, hundredths, etc., decimal point*

| Content Branches | Suggested Grade-Level Timing* | | | Embedded Concepts | Performance Indicators/ Assessment Expectations |
|---|---|---|---|---|---|
| 107. Using decimals for money | 2 | 3 | 4 | Money is made up of dollars and cents. A dollar is equal to 100 cents. When we write the decimal symbols for cents, the cents come after the decimal point to show that the value is less than a dollar: 100 cents is always written as 1 dollar and zero (00) cents or $1.00. The dollar sign also is used. | Ability to transcribe word sentences to symbols for dollars and cents |

*NOTE: A = Exploration, B = Concept Mastery, C = Algorithmic or Procedural Mastery

(Continued)

**Number System/Operations/Patterns: Decimals**
*Language check: tenths, hundredths, etc., decimal point*

| Content Branches / Major/minor | A | B | C | Embedded Concepts | Performance Indicators/ Assessment Expectations |
|---|---|---|---|---|---|
| 108. Decimals as an alternate form of common fractions: <br> (a) tenths <br> (b) hundredths | <br><br>3<br>4 | <br><br>4<br>5 | <br><br>5<br>6 | The fractions 1/10 and 1/100 can be written as decimal fractions or parts less than one whole by placing a decimal point after the smallest whole numeral place (the ones place): 3.1 is 3 wholes and 1/10 of one whole. One hundredth is one tenth of one tenth, or one hundredth of a whole. 3.01 is 3 wholes and 1/100. The zero is used as a placeholder to tell .1 from .01. | Ability to symbolically rename tenths and hundredths in decimal form <br> Ability to compare relative decimal and whole numbers in inequalities e.g., <br> 2 > .2 <br> .2 > .02 |
| 109. Comparing and ordering decimals <br> (a) tenths <br> (b) hundredths | <br>3<br>4 | <br>4<br>5 | <br>5<br>6 | Decimals can be renamed. Fifteen hundredths is the same as one tenth and five hundredths. One tenth is the same as ten one hundredths, and is one hundredth more than nine one hundredths. | Ability to order tenths and hundredths |
| 110. Rounding decimals to whole numbers | 4 | 5 | 6 | Sometimes we need only whole numbers. Five tenths or more (1/2 or more) is usually rounded to the next whole number; less than .5 or 1/2 to the lower whole number. | Ability to round off to whole numbers from tenths |
| 111. Addition-subtraction: <br> Tenths, <br> Hundredths, <br> Thousandths | <br>3<br>4<br>5 | <br>4<br>5<br>6 | <br>5<br>6<br>7 | Decimals can be added and subtracted like whole numbers, but like denominations must be added or regrouping must be done; e.g., five tenths can be subtracted from one whole if the whole is regrouped for ten tenths. <br> Ten hundredths = 1 tenth <br> Ten thousandths = 1 hundredth <br> Thousandths are one tenth as large as the same number hundredths. | Ability to estimate and add and/or subtract decimals to tenths, hundredths; ability to rename ones, tens, and hundredths as thousandths (decimal and common fraction) |
| 112. Place value system connections: Right and left shift for multiplication and division by whole multiples of ten | 4 | 5 | 6 | Each digit in a decimal place is ten times larger than the same digit in a place on its right and ten times smaller than one on its left. To make a decimal value ten times larger, shift it one place to the left; to make it ten times smaller (divide it by ten), shift it to the right. | Ability to multiply and divide any decimal number by 10 or 100 mentally by shifting place (Note: students may also choose the alternative of moving the decimal point, but only after understanding the connections to place value) |
| 113. Decimal parts of an area | 4 | 5 | 6 | Parts of a whole or area can be renamed as decimal parts. | Ability to describe parts of an area in decimal terms |

*NOTE: A = Exploration, B = Concept Mastery, C = Algorithmic or Procedural Mastery

## Number System/Operations/Patterns: Decimals
*Language check: tenths, hundredths, etc., decimal point*

| Content Branches / Major/minor | Suggested Grade-Level Timing* A | B | C | Embedded Concepts | Performance Indicators/ Assessment Expectations |
|---|---|---|---|---|---|
| 114. Multiplication of decimals: concept ideas whole numbers by tenths | 5 | 6 | 7 | Multiplying by a decimal is like multiplying by a fraction. The product of any number multiplied by a decimal is going to have a lesser value than the original number. Multiplying a whole number by 1/10 or .1 results in the same value as dividing it by ten. Multiplying it by .2 is like multiplying it by 2/10; you multiply by 2 and divide by 10; .5 times a number is the same as 5/10 or 1/2 times the number. | Ability to estimate multiplication of whole numbers by decimals; ability to compute products |
| 115. Multiplication of decimals without regrouping | 5 | 6 | 7 | One tenth × one tenth equals one hundredth; (.1 × .1 = .01) because 1/10 of 1/10 is 1/100. Tenths times units = tenths; tenths times tenths = hundredths; hundredths times tenths = thousandths; .06 × .3 = .018. | Explanation for generalizations for products of multiplication of decimals by decimals |
| 116. Multiplication by two-place decimals with regrouping Multiplication algorithm | 5 | 6 | 7 | Decimals can be multiplied using an algorithm based on the distributive principal like the one for whole numbers. When combining the partial products, like denominations can be added (regrouping may need to come first). | Correct computation using algorithm; analysis and solution of problems Correct placement of decimal points |
| 117. Percentage | 5 | 6 | 7 | A common use of decimal fractions is percentage. Parts of a whole value are expressed in hundredths. Percentage means parts of one hundred: 25% is the same as 25/100 or 1/4. If the percentage is less than 100%, the value will be less than the whole value; 100% of a value is the same as the whole, more than 100% of a value is more than the whole value. | Ability to change percentages to decimals and common fractions; ability to estimate percentages of whole values, especially when more or less than the original value |
| 118. Finding percentages: Ten percent and one percent; other percentages | 5  6 | 6  7 | 7  8 | We can find ten percent or 10/100 or 1/10 of a value by shifting the whole value to the next smaller place. One percent of a number is the whole value shifted two places to the right (or move the decimal point to the left to accomplish the same thing). Even multiples of 10% or 1% can also be mentally computed. For other percentages, change the percentage to a decimal and multiply the whole number by it. | Ability to mentally compute 10% and 1% of a number; ability to mentally compute 20% and 2% of a number and make other percentage estimates; ability to compute exact percentage of a number by changing to a decimal and multiplying |

| Content Branches | Suggested Grade-Level Timing* A | B | C | Embedded Concepts | Performance Indicators/ Assessment Expectations |
|---|---|---|---|---|---|
| Major/minor | A | B | C | | |

**Number System/Operations/Patterns: Decimals**
*Language check: tenths, hundredths, etc., decimal point*

| | A | B | C | Embedded Concepts | Performance Indicators/ Assessment Expectations |
|---|---|---|---|---|---|
| 119. Division of decimals by whole Multiples of 10 Estimating quotient size | 5 | 6 | 7 | For exact division of decimals by whole numbers 10, 100, 1000 you can use a right place position shift. We get quotients more than one whole when we divide a whole number or a decimal fraction by a smaller valued decimal or fraction. We get quotients less than one whole when we divide a whole number or a decimal number by a value that is larger (e.g., 2.5 ÷ 1.2 is going to be more than one whole or about 2, but the quotient for 1.8 ÷ 2.0 is less than one whole or .9). | Ability to divide or shrink decimals by multiples of ten using a right shift of place position; ability to conceptually estimate quotients for problems with one digit decimal divisors; ability to *predict whether answers will be more or less than one* |
| 120. Division of decimals by whole numbers: Exchanging decimals for their smaller size equivalents so that division is easier | 5 | 6 | 7 | We can regroup decimal dividends into their smaller size equivalents so that division is easier. Then we can use the whole number division algorithm form to find the quotient. | Ability to use the division algorithm for division of decimals by whole numbers Ability to explain the regrouping process involved in the above |
| 121. Conversion of common fractions into decimals by dividing numerator by denominator | 5 | 6 | 7 | Any fraction can be converted to its decimal form through the process of dividing numerator by denominator: 24/6 is the same as 24 wholes ÷ 6, or equal to 4. When we convert a common fraction like 5/6 to decimals, we use the division algorithm and regroup or trade indivisible digits and remainders for their smaller sized decimal equivalents. We can also use our calculators. | Ability to use the division algorithm for finding the decimal equivalent of improper and proper fractions Ability to relate the conversion of fractions to decimals to the division meaning of fractions and explain the regrouping process involved |

**Measurement/Patterns/Operations**
*Language check: same as, more, less, shorter than, longer than, heavier than, wider than, holds more than, object/property/attribute, unit, standard/nonstandard, customary, metric, square unit, mass/weight*

| | A | B | C | Embedded Concepts | Performance Indicators/ Assessment Expectations |
|---|---|---|---|---|---|
| 122. Vocabulary of measure equalities | K–2 | 3–4 | 5 | Different words help us describe and compare objects so that we can communicate about them. These are measures. | Ability to match descriptive measure words and real objects or pictures |

*NOTE: A = Exploration, B = Concept Mastery, C = Algorithmic or Procedural Mastery

| Content Branches | Suggested Grade-Level Timing* | | | Embedded Concepts | Performance Indicators/ Assessment Expectations |
|---|---|---|---|---|---|
| | A | B | C | | |

**Measurement/Patterns/Operations**

*Language check: same as, more, less, shorter than, longer than, heavier than, wider than, holds more than, object/property/attribute, unit, standard/nonstandard, customary, metric, square unit, mass/weight*

| Content Branches | A | B | C | Embedded Concepts | Performance Indicators/ Assessment Expectations |
|---|---|---|---|---|---|
| Major/minor | | | | | |
| 123. Nonstandard units of measures as equalities | K | 1 | 2 | We can use things we know to help us measure things we don't know the size of. We know how big a block is, and we can measure our desks with blocks. | Ability to estimate and make measurements expressed in nonstandard units as equalities |
| Estimating and measuring in nonstandard units | 1 | 2 | 3 | We must be careful not to leave spaces. We can compare measures of length and weight to show which is the larger or smaller measure using words and symbols (< and >). | As above with increased precision for length and expression in words as inequalities; e.g., The desk is more than five hands long |

**Length: Area, Perimeter**

*Language check: inch, foot, yard, centimeter, meter, millimeter*

| Content Branches | A | B | C | Embedded Concepts | Performance Indicators/ Assessment Expectations |
|---|---|---|---|---|---|
| 124. Estimating, measuring in: whole feet, inches, yards, whole cm, whole meters, millimeters; rounding to the nearest unit | 1<br>2<br>1<br>2<br>3<br>3 | 2<br>3<br>2<br>3<br>4<br>4 | 3<br>4<br>3<br>3<br>5<br>5 | The centimeter and the inch are standard measures. Standard measures are useful because everyone's hand or foot is different. Governments decide standards. Items measured with these units will always be the same measured length and understood by others. The standards have special names and abbreviations. If an object does not have an exact measure, we can round it to the nearest smaller or larger unit, depending upon whether it is more or less than half of the larger one. | Ability to estimate the size of common objects using metric and customary standards alternately; ability to measure using these units; ability to round off to the nearest whole unit; ability to record measures using appropriate units and abbreviations |
| 125. Standard equivalents: American | 2 | 3 | 4 | Standard units can be combined into larger units. The equivalents are also standards. Larger units are better for measuring larger objects or spaces. The larger the unit size, the fewer the number of units. For example: 1 foot = 12 inches, 3 feet = 1 yard, 100 cm = 1 m, 1 cm = 10 mm, 5680 ft. = 1 mile. To convert measurements from the smaller size unit to the larger you divide by the standard equivalent; to convert from the larger size unit to the smaller you multiply by the equivalent. | Ability to describe standard equivalents in same system from larger to smaller and vice versa; ability to justify use of larger or smaller unit; ability to connect measures to real-life applications |
| Metric | 3 | 4 | 5 | | |

NOTE: A = Exploration, B = concept Mastery, C = Algorithmaic or Procdeural Mastery

*(Continued)*

## Length: Area, Perimeter
*Language check: inch, foot, yard, centimeter, meter, millimeter*

| Content Branches Major/minor | Suggested Grade-Level Timing* | | | Embedded Concepts | Performance Indicators/ Assessment Expectations |
|---|---|---|---|---|---|
| | A | B | C | | |
| 126. Equivalent measures: feet, yards, miles; m, cm, km | 2 3 | 3 4 | 4 5 | Metric conversions can be made by multiplying or dividing by multiples of ten. Remainders are the smaller unit. | Ability to *explain* conversion *generalization*; ability to convert metric and customary measurements from smaller to larger and larger to smaller units: m, cm, km, mm; in., ft., yd. |
| 127. Equivalent measures: across common system conversions | 3 | 4 | 5 | A meter is a little more than three feet. There are about 2½ cm in an inch, and a little more than 2 km in a mile. | Ability to estimate metric and customary equivalents |
| 128. Estimating and measuring perimeter in inches and centimeters: square, rectangle, triangle, pentagon, hexagon | 2 3 | 3 4 | 4 5 | The perimeter of an object is the distance around its edges. Distance tells how far you must go to walk around the edge. We add all the separate measures to find the total. | Ability to estimate and solve real-life word problems (e.g., fencing) and diagrams for perimeter (use geoboards) |
| 129. Estimating and measuring area (square and rectangle) | 3 | 4 | 5 | Area is the amount of space on a flat surface as measured by square units (or the amount of square units needed to cover it). Multiplication is a shortcut for adding repeated similar groups of square units (use geoboards and centimeter graph paper). | Ability to define a square unit and to use a grid to measure area; ability to write multiplication sentences for repeated similar groups |
| 130. Area of a right triangle | 5 | 6 | 7 | Not all areas have repeated similar groups of units, but we can use our geometric knowledge to help us measure these areas. The area of a right triangle is half the area of a rectangle that can be formed by putting together two identical right triangles. | Ability to describe how the area of the right triangle is half the area of the rectangle formed; ability to compute area of given right triangle |

*NOTE: A = Exploration, B = Concept Mastery, C = Algorithmic or Procedural Mastery

| Content Branches | Suggested Grade-Level Timing* | | | Embedded Concepts | Performance Indicators/ Assessment Expectations |
|---|---|---|---|---|---|
| | A | B | C | | |
| Major/minor | | | | | |

**Mass/Weight** Note: Use the term "weight" until Grade 3 or 4; then begin to use the term "mass" as an alternate with the understanding that weight depends on gravity but mass is independent (our weights are different on the moon and Mars, but our masses are the same).
*Language check: ounce, pound, ton, gram, kg, mass, weight, balance*

| Content Branches | A | B | C | Embedded Concepts | Performance Indicators/ Assessment Expectations |
|---|---|---|---|---|---|
| 131. Finding mass in nonstandard units | 2 | 3 | 4 | We use what we know (coins, washers, cubes) to weigh and compare what we do not know. Balances help us measure weight. Equal weights balance. | Ability to use balance to measure unknowns in nonstandard units |
| 132. Ordering of mass in nonstandard units | 2 | 3 | 4 | The larger the mass (weight) of an object, the greater the number of nonstandard units. | Ability to estimate and order mass quantities when compared to nonstandard units |
| 133. Customary standards of weight Measuring mass in ounces and pounds; grams and kilograms | 3 | 4 | 5 | The mass of an object can be determined by comparing it to standard units. The standards of measure for mass (use "weight" until Grade 4) are the pound (lb.) and kilogram (kg). | Ability to estimate and order measured masses; prove measures with the balance |
| 134. Reading scales and balances | 3 | 4 | 5 | A bathroom or butcher's scale uses a spring instead of balancing unknown weights with known standard weights like the balance. The standard for the spring scale is in the give of the spring; heavier weights pull the spring more (use spring scales). | Ability to predict relative give of spring for different standard weights; accurate use of the balance and spring scale |
| 135. Comparing mass of familiar objects to standards: 1 kg, 1 lb. | 2 | 3 | 4 | The standards of measure for mass (use "weight" until Grade 4) are the pound (lb.) or kilogram (kg). A pound is about the weight of a large bag of M&M's. A kilogram is a little more than the weight of two bags. | Ability to name standard and its abbreviation, estimate weight based on pound or kilogram standard; compare pound and kilogram as an inequality |
| 136. Equivalent standards | 4 | 5 | 6 | Standard units can be combined into larger units. The equivalent heavier units are better for measuring heavier objects. The larger the unit size, the fewer the number of units. For example: 1 lb. = 16 oz., 1 ton = 2000 lbs., 1 kg = 1000 gm | Ability to explain conversion generalization; ability to describe metric and customary standards for units and to change from smaller to larger and larger to smaller units |

*NOTE: A = Exploration, B = Concept Mastery, C = Algorithmic or Procedural Mastery

*(Continued)*

(Continued)

| Content Branches | Suggested Grade-Level Timing* | | | Embedded Concepts | Performance Indicators/ Assessment Expectations |
|---|---|---|---|---|---|
| Major/minor | A | B | C | | |
| **Mass/Weight** Note: Use the term "weight" until Grade 3 or 4; then begin to use the term "mass" as an alternate with the understanding that weight depends on gravity but mass is independent (our weights are different on the moon and Mars, but our masses are the same). _Language check: ounce, pound, ton, gram, kg, mass, weight, balance_ | | | | | |
| 137. Equivalent standard conversions:<br>oz. ↔ lbs. ↔ tons<br>kg ↔ gm ↔ mg | 6 | 7 | 8 | To convert from the smaller size unit to the larger you divide by the standard, and to convert from the larger size unit to the smaller you multiply. The larger the unit size, the fewer the number of units. We can use function equations: (oz.) = 16 × (lbs.), (lbs.) = (oz.) ÷ 16. For metrics, conversions can be made by multiplying or dividing by multiples of ten: (# of gms) = 1000 (# of kgs),(# of kgs) = (# of gms) ÷ 1000. | Ability to make exact correct equivalent conversions from grams to kilograms or ounces to pounds using equations and to solve problems that require it |
| 138. Conversions between different standard systems | 6 | 7 | 8 | A kg is a little more than 2.2 lbs. | Correct estimations from metric to English (customary) standards and exact across standard system conversions with a calculator |
| **Capacity/Volume** *Capacity is usually applied to liquids and small-particle solids because they fill their containers. Volume is applied to rigid objects that do not fill containers. _Language check: pint, quart, cup, gallon, liter, milliliter, standard measure_ | | | | | |
| 139. Conservation of capacity | K | 1 | 2 | The shape of a container does not determine its capacity. Equal amounts of liquid can look different in different containers, but there is no loss of quantity when containers are changed. | Ability to correctly judge Piagetian conservation tasks |
| 140. Estimating and comparing (capacity) | 1 | 2 | 3 | Different sized containers have different capacities. A full container of liquid will not fill a larger container. | Estimation of capacity; ability to predict whether or not a container will be filled. Capacity expressed as equalities and inequalities |
| 141. Standard units of cups, pints, quarts<br>Liters | 2<br>4 | 3<br>5 | 4<br>6 | Standards of capacity help us measure more exactly. We measure liquids by pouring the liquid into the standard. | Estimation of capacity; ability to measure by pouring liquid into standard and recording |

*NOTE: A = Exploration, B = Concept Mastery, C = Algorithmic or Procedural Mastery

| Content Branches | Suggested Grade-Level Timing* | | | Embedded Concepts | Performance Indicators/ Assessment Expectations |
|---|---|---|---|---|---|
| Major/minor | A | B | C | | |

**Capacity/Volume** *Capacity is usually applied to liquids and small-particle solids because they fill their containers. Volume is applied to rigid objects that do not fill containers.
*Language check: pint, quart, cup, gallon, liter, milliliter, standard measure*

| Content Branches | A | B | C | Embedded Concepts | Performance Indicators/ Assessment Expectations |
|---|---|---|---|---|---|
| 142. Equivalent conversions: cups, pints, quarts, gallons | 3 | 4 | 5 | Equations describe conversions: 1 cup = 16 fluid ounces, 2 cups = 1 pint, 4 quarts = 1 gallon, 2 pints = 1 qt. = 4 half pints, 2 quarts = 1 half gallon. 1 liter = 1000 ml. | Correct solutions to problems that require equivalent conversions within standard systems |
| Above for ml, liters | 4 | 5 | 6 | | |
| 143. Conversions across standard systems | 4 | 5 | 6 | A quart is just a little less than a liter. A half-gallon or 2-quart milk container is slightly less than a 2-liter soda bottle. Estimate only for across-standards conversions or use a calculator. | Ability to solve problems that require across-standard system conversions; ability to estimate common conversions including quart to liter and liter to gallon (use calculator for exact conversions) |
| 144. Estimating volume; counting cubes to find volume (nonstandard units) | 3 | 4 | 5 | Volume is the amount of space taken up by solid (3-D) objects. We measure volume by adding up cubes as units. Structures of varying volumes can be built on the same area. The metric standard unit of volume is the cubic centimeter. The customary standards would be cubic inches, etc. | Ability to make estimates of volume in nonstandard units; measurements using cubes |
| 145. Computing volume | 4 | 5 | 6 | The volume of an object is the product of its three dimensions: length, width, and depth. Area is measured in square units (multiples of the product of length times width) on a 2-dimensional surface. Three-dimensional volume is measured in cubic units (multiples of the product of length × width × depth). | As above, using standard metric units and useful customary ones such as the cubic foot for the size of a box (see section on geometry for more complex computations) |

**Money**

| Content Branches | A | B | C | Embedded Concepts | Performance Indicators/ Assessment Expectations |
|---|---|---|---|---|---|
| 146. Vocabulary of coins, bills; American money | K | K | 1 | Different coins represent different amounts of money. Different countries use different money standards; connect to exchange values and new Euro. | Correct identification of coins; explanation of exchange value |
| Foreign money examples/dollar value | 6 | 7 | 8 | | |

*NOTE: A = Exploration, B = Concept Mastery, C = Algorithmic or Procedural Mastery

(Continued)

| Content Branches Major/minor | Suggested Grade-Level Timing* | | | Embedded Concepts | Performance Indicators/ Assessment Expectations |
| --- | --- | --- | --- | --- | --- |
| | A | B | C | | |
| **Money** | | | | | |
| 147. Estimating and counting (in line with number sequence) | 1 | 2 | 3 | Each dime counts as ten pennies, each nickel is five pennies, etc. (Grade 1); quarters and half dollars (Grade 2) | Ability to total real and pictured coins |
| 148. Place value connections: (a) whole dollars (b) dollars and cents | 1–2 2–3 | 2–3 3–4 | 4 5–6 | Dollars come in units and multiples like our number system. See decimals for place value connections. Cents are parts of dollars. One hundred cents = 1 dollar. | Ability to rename dollar multiples from word problems |
| 149. Making change | 1 | 2–3 | 4 | We make change by counting up from cost to given quantity or down (whichever is easier). We start with the coin that brings us to multiples of the next largest coin or dollar. There is more than one way to give exact change. | Ability to estimate change; ability to give change by counting up or down without subtraction algorithm; pennies or nickels to nearest dime (Grade 1); pennies and/or nickels and/or dimes to nearest quarter, to nearest dollar (Grade 2+) |
| 150. Operations adding/ subtracting with money | 1 | 2–3 | 4 | Money can be added most easily by renaming or regrouping cents up to larger units if addends total ten. Money can be subtracted by renaming or regrouping dollars or larger coins to pennies (hundredths of a dollar). | Ability to estimate totals, form properly placed algorithms from money word problems, and solve them with and without calculators |
| **Time** *Language check: rotary, digital, A.M., P.M.* | | | | | |
| 151. Comparative time only, telling time | K | K | 2 | Words such as "longer," "less," "more," and "as much as" can be used to compare time. Hours and minutes are amounts of time. Clocks help us keep track of time in hours and minutes. They move with time! Larger amounts of time are days, weeks, months, and years. | Ability to recognize whole hours on the rotary clock and the digital clock; ability to relate specific times such as morning, noon, afternoon, and evening to activities and absence or presence of daylight |

*NOTE: A = Exploration, B = Concept Mastery, C = Algorithmic or Procedural Mastery

**Money**

| Content Branches | Suggested Grade-Level Timing* A | B | C | Embedded Concepts | Performance Indicators/ Assessment Expectations |
|---|---|---|---|---|---|
| Major/minor | | | | | |
| 152. Telling time: Whole hour | 1 | 1 | 2 | Time measures are related to how long it takes for the earth to turn completely around, toward and away from the sun (earth rotation). There are twenty-four whole hours in the day, twelve before and twelve after noon. The digital clock shows us the hour first and then minutes. The rotary clock shows us each whole passed hour by pointing to the number with its smaller hand. The larger hand shows minutes (see Chapter 3 for details). | Ability to tell whole hour time from digital and rotary clocks |
| 153. Telling time: Beginning, end, noon; A.M./P.M. | 2 | 3 | 4 | The day begins at midnight. It is divided into twenty-four hour parts; twelve before noon (A.M.) and twelve after noon (P.M.). Noon is when the sun is highest in the sky (or at the meridian). Morning is before noon, and afternoon is after it (A.M. stands for ante meridiem and P.M. for post meridiem). | Ability to estimate and describe comparative amounts of elapsed time; ability to relate specific hours (e.g., 9:00 A.M.) to the position of the sun, and the terms *morning*, *afternoon*, *midnight*, and *noon* |
| 154. Telling time: Half hours Quarter hours Minutes | 1 1 2 | 1 2 2 | 1 2 2 | Each whole hour can be divided into two parts (halves or 1/2), four quarter parts (1/4 hours), or 60 minute parts. There are four quarter hours in a whole hour. Half an hour is the same as two quarters, or thirty minutes (half of 60 minutes). We tell the time by naming the hour and the fractional part after it in halves or quarters or in minutes. | Ability to *explain* the rotary clock in terms of its fractional parts; ability to rename half hours and quarter hours as minutes; ability to read digital and rotary clock time to the exact minute |
| 155. Time variations | 4 | 5 | 6 | Because the earth rotates, the time of day is different at different places on the earth. When it is midnight at one point on earth, the place on the completely opposite side, or 180 degrees of longitude away, is at noon. | Ability to *explain* the variations in time around the world; ability to explain why there are changes in standard time as the earth rotates |

*NOTE: A = Exploration, B = Concept Mastery, C = Algorithmic or Procedural Mastery

*(Continued)*

(Continued)

| Content Branches | Suggested Grade-Level Timing* | | | Embedded Concepts | Performance Indicators/ Assessment Expectations |
|---|---|---|---|---|---|
| Major/minor | A | B | C | | |
| **Time** | | | | | |
| | | | | The earth rotates toward the east, so we lose time when we travel to the east faster than the earth moves. The time in the east is ahead of us. The west is behind us. Because the earth is tilted on its axis, the number of hours of daylight changes with the seasons. We, therefore, change the clocks during the year in order to start the day an hour earlier in the spring when the sun rises earlier. In the fall, when the sun rises later, we move the time an hour back to where it was. | |
| 156. Calculating elapsed time in hours, but not passing 12 | 2 | 3 | 4 | When the clock has moved from 1 to 3, there is a difference of two hours; it is two hours later. | Ability to calculate elapsed time (not passing 12) and solve word problems |
| Calculating elapsed time in hours, passing 12 | 3 | 4 | 5 | To find the elapsed time passing 12 you must find two differences, before the twelve and after it, then add them together. When the clock has moved from 11 to 3 there is a difference of four hours; one hour before noon and three hours from noon to 3. | Ability to solve *and pose* problems that require calculation of elapsed time from clock diagrams, and then from digital readings |
| 157. Calculating elapsed time in minutes | 2 | 3 | 4 | To calculate the difference when you pass the hour you must find two differences, before the hour and after it, and then add them together. | As above, but passing the hour; then passing 12 |
| 158. Calendar: days in the week in sequence months | K | 1 | 2 | There are seven days in the week (*they are.*). There are twelve months in the year (*they are.*). There are 365 days in most years. Calendars help us keep track of larger amounts of time. | Ability to recall number and name of days of week and months of the year; identify present, previous, and next day of week and month; connect to events |
| 159. Calendar: time of the year | 1 | 1 | 2 | Days of the month and year are shown on a calendar that also shows the weeks. Different days are related to different activities. | Ability to identify day, month, year on calendar, recall months and *connect* to seasons, other events |

*NOTE: A = Exploration, B = Concept Mastery, C = Algorithmic or Procedural Mastery

| Content Branches | Suggested Grade-Level Timing* | | | Embedded Concepts | Performance Indicators/ Assessment Expectations |
|---|---|---|---|---|---|
| Major/minor | A | B | C | | |
| **Time** | | | | | |
| 160. Variations in calendar; days of month, year | 2 | 3–4 | 5 | Different months have different numbers of days. Each year the days of the year may happen on different days of the week. Leap year has one more day in the year. | Ability to recall number of days in each month |
| 161. Calculating elapsed time in weeks, months | 3 | 4 | 5 | One week from Thursday is the following Thursday. If the 23rd is on Thursday, then the 30th is on Thursday. | Ability to identify one week before or after on the calendar; ability to predict day of the week given two dates seven days apart—but only in the same month |
| 162. Determining days and dates of the week | 3 | 4 | 5 | Monday is two days before Wednesday and three days after Friday, etc. (let them use their fingers if they wish). | Ability to mentally calculate day of week given two dates up to seven days apart and day of the week for one date (e.g., If the 23rd is on Tuesday, on what day is the 26th? If the 26th was on Friday, what day of the week was the 23rd?) |

**Temperature**
*Language check: degree, temperature, thermometer, Fahrenheit, Celsius*

| Content Branches | A | B | C | Embedded Concepts | Performance Indicators/ Assessment Expectations |
|---|---|---|---|---|---|
| 163. Comparative temperature only | K | 1 | 2 | Temperature tells us how warm or cold something is. | Ability to compare perceived or felt temperature to room temperature |
| 164. Fahrenheit reading Celsius reading (whole degree) | 2 3 | 3 4 | 4 5 | A standard unit of measure for temperature is the degree. The warmer it is, the higher the temperature. Water freezes at 32°F (0°C) and boils at 212°F (100°C). Room temperature is about 70°F (21°C). | Ability to read and record temperature from a thermometer to the nearest degree; estimate colder or warmer than room temperature from reading; compute changes |

*NOTE: A = Exploration, B = Concept Mastery, C = Algorithmic or Procedural Mastery

(Continued)

(Continued)

| Content Branches | Suggested Grade-Level Timing* | | | Embedded Concepts | Performance Indicators/ Assessment Expectations |
|---|---|---|---|---|---|
| | A | B | C | | |
| Major/minor | | | | | |

**Geometry: Visualizing Shapes and Patterns, Models**
*Language check: horizontal, vertical, perpendicular, polygon (and derivatives such as hexagon), symmetry, bilateral, radial, transform, flip, rotation, slide, congruent, plane, angle, vertex, circumference, radius, diameter*

| Content Branches | A | B | C | Embedded Concepts | Performance Indicators/ Assessment Expectations |
|---|---|---|---|---|---|
| 165. Comparing and naming two-dimensional shapes (areas on a surface): Square, circle; Triangle; Rectangle; Pentagon, hexagon; Quadrilateral | K 1 3 4 5 | K 2 4 5 6 | 1 3 5 6 7 | Shapes or forms on flat surfaces like paper have different properties. Most of the shapes have straight (flat) sides and corners, but the circle and oval do not have any corners and no straight (flat) sides. Different shapes have different numbers of sides and corners and form different patterns. There are many different shapes and combinations of shapes in the environment. The names of shapes are derived from their properties. Familiar items are named after their shapes (e.g., the Pentagon, a traffic circle). | Identification of shapes on paper and in the environment, at appropriate level; ability to count sides and corners, find patterns, reproduce shapes; ability to explain prefix-suffix meanings: e.g., polygon, hexagon |
| 166. Definition of a circle | 3 | 4 | 5 | All the points on the curved line that forms a circle are the same distance from the center of the circle. | Ability to identify and describe a circle |
| 167. Making patterns, designs | K | 1 | 2 | Repeating similar shapes creates a pattern. | Construction and identification of repeat unit in a pattern |
| 168. Naming and comparing shapes of solid forms (3-D objects) that take up space | 1 | 2 | 3 | Solid forms are three-dimensional (3-D) objects that take up space. Solid forms have faces, edges, and corners. Different forms have different numbers of sides (edges) faces, and corners. The size of the edges of a solid form may be the same as or different from each other. The number of faces and number of corners form patterns. | Identification of solid forms: cube, cylinder, sphere, prism, cone; counting faces, edges, corners; comparing shapes, finding patterns |
| 169. Bilateral (mirror) symmetry | 1–2 | 3 | 4 | The same pattern in reverse on either side of a line creates mirror symmetry (use a Mira here). Mirror symmetry can be created by reflecting across an imaginary line. We can find these patterns in the environment. | Identification of mirror symmetry; identification of mirror symmetry with a string and in environment; *proof* with a Mira |

*NOTE: A = Exploration, B = Concept Mastery, C = Algorithmic or Procedural Mastery

**Geometry: Visualizing Shapes and Patterns, Models**

*Language check: horizontal, vertical, perpendicular, polygon (and derivatives such as hexagon), symmetry, bilateral, radial, transform, flip, rotation, slide, congruent, plane, angle, vertex, circumference, radius, diameter*

| | Content Branches | Suggested Grade-Level Timing* | | | Embedded Concepts | Performance Indicators/ Assessment Expectations |
|---|---|---|---|---|---|---|
| | Major/minor | A | B | C | | |
| 170. | Drawing symmetrical shapes and relating them to design | 1–2 | 3 | 4–5 | Patterns with mirror symmetry (reflections) can be created with a flip from right to left or top to bottom across a line (use drawings and software applications for practice). | Creation of patterns with mirror symmetry; connections of symmetry to design elements in art projects |
| 171. | Radial symmetry | 3 | 4 | 5 | If you can rotate a form in any way and it still is the same, it has radial symmetry. | Identification of radial symmetry; construction of forms with radial symmetry |
| 172. | Transformations | 5 | 6 | 7 | When you flip or rotate a figure or move it to the side (slip or slide it), it has been transformed in its position on a plane, but the original figure and the one you transformed have the same dimensions and attributes. Transformed figures with the same dimensions are called congruent. Use computer software for this. | Ability to draw transformed figures and identify congruent triangles and parallelograms; solution of problems that require reference to congruent objects; *proof* of congruence using computer-based transformations or cutouts |
| 173. | Symmetry in number tables—triangular and square numbers | 4 | 5 | 6 | Number tables or objects can be constructed with symmetry and/or in shapes (e.g., triangular numbers, 3, 6, 10; or square numbers, 1, 4, 9, 16, 25). | Ability to recognize symmetry in a table, or construct an object triangle from triangular numbers |
| 174. | Definitions: point, line, horizontal, vertical, perpendicular | 4 | 5 | 6 | A *point* is a particular location in space. A *line* is a set of points. Horizontal lines are like the horizon; they go from left to right or right to left. Vertical lines go up and down from the horizon. When two lines meet and form a right angle (see below), we say the lines are *perpendicular*. A *straight line* goes infinitely (endlessly) in only two opposite (mirror image) directions and can be determined by any two points. | Ability to define and construct horizontal, vertical, and perpendicular lines; ability to identify them in the environment and make *connections* to architecture |
| 175. | Definitions: line segment, ray | 5 | 6 | 7 | A *line segment* is part of a line between two particular points. It includes all the points in between the two particular ones. A *ray* is the part of the line that goes in one direction from one point on the line. | Ability to define and construct line segments, rays |

*NOTE: A = Exploration, B = Concept Mastery, C = Algorithmic or Procedural Mastery

(Continued)

(Continued)

**54**

## Geometry: Visualizing Shapes and Patterns, Models

*Language check: horizontal, vertical, perpendicular, polygon (and derivatives such as hexagon), symmetry, bilateral, radial, transform, flip, rotation, slide, congruent, plane, angle, vertex, circumference, radius, diameter*

| Content Branches | Suggested Grade-Level Timing* | | | Embedded Concepts | Performance Indicators/ Assessment Expectations |
|---|---|---|---|---|---|
| Major/minor | A | B | C | | |
| 176. Definitions: planes | 5 | 6 | 7 | A *plane* is a surface determined by three points on that surface that are not on the same straight line. A line between any two points on the determined plane will be on that surface. A tabletop is often thought of as a plane surface, but the plane on which it lies goes on infinitely. The legs of the table are on different planes. | Ability to determine whether a surface is a single plane; identification of different planes in three-dimensional objects |
| 177. Parallel lines Parallelogram | 5 | 6 | 7 | *Parallel* lines are two separate straight lines that go in the same direction in the same plane and never cross. The *parallelogram* has opposite sides that are parallel. | Construction and identification of parallel lines, parallelograms |
| 178. Definitions: angles | 3 | 4 | 5 | When two (rays) come from the same end point, they form an angle. The point where they meet is called the vertex. The rays are the sides of the angle. The larger the opening between the rays, the larger the angle. At the same distance from their endpoints, larger angles will have a greater difference between the rays than smaller angles. The size of the angle determines the direction from the endpoint. | Ability to demonstrate and explain variations in angle size and relate them to differences in direction from an endpoint; ability to draw and compare smaller and larger angles using a straight edge |
| 179. Measuring circles and angles | 5 | 6 | 7 | Measures of angles and circles are related because if you keep increasing the size of an angle by rotating one ray until you are back to where you started, you have rotated all the way around and every point on the ray has described a circle. The standard is to divide the circle into 360 degree units and a symbol (°) is used. A half circle (semicircle) is 180°. A quarter circle is 90°. | Ability to make the *connections* between angles and circles by drawing and explaining; ability to identify degrees in full circle, semicircle, quarter circle; ability to *connect* the structure circles to their radial symmetry and make transformations of semicircles |

*NOTE: A = Exploration, B = Concept Mastery, C = Algorithmic or Procedural Mastery

| Content Branches | Suggested Grade-Level Timing* | | | Embedded Concepts | Performance Indicators/ Assessment Expectations |
|---|---|---|---|---|---|
| | A | B | C | | |
| Major/minor | | | | | |

**Geometry: Visualizing Shapes and Patterns, Models**

*Language check: horizontal, vertical, perpendicular, polygon (and derivatives such as hexagon), symmetry, bilateral, radial, transform, flip, rotation, slide, congruent, plane, angle, vertex, circumference, radius, diameter*

| Content Branches | A | B | C | Embedded Concepts | Performance Indicators/ Assessment Expectations |
|---|---|---|---|---|---|
| 180. Measuring angles | 5 | 6 | 7 | We measure angles or the opening between the rays in degrees. The higher the number of degrees, the greater the difference between the lines (rays). The measure of an angle is the same as the part of the circle it has described. If you rotate a duplicate of a ray halfway around to form a semicircle, the duplicate ray and the original form a straight ray or straight angle of 180°. The total distance rotated is 180 degrees. | Demonstration of angle formation by physical rotation of two straight edges; ability to compare relative size of angles |
| 181. Special angles; measuring angles with protractors | 5 | 6 | 7 | A straight line or straight angle of 180° has two rays going in opposite directions from one point. If we rotate one ray of the straight angle half of the way to 180°, the two rays are perpendicular and form a 90° angle. A 90° angle is also called a right angle. | Ability to use a protractor to draw exact angles; ability to measure angles with a protractor Ability to identify right angles; ability to make right angle transformations |
| 182. Measuring circles | 5 | 6 | 7 | The distance around the edge of the circle is called the circumference. The distance from the center to the edge is the radius, and the distance from one point on the edge through the center to the opposite edge is the diameter. The length of the diameter is always twice the length of the radius. | Ability to describe and compare circles using the terms *diameter*, *radius*, and *circumference* |
| 183. Using compasses to construct circles | 3 | 4 | 5 | Compasses allow you to draw a set of points all equally distant from the center. This is a circle. A protractor allows you to draw and measure specific angles. Explore only relative sizes of circles at this level. | Use of the compasses to draw a circle and the line to the center point; ability to predict relative size of edge of a circle when comparing measured lines to the center point |
| 184. Value of pi | 5 | 6 | 7 | The circumference of a circle is always the same number of times larger than the diameter. It is a constant value of (3.14), which is represented by a Greek letter called pi (p). We can compute pi by measuring the diameters and circumferences of several circles and looking for the relationship between the measures. | Ability to *predict* relative size of circumference from given diameters; ability to estimate and then compute circumference from diameter (see Chapter 3 for activities that construct the meaning and value of pi) |

*NOTE: A = Exploration, B = Concept Mastery, C = Algorithmic or Procedural Mastery

*(Continued)*

(Continued)

| Content Branches | Suggested Grade-Level Timing* | | | Embedded Concepts | Performance Indicators/ Assessment Expectations |
|---|---|---|---|---|---|
| | A | B | C | | |
| Major/minor | | | | | |

**Geometry: Visualizing Shapes and Patterns, Models**
*Language check: horizontal, vertical, perpendicular, polygon (and derivatives such as hexagon), symmetry, bilateral, radial, transform, flip, rotation, slide, congruent, plane, angle, vertex, circumference, radius, diameter*

| Content Branches | A | B | C | Embedded Concepts | Performance Indicators/ Assessment Expectations |
|---|---|---|---|---|---|
| 185. Surface area of three-dimensional figures | 5 | 6 | 7 | The surface area of three-dimensional figures is the sum of the areas of all planes. Different figures have different relationships of volume to surface area. | Analysis and comparison of relative size of surface areas for three-dimensional objects; e.g., cube vs. flat cylinder; sphere vs. cone; ability to compute surface area of cube and cylinder |

**Data/Tables/Graphs: Models/Multiple Representation/Algebra Functions**
*Language check: data, attributes, interval, reference line, coordinates*

| Content Branches | A | B | C | Embedded Concepts | Performance Indicators/ Assessment Expectations |
|---|---|---|---|---|---|
| 186. Data gathering; organization; tallying | 1 | 2 | 3 | Data must be recorded and organized to have meaning for others. Data can be collected and tallied or added up. | Ability to organize loose data; ability to use tallies and tally tables and to interpret them |
| 187. Analysis: Comparison of data | 2 | 3 | 4 | Data can be compared when they are organized. Data gathering is subject to error. | Ability to *analyze* data and predict errors in gathering |
| 188. Data tables | 2 | 3–4 | 5–6 | A data table helps us organize measured attributes or events. It helps us see patterns more clearly and plan for other models. | Ability to *analyze* and construct data tables with appropriate labels and intervals; ability to recognize patterns from tables |
| 189. Simple pictographs | K | 1 | 2 | A graph is a picture or model of measured quantities or data. The pictures help us see values clearly and compare them. We need a key and labels to tell us what the pictures mean. It is useful to have equally measured spaces or intervals on graphs. | Ability to record data and to construct and interpret simple pictographs (with verbalized explanations) |
| 190. Bar graphs (construction/ interpretation) | 1 | 2 | 3 | A type of graph is the bar graph. Two perpendicular lines are used as starting places or reference lines. We label the reference lines to tell what they represent. The distance from one reference line to the end of the bar shows the data value; the other line separates the categories. Bar graphs show data differences well. | Ability to *analyze* and compare quantities from bar graphs; ability to construct bar graphs on paper and on computer from data tables; ability to *justify* choice of bar graph |

*NOTE: A = Exploration, B = Concept Mastery, C = Algorithmic or Procedural Mastery

## Data/Tables/Graphs: Models/Multiple Representation/Algebra Functions

*Language check: data, attributes, interval, reference line, coordinates*

| Content Branches | Suggested Grade-Level Timing* | | | Embedded Concepts | Performance Indicators/ Assessment Expectations |
|---|---|---|---|---|---|
| Major/minor | A | B | C | | |
| 191. Circle (pie) graphs; relative size of parts | 3 | 4 | 5 | A pie graph shows differences between the different elements of a data set, but it also shows how one element is related to the whole. The circle represents the whole data set, and the pie pieces represent the size of each part. | Ability to *analyze* pie graphs and compare relative (more or less than) quantities of elements pictured in a pie graph; ability to estimate size of one element as fractional part of whole |
| Estimation of part to whole | 4 | 5 | 6 | | |
| 192. Simple line graphs | 4 | 5 | 6 | Line graphs can be used to show how often particular measures occur. They give you a good idea about how data are distributed and how data change over time. Stem and leaf plots are also an efficient way to show the distribution of data. | Ability to extract data from a line graph; ability to identify areas where greatest number of events occurred; ability to construct a line graph from a data table |
| 193. Line graphs using coordinates | 5 | 6 | 7 | Line graphs using coordinate points are useful for showing how two variables are related or how a variable changes over time. We call the horizontal reference line the x-axis and the vertical reference line the y-axis. We connect the coordinates that show the related points with lines. | Ability to translate data tables showing two related variables into coordinates and line graphs |
| 194. Using coordinates to locate positions on a grid and follow directions with a map | 3 | 4 | 5 | Coordinates are equally measured spaces like those on a map that can help us show and find things. You need two perpendicular reference lines coming from one point or origin for your grid. Two measured distances on the lines from the origin locate a specific point in a plane. We usually show the value of the measured distances as ordered pairs of values and show distance on the horizontal line first. | Ability to locate points on a grid from an ordered pair of distances from a line (Have each child put a dot on a blank piece of paper and try to describe where it is; then repeat with geoboard or grid paper. This is a good language arts skill as well as social studies articulation point.) |
| 195. Line plots, stem-and-leaf plots, and scatter plots | 4 | 5 | 6 | Line plots, stem-and-leaf plots, and scatter plots help us organize data and understand how data are related and distributed. They can also show data trends. | Ability to construct and interpret line plots, stem-and-leaf plots, and scatter plots; ability to identify relationships and trends |
| 196. Time lines (construction/ interpretation) | 4 | 5 | 6 | Events can be recorded on lines in order of their occurrence either from left to right or bottom to top. Distance between events should relate to the time between their occurrences. | Ability to interpret event sequence from a time line; ability to construct a time line from a story and/or real-life adventure |

*NOTE: A = Exploration, B = Concept Mastery, C = Algorithmic or Procedural Mastery

(Continued)

(Continued)

| Content Branches | Suggested Grade-Level Timing* | | | Embedded Concepts | Performance Indicators/ Assessment Expectations |
|---|---|---|---|---|---|
| | A | B | C | | |

**Data/Tables/Graphs: Models/Multiple Representation/Algebra Functions**
*Language check: data, attributes, interval, reference line, coordinates*

| Content Branches | A | B | C | Embedded Concepts | Performance Indicators/ Assessment Expectations |
|---|---|---|---|---|---|
| 197. Choosing appropriate representations | 5 | 6 | 7 | Different graphs and representations are used to show data. The choice depends on the relationships or trends you wish to take note of or the ideas you wish to communicate. | Ability to explain and *justify* choice of a graph; ability to connect use of different graphs to different sets of data and purposes |

**Probability and Statistics: Models/Multiple Representation/Functions**

| Content Branches | A | B | C | Embedded Concepts | Performance Indicators/ Assessment Expectations |
|---|---|---|---|---|---|
| 198. Chance events, certainty/uncertainty | K | 1 | 2 | Sometimes things are certain to occur, and other times there is only a chance that they will happen. | Ability to distinguish between certain and chance events |
| 199. Equal or unequal outcome possibilities | 3 | 3–4 | 4–5 | Outcomes are not always equally expected. For example, there is a greater chance of a warm day in July than in March—although it could happen. | Ability to identify factors that affect outcome of chance events; ability to compute simple unequal outcome probabilities |
| 200. Expressing probability in fraction form | 3 | 4 | 5 | We express the probability of an event as a fraction. The numerator tells us the number of probable occurrences out of the number of possibilities, which is shown in the denominator. | Know how to express the probability of an event as a fraction |
| 201. Predicting outcomes | 2 | 3 | 4 | Sometimes we can predict the probability of uncertain events. If there are two choices on the spinner, we can predict that each choice will come up half of the time. If there are more choices on the spinner, each choice will happen fewer times. If one die has only the numbers 1, 2, 3 on it, and the other die has 1, 2, 3, 4, 5, 6, which one will land with number 2 on the top most often? | Ability to compare probability of individual events given the number of choices; ability to construct a tree diagram or table of probable events |
| 202. Proof of inferences | 3 | 4 | 5 | We can prove our predictions by collecting data, but the data will not always be exact. The more data we collect, the closer they will be to our prediction. | *Proof of prediction by collecting and collating data* |

*NOTE: A = Exploration, B = Concept Mastery, C = Algorithmic or Procedural Mastery

| Content Branches | Suggested Grade-Level Timing* A | B | C | Embedded Concepts | Performance Indicators/ Assessment Expectations |
|---|---|---|---|---|---|
| Major/minor | | | | | |

**Data/Tables/Graphs: Models/Multiple Representation/Algebra Functions**
*Language check: data, attributes, interval, reference line, coordinates*

| Content Branches | A | B | C | Embedded Concepts | Performance Indicators/ Assessment Expectations |
|---|---|---|---|---|---|
| 203. Combinations: Order independent | 2 | 3–4 | 4 | Different objects can be combined into different groups or sets, but a given number of objects can be combined in only a certain number of ways. Tree diagrams and tables record combinations. You can make six different combinations of any two objects out of four different objects if the way or order of how the objects are combined doesn't matter (e.g., for objects R, W, Y, and B, there can be RW, WY, YB, RB, WB, and RY). | Ability to explain that objects can be differently arranged; ability to compute number of sets of two from three or four different objects using real objects and tables; ability to construct a tree diagram or table of possible events |
| 204. Permutations: Order dependent combinations of two objects | 4 | 5 | 6 | Sometimes the order does matter. Then there are more different possibilities for combining objects because a switched order of the two objects makes a different case. We call these permutations. | *Proof of inference using tree diagrams as real data* |
| 205. Central tendency: Finding the average or mean | 5 | 6 | 7 | The average (mean) of several measured quantities helps you interpret the data. An average makes it easier to consider the whole group or data set rather than many different separate measures. We find the mean by adding up all the separate quantities in a set of data and dividing by the number of quantities. Values that are very different from most values are called outliers, and sometimes they affect the mean too much and may be incorrect data. | Ability to estimate and compute means and explain them; explanation of how outliers affect mean (Batting averages are also ratios. They tell us what proportion of the times at bat resulted in hits. The total number of a player's hits is divided by the number of times at bat. Why is a batting average usually less than one? What other kinds of data could give us an average less than one?) |
| 206. The median and the mode | 5 | 6 | 7 | Medians also tell us something about the whole group. The median is the value in the middle. You find the median by lining all the data in order; counting the number of entries, and then finding the middle score, which has an equal number of scores above and below it. If the number of scores is even, then you have to find the average of the two middle scores. Medians and means are sometimes close but not the same. Outliers do not make a difference in medians. The mode is the item or value that is repeated or occurs most frequently. | Ability to compute median and mode with explanations of how each value was obtained |

*NOTE: A = Exploration, B = Concept Mastery, C = Algorithmic or Procedural Mastery

*(Continued)*

# 3

# Scaffolds for Teachers and Problems for Students

## A GUIDE TO CHAPTER 3 ■

Chapter 3 is designed as a supplement to Chapter 2. It provides some of the instructional ideas for achieving the concepts listed by number in Chapter 2. The ideas presented are based on the work of many mathematics education researchers (some of whom are listed in the references), my own observations of children and preservice teachers as they learned, and those of the experienced teachers with whom I work. The item numbers in Chapter 3 correspond to the item numbers of the skills and concepts in Chapter 2. In some cases, the numbers have been consolidated into groups in order to demonstrate the opportunities for review and conceptual connections within the scaffolds and illustrative problems.

Each item begins with a discussion of the skills and concepts presented in Chapter 2 and an analysis of the challenges of helping students learn them. There are specific suggestions for scaffolding dialogue and manipulatives to help in the process. The discussion is followed by articulated exemplar problems that can be used for both concept development and proximal (classroom) assessment purposes. The illustrative examples are almost entirely original and somewhat different from textbook problems in the way that they are presented. They may take students over several development levels and connect to other concepts. They are meant to be used as an interactive support in the scaffolding process as the teacher guides and assesses the progress of students in the construction of new knowledge.

Teachers may wish to copy the exemplar problems for use with their students, but they may need to adapt some of them to the developmental level of their students. Many of the exemplars involve group activities. They represent only a limited sample of the kind of challenges teachers will need to help students develop a wide range of problem-solving skills. Teachers should consult the many additional scaffolding ideas and sample problems in the National Council of Teachers of Mathematics (NCTM, 1989, 2000) standards documents and other sources listed in this book's References. Mathematics textbooks meant for use by children also have many problems and activities that can be used along with these examples for further practice and challenges.

Since the publication of the first edition of this book, my attention has been called to the growing need for students to be able to quickly retrieve (automatize) some basic facts. Cognitive research tells us that memorization is easier at younger ages, and automatized facts enable a better focus on the understanding of algorithms. Although calculators should be encouraged for complex calculations, the basic facts (as suggested in Chapter 1) need to be automatized as soon as possible. The pattern recognizing activities and scaffolding presented in Chapter 3 should facilitate the process.

The algorithms for which scaffolding is suggested are, for the most part, the standard algorithms. Technology makes most algorithms less important, but they are fast, accurate, and powerful, and they provide a written record (Usikin, 1998). We also need to recognize that different algorithms are standards in other places or have been the standard form at different times.

Learned with meaning, algorithms may also help students understand relationships and patterns. Concurrently, students should be encouraged to try to develop their own algorithms and perhaps share them with others. The value of student-invented algorithms is that the process of invention firmly constructs mathematical concepts. This value is further enhanced by opportunities to describe the invented procedure. Even if the invention is not as efficient as the standard procedure, it should be recognized as valid. Student attention, however, should be called to the relative efficiency of standard algorithms. In any case, teachers should avoid spending too much time on drill and practice with algorithms; there are too many other useful mathematics ideas that students have to learn.

Most of the concrete manipulatives suggested are among those in most common use, available from educational supply companies, and there are many additional forms that are useful. Some of the other manipulative suggestions—such as the shoebox roll with pom-poms and egg carton fractions—may not be as familiar to teachers. They are, however, easily constructed.

The suggested technology applications are just the tip of the iceberg. Many of the new-generation software applications can be used as supplements to help provide additional experiences. Using common drawing applications, students can construct their own chips and duplicate and manipulate them. They can create figures, rotate them, and transform them. They can use interactive probes to collect original data on temperature or light, organize the data into tables, plot graphs, and perform operations with handheld calculators. Over the Internet students can retrieve data such as seismographic readings, temperature, distances, and annual rainfall from all over the world.

The overriding concept, however, is that we all learn by "doing" mathematics.

1 Counting begins as a rote repetition of the number words, but learners soon develop concepts of quantity such as "more," "less," "many," "few," "a whole bunch." They then begin to understand the sequence as an increasing number line. One-to-one correspondence is the understanding that each item

counted has a different number word in the counting sequence and represents a different position on the number line. Pointing to or touching the item as it is counted is both good practice and an indicator of concept construction. Use real things and manipulatives such as beads and chips as well as pictures. To help develop the concept of increasing quantity, ask in reference to the figure: "One more horse would be how many, and one more than that would be . . . ?"

Count the horses; touch each one and say the number name.          **Figure 1**

Touch the horse with the number name two.

Touch the number four horse.

Put a circle on the numbers 2 and 4 on the number line.

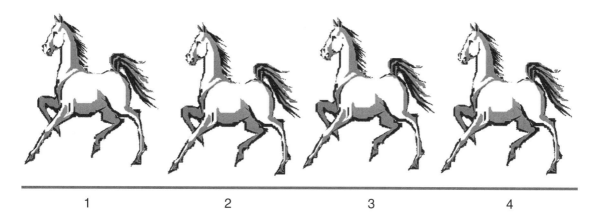

| 1 | 2 | 3 | 4 |

Make your own bead frames. Bead frames are great because they stay in place. Each child should have one in his or her desk. Use a 10"-by-12" piece of pegboard and plastic cord to string 10 beads at a time. Let the children make them. I like using beads of all the same color for several conceptual reasons. You can also make a bead frame for the overhead projector by drilling holes in a sheet of clear hard plastic and stringing it.

Count the balls. Count the jacks.          **Figure 2**

Count them on the number line.

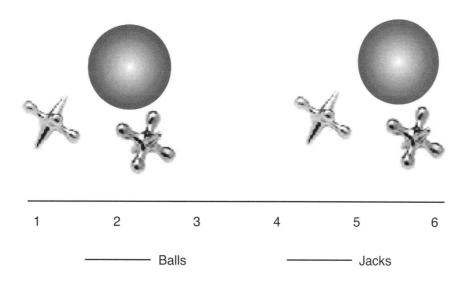

| 1 | 2 | 3 | 4 | 5 | 6 |

——— Balls                    ——— Jacks

• Manipulatives are analogies for the real things. You can help students make the analogy transition to the manipulatives by asking questions such as: *"What does each bead mean?"* or *"What does each bead stand for?"*

**2** Some children will not attain *cardinal principle* or the concept that the last number counted represents the size of the group until the second or third grade. Not having the concept will delay their ability to add and subtract with meaning. Teachers will note that children without the concept always recount each item when adding. They can see addition as an increase in the number line, but do not start from the last number counted.

Try using two-sided chips, turning each as it is counted.

Cover up a just-counted group and ask: *"How many did you count?"* Keep extending the wait time before asking the question. Or have the children count items in their hands and then put their hands behind their backs and ask them the *"how many"* question. Counting without the number line and in various arrangements will also help.

**3** Practice in counting objects spaced differently and in different arrangements should help the **conservation** of number concept develop. The conservation concept may also be strengthened by simultaneously providing opportunities for students to pour liquids into different containers and asking them if the amount of liquid changed.

**Figure 3**     How many yo-yos?

How many yo-yos?

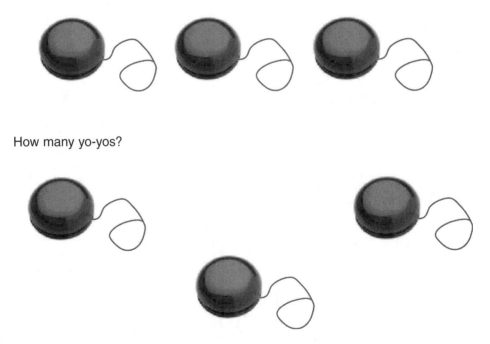

4 Sorting and **seriation** are related, and both require the ability to distinguish between the name of the object and its properties. Seriation seems to be more intrinsically related to natural development of magnitude. Strong **seriation** and sorting concepts will help with more complex kinds of attribute and pattern recognition. Use size and other attributes to help students develop this concept as they put real objects in order of the changing amount of a single property, and always ask for identification of the property. The critical scaffolding questions for seriation are:

Number all the helmets according to size. Number the smallest helmet (1) and the largest helmet (3). 

**Figure 4**

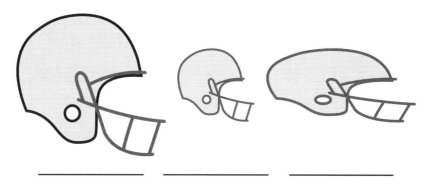

Do you see any other differences?

*Here are some eight balls. How are they the same? How are they different? Can we put them in order of how dark they are? Is there any other order we can use?*

**Figure 5**

Number all the eight balls according to how large they are. Number the smallest (1) and the largest (3). Do you see any other differences? Can you number them differently for other properties?

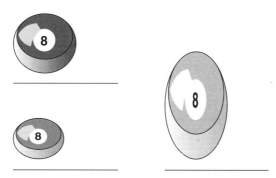

• Let the children learn to use a computer drawing program to repeat the same object, change the size of each object, and then put their objects in size order.

Follow the seriation of different sizes of single objects to the seriation of different sized groups or sets of the same object. Use the alternate terms "smaller group"/"fewer," "larger group"/"more," as they compare and count the number of elements in the groups.

**Figure 6**

    (A)   Put a circle around the larger group of cookies.

    (B)   How many cookies are in the group that has more?

    (C)   How many cookies are in the group that has fewer?

Circle the set that has fewer shapes.

How many shapes are there when you add the two sets together?

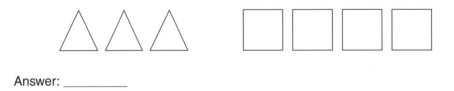

Answer: _____

**5** The critical scaffolding questions for sorting are:
*What makes these the same? What makes them different?*

For distinguishing between an object and its properties, the critical questions are the following:
*Can you think of another object with a different name that has the same property? What property makes them the same? Put all of the things that have that property together in a group. Why are some things not in the group? Are there other ways to sort these same items?*

There are many commercial sorting materials available, but you can use common items such as beans, toys, and foods. Make connections to language arts by sorting words according to their properties, and then stories according to their common themes. Make connections to social studies by grouping cities, states, and countries. Make connections to science by sorting living and non-living things.

**6** Beyond rote repetition of the number names, the teen numbers are sometimes difficult conceptual hurdles for students. Use a bead frame to build the concept of ten and one more, two more, three more, and so on. Popsicle sticks that children can tie into groups of ten with rubber bands are useful here. Ten frames and counting tables are also helpful.

Number all the animals from (1) to (3).

Number the slowest runner (1) and the fastest (3).

How are the animals the same? How are they different?

**Figure 7**

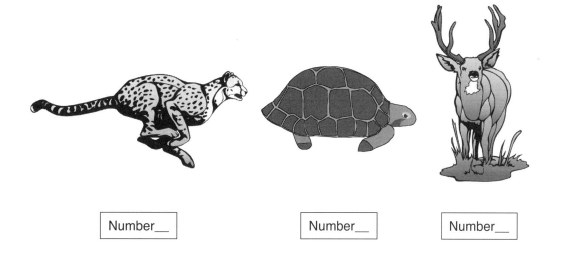

| Number__ | | Number__ | | Number__ |

What properties make them the same?

What properties make them different?

Which two are the most alike? Why?

**Figure 8**

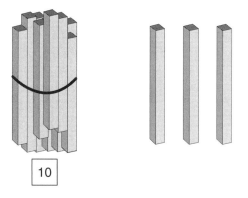

How many sticks are there altogether?

Look quickly at the happy faces. Try not to count them one by one.

**Figure 9**

*How many are there? Explain how you knew that.*

**7** Being able to visually recognize the size of a small group without counting each item (subitizing) is a useful skill. Let the children come up with their own schemes for doing this, but encourage them to verbalize and share.

**8** Counting by ten and an introduction to place value should come together. "Base-ten" blocks, stacked Unifix Cubes, packages of sticks, and other groups of materials (money also can be used; see Number 12) should be used simultaneously with a number table up to 100. The critical transition is from the rote repetition of the decades to the understanding that ten is added each time. Adding ten with a calculator is also helpful.

*How did we get from ten to twenty, from twenty to thirty?*

*Give me twenty. Give me ten more.*

*How many did you give me?*

*Count the blocks by ten. Find the total on the number table. How many tens did you count? How many ones?*

**Figure 10**   Count the blocks by tens. Find the total on the number table. How many tens did you count? How many ones?

| 1 | 2 | 3 | 4 | 5 | 6 | 7 | 8 | 9 | 10 |
|---|---|---|---|---|---|---|---|---|---|
| 11 | 12 | 13 | 14 | 15 | 16 | 17 | 18 | 19 | 20 |
| 21 | 22 | 23 | 24 | 25 | 26 | 27 | 28 | 29 | 30 |
| 31 | 32 | 33 | 34 | 35 | 36 | 37 | 38 | 39 | 40 |
| 41 | 42 | 43 | 44 | 45 | 46 | 47 | 48 | 49 | 50 |
| 51 | 52 | 53 | 54 | 55 | 56 | 57 | 58 | 59 | 60 |
| 61 | 62 | 63 | 64 | 65 | 66 | 67 | 68 | 69 | 70 |
| 71 | 72 | 73 | 74 | 75 | 76 | 77 | 78 | 79 | 80 |
| 81 | 82 | 83 | 84 | 85 | 86 | 87 | 88 | 89 | 90 |
| 91 | 92 | 93 | 94 | 95 | 96 | 97 | 98 | 99 | 100 |

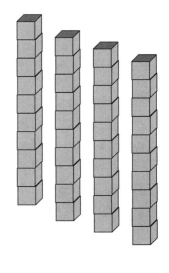

**9** There are two phases for **skip counting**. The first phase is an understanding of skip counting as it relates rote repetition of counting tables to the number line. Do not completely discount the rote memorization or automatization of the counts. Rhythmic language patterns will help students automatize the counts. However, instead of just memorizing the counting tables, students can see the sequence as a pattern of skipping numbers on the number line.

*Begin with skip counting by two and its relationship to odd and even numbers.*

*Make a connection to sharing division. Line up a variety of manipulatives and divide them into two groups to allow students to discover why numbers are odd or even. Relate the mathematical terms to their common language usage.*

Children can act the skip counts out by arranging themselves in a line and actually "skipping out" by two and by three. Musical rhythms also can be useful. They learn the concept that skip counting omits numbers on the line or emphasizes beats on the drum. Skip counting can also show doubling patterns. For example, counting by four skips a count by two, but the doubling concept may be more readily developed after the transition to multiple groups has been made.

The second phase for skip counting is a transition from the number line concept to multiplication as repeated addition or the idea that each time you skip to the next number you add on a group of two, three, or four, and so on. Scaffolding questions for this transition include: *How did you skip count 0, 3, 6, 9, 12? How did you get from 6 to 9? How much more is 6 than 3, 9 than 6, 12 than 9? How many skips of three are there from 0 to 12? How many times did you add three? How much is four times three?*

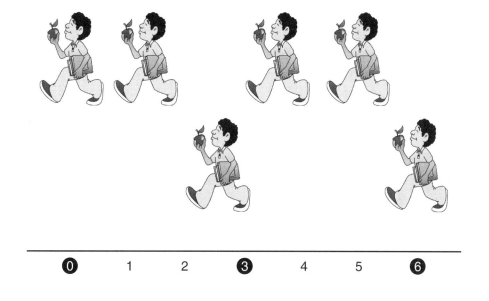

**Figure 11**

We started at zero.

How many boys did we skip before we got to three?

How many from three to six?

How do we get to nine?

**Figure 12**

Let's put the boys in groups.

How many groups to get to six?

How many in each group?

This is also a good place to introduce doubling patterns for multiplication. Bead frames and calculators can also be used to support the skip counting concept.

*How can we use the calculator to find how much four times three is equal to? How many times would you have to hit the number three key on the calculator? What was your total? How much does four times three add up to? How much would five times three equal?*

**Figure 13**

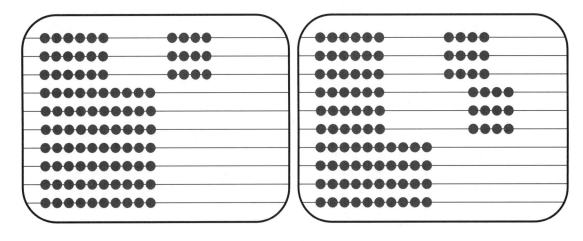

Count by four. Four, one time, is four. Four, two times, is eight. Four, three times, is twelve. Three times four is _____.

Double the count. Four, six times, is _____. Six, four times, is _____.

**10** Make the connection between the word "ordinal" and the fact that the order in which items are arranged counts for ordinal numbers. Children grasp this concept easily—perhaps because it has so much application in sports, their games, and personal competition.

*Evan said that the third person on the stage was his friend Fred. Jim said that Fred was the sixth person on the stage. Explain why they are both right. Can you tell how many people were on the stage?*

The boys left school in a line. The third boy and the fifth boy got on a bus. Put a circle around the boys who got on a bus.

**Figure 14**

**11** Place value concepts are very critical for understanding, but often incompletely developed. There are several conceptual transitions that must be made.

- The move from one-to-one correspondence to cardinal principle should be followed quickly or accompanied by the idea that we can think of groups or sets of individual items or values as a whole.
- The next step is combining sets that are the same and counting by ten (see above). *We counted three tens. How many do we have?*
- A sometimes overlooked transition is the ability to *visualize one single item as a symbol for a group of ten (or more). This is the concept of one-to-many correspondence.*
- The next and important transition is understanding that the value of a symbol can *change with its position.*

Manipulatives can help with each transition. For the first two steps, any kind of grouped materials work well. Grid sheets and base-ten blocks can be introduced here, but *be careful to make the analogy of the manipulative to the real thing.* This is also a good time to make the money connections. One dime represents 10 pennies, and one dollar represents 100 pennies. One 10-dollar bill is the same as 10 singles. Card trading games are also applicable (Ross, 1989).

Base-ten blocks are also useful for one-to-many correspondence, but, because you can still see the individual ones, I like to use different sizes of pom-poms for the transition to seeing a single symbol as representative of many. Pom-poms are excellent for the shoebox roll activities for place value and combinations because they are inexpensive, varied, soft, and quiet. You can, however, also use large and small lima beans.

**Figure 15**

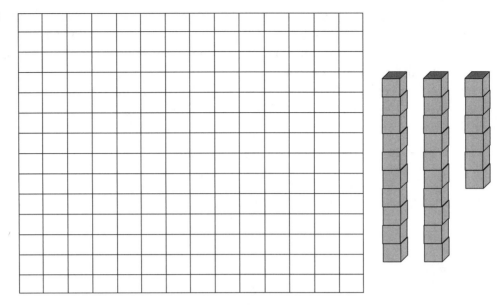

Color in the tens grid to show the number of ones cubes.

_____ tens and _____ ones = _____

**Figure 16**

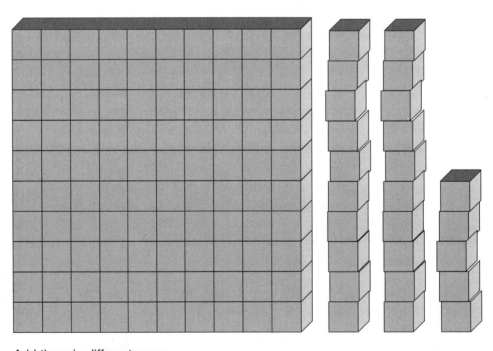

Add them in different ways:

_____ hundreds, _____ tens, and_____ ones = _____

_____ tens and _____ ones = _____

Follow a developmental sequence of concepts with the pom-poms.

- Begin by using large and small pom-poms with the single large pom-pom a symbol for ten.
- Follow this with different colored pom-poms for ones and tens.

- For the final transition to position as the value indicator use the same color and size pom-poms because you want students to develop the idea that the same symbol in a different position has a different value.
- Students can also construct their own images of the shoebox roll using drawing programs on the computer.
- Let students discover that using the same number of pom-poms can create different values and larger numbers of pom-poms can show lesser values.
- Let students discover why zero is needed as a place holder as they see an empty center box and try to express the quantity in number symbols.

Make a shoebox roll by dividing an ordinary empty shoebox into two sections with a piece of construction paper, and label the sections "ones" and "tens." Leave enough room on top of the partition for the pom-poms to roll over it. Cover the box and shake it to achieve various values. The children can work with individual boxes in pairs, and you can also use a clear plastic box on the overhead projector. Then divide the boxes into three sections, adding a section for hundreds.

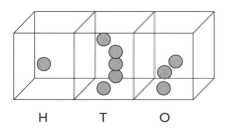

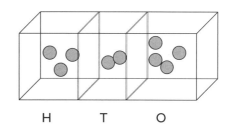

**Figure 17**

153 = 1 hundred + 5 tens + 3 ones

324 = 3 hundreds + 2 tens + 4 ones

Nine pom-poms roll in the place value shoebox in different ways.

Show how nine pom-poms can add up to 234.

Could you add nine more pom-poms and only show a value of 99?

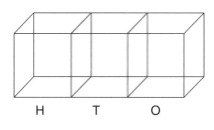

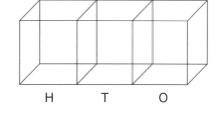

__ hundreds + __ tens + __ ones = 234

__ hundreds + __ tens + __ ones = 99

Can you use the same number of pom-poms to show 909?

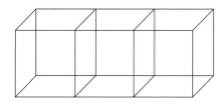

__ hundreds + __ tens + __ ones = 909

**12** Practice with base-ten blocks combined with simultaneous notation of symbolic forms is useful as students develop the concept of a systematic one-to-many pattern of equalities in our number system. Trading games with the blocks and with money are supportive. Making these simultaneous with the renaming of the number symbol form for quantities in different ways will strengthen student ability to deal with complex computations and develop number sense: 1232 is 1 thousand, 2 hundreds, 3 tens, and 2 ones, but it is also 12 hundreds, 3 tens, and 2 ones, and it is also 123 tens and 2 ones, or just 1232 ones. Ask questions such as: *When are larger units necessary? When are smaller units needed?* Again, connections to money, baseball cards, or other card trading games can be helpful as familiar analogies to the process (Fuson et al., 1998).

**Figure 18**    Make even trades.

Trade the blocks below for: 12 hundreds and _____ tens and _____ ones.

Trade them for: one thousand, and _____ tens and 4 ones.

Trade them for: _____ ones.

Can you find another even trade?

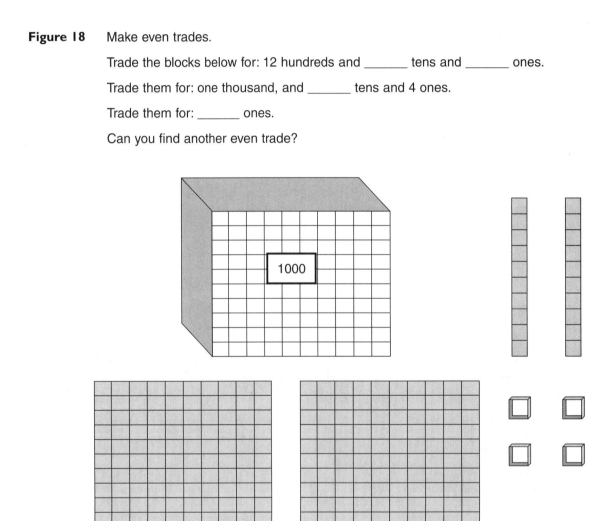

**13** The next place value transition is the shift from the concept of equality to the concept of multiple. One ten is equal to ten ones, but it is also ten times larger. When asked, "*How much larger is the ten than the one?*" children will correctly say that the ten is nine more. The enlargement concept of multiplication as it is related to place value needs careful scaffolding. "*How many times larger?*" is better. Use the base-ten blocks to demonstrate this concept, carefully beginning with just the units and showing groups that are one time larger, two times larger, and three times larger before shifting to: *"How many times larger is the ten than the one?"*

Blowing up balloons is also effective here. Equal sizes of balloons have one time as much air as the original. Two times as much air is in a balloon twice as large. Use the balloons or drawings, or have students enlarge a diagram made with a computer-based drawing program. They can make a copy for comparison and then enlarge the original several times, simultaneously writing the number sentence for each enlargement.

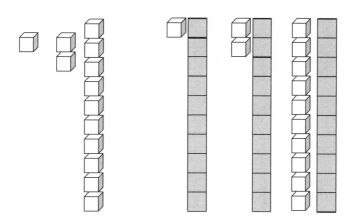

**Figure 19**

1 time, 2 times, ten times as many ones.

1 time, 2 times, ten times as much air.

Each unit in a place is 10 times larger than the same unit to its right. To make a unit 10 times larger, you shift it to the left; to make it 10 times smaller, you shift it to the right. Let the students play shift games, lining themselves up like the number symbols. Each student is given a unit value, and competing teams try different line-ups to see which has the greatest total value. Be sure to use zero values and to record symbols for different regroupings (e.g., 1 hundred, 2 tens, and 3 ones; or 12 tens and 3 ones; or 123 ones). Then multiply the values by using a left-shift as a bonus for quick arrangements of given quantities and division by right-shift as a penalty for the slowest.

The shoebox roll is also excellent for this concept, and students should discover both the need for zero as a place holder and the effect of left and right shifts.

Move quickly to multiplication of number symbols by 10 and 100 and division by 10 and 100.

**Figure 20**

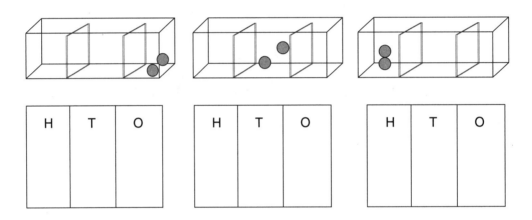

Fill in the right number symbol. Be sure to use zero as a place holder.

Make this value ten times larger.

| H | T | O |
|---|---|---|
|   | 3 | 1 |

| H | T | O |
|---|---|---|
|   |   |   |

**Figure 21**    Make this value ten times smaller.

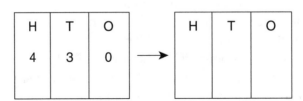

**14** Decimal place value concepts should follow review activities with whole numbers as above.

The question of how to divide ones by 10 should lead to the concept of decimal fractions, and the extension of the place value system to values less than one whole. *What fraction is one tenth of one whole? What fractional part of a whole is 10 times smaller than the whole? How can we show values less than one whole? Shifting one place to the right makes a unit 10 times smaller. Why do we need a decimal point?* Read the decimal point as "and," and the decimal values as the smallest place (read 25.23 as "twenty-five and twenty-three hundredths").

The concept of decimal place values can be connected concurrently to the division application of fractions (partition form). *Dividing a number by ten is like finding what fractional part of it? How can we find one tenth of a number by shifting places? And how can we find 10 percent of a number by shifting places?*

Make this value ten times smaller.

**Figure 22**

| H | T | O |
|---|---|---|
| 4 | 3 | 2 |

→

| H | T | O | tenths |
|---|---|---|--------|
|   |   |   |        |

Make this value ten times larger.

| H | T | O | tenths |
|---|---|---|--------|
|   | 3 | 6 | 5 |

→

| H | T | O | tenths |
|---|---|---|--------|
|   |   |   |        |

Find one tenth of this value.

| H | T | O | tenths |
|---|---|---|--------|
|   | 6 | 5 |        |

→

| H | T | O | tenths |
|---|---|---|--------|
|   |   |   |        |

**15** Conventional rounding is an important number sense skill, but it should be considered in the context of other estimation approaches. The kind of estimations we make depends upon the purpose of the computation or use of the value. Sometimes just front-ended estimation (using the highest place value) is good enough. If the attendance at a series game is 10,346 on day one and 12,765 on day two, it may be good enough to estimate 10,000 and 12,000 for a

2000 difference—even though conventional rounding would produce a different figure. If I were estimating the sum of 1438 and 1247 to the nearest hundred, I would estimate it as 2,700, quickly noting that the sum of the tens would be close to one hundred and adding that to the sum of the hundreds without thinking of rounding. If the numbers had been rotely rounded to the nearest hundred first, the estimate would have been 2,600.

**16** Some of the difficulty students have had with the rounding convention for larger numbers may be because of the traditional focus on just the number 5 rather than on the concept that five tens are half of one hundred and five hundreds are half of one thousand. Scaffolding can help. For rounding a number such as 363 to the nearest ten ask, *How many ones for half a ten? Do we have more or less than five ones? What do we do with less than five ones?*

**17** For rounding numbers more than one place such as a frequently mishandled quantity like 2647 to the nearest hundred ask, *What is the next smallest place after the hundreds? How many tens for half a hundred? Do we have more or less than five tens? Since we have less than half a hundred, what should we do with the tens and ones? What should take their place?*

A variety of estimation approaches should be encouraged to accompany calculator computations. *Estimation is the calculator check, but do it first.*

**Figure 23**

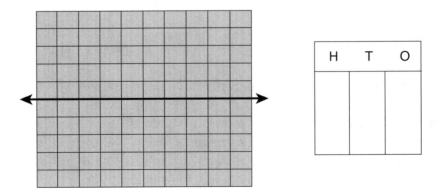

Change each value to one half the size.                    **Figure 24**

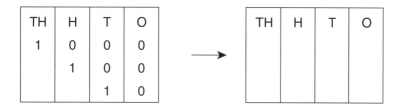

Look at the values in the box below.

Put an X over the values in the tens place that are more than half of a hundred.

Circle the values in the hundreds place that are more than half of a thousand.

Round the first number to the nearest thousand.

Round the second number to the nearest hundred.

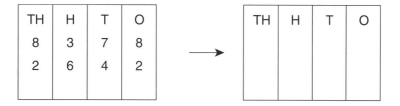

**18** There are several transitions in the development of the operations concepts of addition and subtraction. Some children will quickly move through them or skip them entirely. Others will need more time and manipulative experience or drill and practice. At first children see addition as an increase in the number line. When confronted with a *"How many more?"* problem, they will not add on to the last number counted but simply start from one again and *count all,* including the added value. Once students realize that the last number counted represents a total group or have attained the **cardinal principle,** they are ready to add on from the last number counted. Teachers can help make this happen by scaffolding sequences such as this:

*Count the candies. How many candies did you count? Cover the candies with your paper. How many candies are there? Let's add on three more on top of the paper. How many are under the paper? How many do we have all together?*

See Numbers 1–4 for additional counting activities.

**19/20** When solving problems in addition, students will at first follow the sequence of the problem: counting on from the first quantity mentioned (COF) and disregarding the possibilities of an easier approach. For example, they will add 8 to 2 by starting with the 2 instead of adding the 2 to the 8. Before students can move to the next step of counting on from the largest quantity (COL), they may need to see the quantities as individual wholes or parts that can be combined into a new whole—and recognize that they can be combined in any order (commutative principle of addition). They will do the same thing with subtraction problems, not realizing that, for example, when taking 6 away from 8 that it is easier to count up from the 6 to the 8 to find the difference. Encourage them to consider alternate methods.

**Figure 25**    Circle the set that has fewer shapes.

How many shapes are there when you add the two sets together?

Where is the best place to start adding?

Add them on the number line.

Write a number sentence for this picture.

_____ + _____ = _____

There are 5 turtles.

3 crawl away.

How many are left?

Use the number line to count back and find the answer.

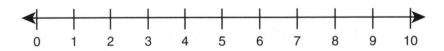

Write a number sentence for what happens when they walk away.

_____ – _____ = _____

The turtles that walked away turned around and came back.

Write a number sentence for what happened when they came back.

_____ + _____ = _____

**21** The recognition that addition is a combination of parts to find the whole is a critical concept that requires careful scaffolding. Problem-solving activities using real objects and manipulatives such as Unifix Cubes and bead frames can help develop the concept. For graphic representations, use specific directions such as: *Put a circle around each part and a bigger circle around the whole* (Lamon, 1996; Resnick, 1983).

**22** It may be useful to simultaneously develop the concept that subtraction is a separation of the part from the whole, and that addition and subtraction are inverse operations. *If you added two parts together to form a whole, what happens when you take away one part? What is left?*

**23** The equalities concept—that in order to keep the same size whole a change in size in one part requires a change in the other—should be clarified before going on to further regrouping concepts. If one part increases in size, then the other decreases and vice versa. This is also an opportunity to automatize the valuable combinations of 10. Two-sided chips and the shoebox roll work well here. Students can discover as they flip chip sides that, for the same whole, as the number of red sides increases the yellows decrease and vice versa. Scaffolds include the following:

*How big was Jon's part? How big was Mark's part?*

*Put them together. How many do they have all together? Can you put them together in a different way?*

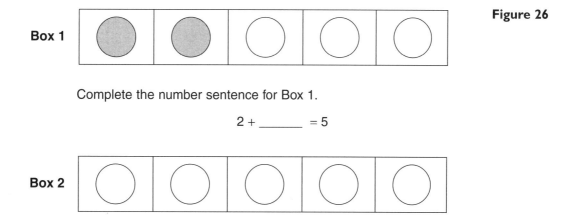

**Figure 26**

Box 1

Complete the number sentence for Box 1.

$$2 + \underline{\hspace{1cm}} = 5$$

Box 2

Use two colors of crayons to show the number 5 in a **different way** than it is in Box 1.

Complete the number sentence for Box 2.

$$\underline{\hspace{1cm}} + \underline{\hspace{1cm}} = 5$$

After the students have had a chance to use constructed shoebox rolls, let them draw their own shoebox rolls using a computer drawing program. Then encourage them to invent other graphic ways to show combinations of parts joined to form wholes.

**Figure 27**    Jane and Lisa each had some baseballs to bring to the game for their team. Jane had six, and Lisa had four. Put a circle around Jane's part. Draw Lisa's part in the box. How many did they have together?

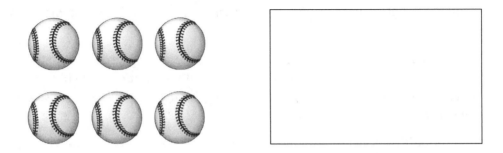

April and Meg are on another team. Meg had four baseballs, and April had six. Draw April's baseballs in the box. How many baseballs did Meg and April have together?

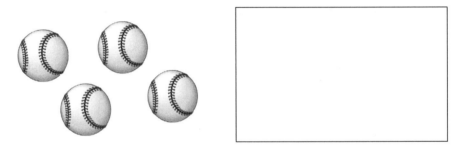

Explain why both teams had the same whole number of baseballs when they got to the game.

Complete the number sentences.

6 + 4 = _____          4 + _____ = 10

**24** An understanding of the (part/part whole) concept can then be extended to the possibility of different groupings of more than two parts to form the same whole (associative principle). Color tiles work to show three parts with three different colors. Activities with the balance will reinforce the concept.

*How many different ways can we use red, green, and yellow tiles to make a total of seven, eight, nine, and ten? What happens when we trade a yellow for a red?*

*I have different packages of Popsicle sticks. They have twelve, eight, six, four, or two sticks in them. If I put the package of twelve on a balance scale, how can I balance it with other packages?*

Regrouping an addend into smaller parts to make adding easier is a valuable skill that should quickly follow. Begin with a real problem. *There are four students from one class and eight from another who are going on a trip in two minivans. Each minivan holds only six students because children are not allowed in the front. How can we regroup the students to fit?*

**Figure 28**

Roll the pom-poms for combinations of 10.

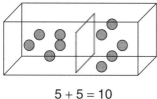 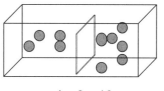 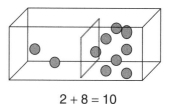

5 + 5 = 10          4 + 6 = 10          2 + 8 = 10

Draw the pom-poms to match the number sentence.

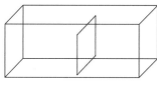  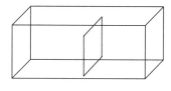

6 + 4 = _____          8 + 2 = _____          1 + 9 = _____

Billy has 2 cookies. Jim has 8 cookies. How many do they have together?

Add them on the number line.

Can you add them in an easier way?

Finish the number sentences.

2 + 8 = _____                                                8 + 2 = _____

**25** The ability to regroup addends to form the easily memorized combinations of ten is a useful number sense skill. Provide practice with the bead frame. *Think about the following:*

$$8 + 2 + 7 = \Box \; ; \; 8 + 9 = 8 + 2 + \Box \; ; \; 5 + 8 = 5 + \Box + \Box$$

*How is the first problem like the second and the third?*

**Figure 29**    John got ten Yu-Gi-Oh cards in his new package that he already had.

He traded the extra cards one at a time for ones he didn't have. Use your two-sided chips to make a record of his trades from the new package. Turn one over for each trade.

John traded for one new card and still had _____ extras.

John traded for three new cards and still had _____ extras.

John traded for six new cards and still had _____ extras.

Explain what happened to the number of new cards and the number of extras whenever he traded.

Why did they always add up to ten?

Can you think of other parts that would add up to ten?

**Figure 30**    Cindy loved tee shirts. Her favorite colors were blue, red, and yellow.

She had thirteen shirts. How many yellow shirts did she have if she had four blue ones and six red ones? Use your color tiles to discover new ideas.

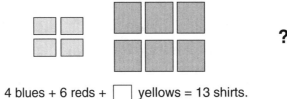

4 blues + 6 reds + ☐ yellows = 13 shirts.

Can you think of other combinations of blue, red, and yellow shirts that would add up to 13?

Can you think of combinations of just blue and yellow shirts that would add up to 13?

Why do three parts sometimes add up to the same amount as two parts?

Can you make three parts out of these two? 8 + 5

Can you think of why it may be useful to change two parts into three parts?

Later let students discover the value of regrouping for multi-digit addition.

$$27 + 8 = 27 + 3 + 5, \text{ and}$$

$$27 + 38 = 20 + 30 + 7 + 3 + 5,$$

$$\text{and then} = 20 + 30 + 7 + 8$$

$$\text{or} = 20 + 30 + 15 = 65$$

Stacey had eight PlayStation games, and Anna had five. How many did they have together?     **Figure 31**

Try making tens: 8 + 5 = 8 + 2 + 3 = ☐

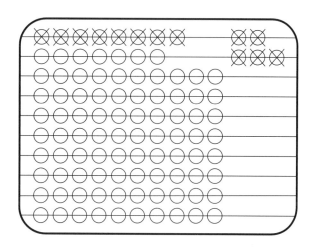

**26** Use missing addend problems and number sentences as an introduction to algebra.

*I need 17 dollars to buy the game, I want. I have 10 dollars. How many more dollars do I need? 10 + ☐ = 17. Then show the inverse subtraction. 17 − 10 = ☐*

**27** The shift to double digit addition without regrouping rarely causes a problem if place value understandings are strong (see Numbers 12–15). The first critical concepts are that like things must be added to like things and that numbers in different positions are not like things. Move quickly to three-digit addition without trading.

Some students will not need much time with manipulatives for this transition, but always use the triad of manipulative, words, and written symbols when solving the initial problems. Use packages of Popsicle sticks or base-ten blocks. Place these on back sheets of tens and ones columns. Later it may be useful to let students prove their answers to others by demonstrating with manipulatives.

Front-end estimation should precede exact calculations. Students can discover that the sum of two 2-digit numbers will have to be the same or larger than the sum of the tens place digits.

*Sour balls came in packages of 10. Jane had 2 packages of grape balls and 3 loose grape ones. How many grape balls did she have? She also had 3 packages of lemon balls and 6 loose lemon balls. How many lemon balls did she have? How many sour balls did she have altogether? How did you find your answer? Did you add the packages or the loose ones first? Does it make a difference? Evan had 43 lemon sour balls and 35 strawberry sour balls. About how many sour balls did he have? Would a good estimate be more than 70? Why? Use your Popsicle sticks to show us how you got your answer.*

**Figure 32**   The pet store has 33 puppies and 16 kittens. How many puppies and kittens did they have all together?

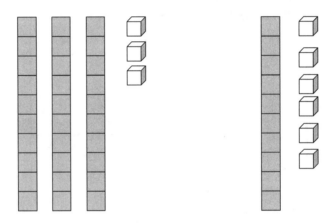

Sean was collecting baseball cards. He had two books of cards with 225 in one book and 123 in another. How many cards did he have all together?

**28** Let students discover the value of regrouping for multi-digit addition.

$$27 + 8 = 27 + 3 + 5 \text{ and}$$
$$27 + 38 = 20 + 30 + 7 + 3 + 5$$
$$\text{and then} = 20 + 30 + 7 + 8$$
$$\text{or} = 20 + 30 + 15 = 65$$

**29** The concept of *regrouping* (sometimes called *trading*) replaces (and makes more sense than) *borrowing*. Trading is critical to an understanding of all the common operation algorithms. Try to let students discover for themselves the structural limitation of ten symbols in a place in our number system. And then let them discover the trading option. Use the calculator as a manipulative to help them discover this, or use a two- and then three-part shoebox roll.

*How can we make our shoebox like our number system? What should we do if there are ten pom-poms in the ones place?*

**Figure 33**

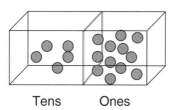

Tens      Ones

How many pom-poms are there in each side of our shoebox?

Can you write this total in our number system symbol form?

What would we have to do with the pom-poms in our shoebox to make it like our number system?

**30** Follow up with addition activities with base-ten blocks or packages of Popsicle sticks. Use a back sheet that indicates tens and ones or hundreds, tens, and ones. Always accompany the manipulative operation with the symbolic form. You may even try trading in systems that are other than base ten to reinforce the multiple representation idea. Baseball cards and other popular trading cards are possible connections. As soon as students have constructed the trading concept as a practical way to handle numbers, move quickly to the hundreds place.

Once the concept is clearly developed children may not wish to bother with the manipulatives, which become cumbersome with large numbers—even distracting from the concept. Let them use the symbolic form or computer graphics, but from time to time ask them to prove their answers with the manipulatives. Use manipulatives again at the beginning of transitions to the next larger place value.

Kelly had 17 hits before this game, and now she got six more. How many does she have all together? Show how you got your answer with your base-ten blocks, and complete the number sentence.

**Figure 34**

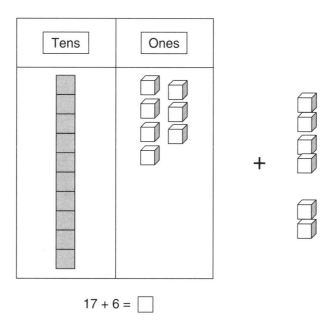

17 + 6 = ☐

**31** Identification of the patterns created when the same number is repeatedly added (addition series) can be useful in developing number sense.

**Figure 35**   Jane has $30. Movie tickets cost $7 each. How many tickets can Jane buy?

Finish the table to help solve the problem.

| 1 | 2 | 3 | 4 | 5 |
|---|---|---|---|---|
| $7 | $14 | | | |

Find the number sequence in the cards.

Write the missing numbers on the blank cards.

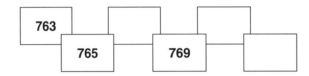

Try more complex series. Build geometric forms to match the series to see the pattern connections.

*Build a series of triangles with your blocks. Make the bottom row one block larger each time. What happens to the total number of blocks each time?*

**Illustration 3.1**

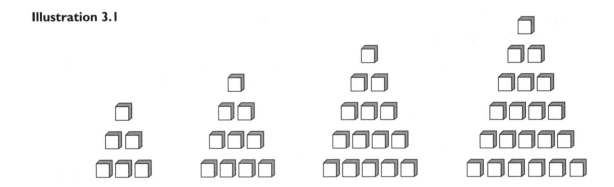

**32** Subtraction presents the first great challenge for some students. The first subtraction concept: counting backward on the number line is easily followed by a transition to subtraction as *"take away."*

*Billy had 8 cookies. He ate 3. How many does he have left?*

The difficulties in learning the subtraction process arise because problems that require the subtraction operation do not all involve the concept of *"take away."* Students who understand traditional or *canonical* take-way problems find it more difficult to solve *non-canonical* problems that involve comparison and problems where the result is given but the change or start is not known (see Number 34). It may be wise to move more quickly beyond take away and think of subtraction as *finding the difference* because each form of subtraction problem can be translated into this concept. For example, when you take a part away from a whole number you are left with the difference between the whole and the part you took away.

The concept of *inequalities* may be a good way to introduce the finding-the-difference concept. Children are always comparing things, and it may be a natural approach. The balance beam is excellent for inequalities, and it allows a focus on subtraction as finding the difference.

*Eight is greater than five: 8 > 5. How are eight chips and five chips different? What do you have to do to make them balance? The difference between 8 and 5 is 3, but can you make the values equal in more than one way?* (either by adding 3 to the smaller or taking 3 away from the larger)

Find the difference.
Balance the scale.

$8 - 3 = \square$

$3 + \square = 8$

**Figure 36**

*When subtraction is a comparison between two wholes*, the concept is clearly to find the difference, but it can be applied to other problems as well. Students will need to discover that, unlike addition, the subtraction operation is not commutative and it is common practice to subtract the smaller value from the larger value (to avoid negative differences). However, they should discover that sometimes it is easier to count up in a subtraction problem than it is to count down. The *take-away* concept makes this transition of making the easier *choice* difficult, but subtraction as *finding the difference* helps.

Billy has 2 cookies. Jim has 8 cookies. How many more does Jim have?     **Figure 37**

Use the number line to find the difference.

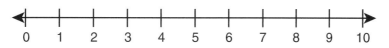

How did you find the difference? Is there an easier way?

**33** Relating the subtraction operation to the part/part whole relationship, subtraction is when you know the whole and one part but not the other part. The unknown part is the difference between the whole and the part you know. Even take-away problems can be described with this concept.

*Sally had eight computer games. She gave three to her friend Jane. What is the whole that Sally had before she gave any away? What is the part she gave to Jane? What is the part she has left? What is the difference between what she had before and now?*

*Sandy had 8 fish in her tank and she gave Fran 6. What she had left was the difference between what she had at the beginning and what she had after she gave the fish away. How many did she have left? How did you find your answer? Can you think of an easier way? Suppose she had eighteen and gave away sixteen. What would be the easiest way to find the difference?*

**Figure 38** James used twenty tracks for his train set-up. Sixteen of them were straight tracks. How many were curved?

THINK: How many tracks in the whole? How many in the straight part? What is the difference between the number of tracks in the whole set-up and the number of straight tracks?

Complete the number sentence: 20 – 16 = ☐

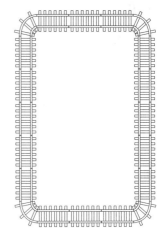

What is the easiest way to find the difference between eight and eleven? Can you think of a problem that makes you find the difference between eight and eleven? Write a number sentence for finding the difference between eight and eleven.

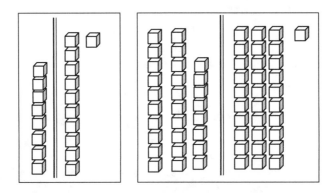

How would you find the difference between 28 and 31?

Write a number sentence for this.

**34** The "finding the difference" concept also works for non-canonical start-unknown problems and is helpful for developing understanding of beginning algebra concepts. For example:

*John has eleven action figures. He got four for Christmas. How many did he have before Christmas? What is John's whole number of action figures? What is the part he got for Christmas? How can we find the other part, the part he had before Christmas? What is the difference between the number he had before and after Christmas?*

$$4 + \square = 11$$
$$11 - 4 = \square$$

The word "equation" can be introduced as an expression that has an equal sign, which shows that the total of the values on each side of the sign are equal to each other.

Beginning in the fifth grade, the terms "variable" and "constant" can be substituted for the empty boxes that represent missing or unknown values in an equation.

$$4 + \square = 11$$

*What are the variables in the equation above? What are the constants?*

Finding the difference also works for change-unknown problems.

*Judy has 27 action figures. She had 19 before Christmas. How many did she get for Christmas? What is Judy's whole number of action figures? What is the part she had before Christmas? How can we find the other part, the part she got for Christmas? What is the difference between the number she had before and after Christmas?*

Evan collected 22 new rock specimens and put them in a special box with other rocks he had collected last year. He now has 34 in his box. How many specimens did he collect last year? THINK: What is the difference between what he had last year and what he has now?

**Figure 39**

Complete the number sentences:

$$22 + \square = 34$$
$$34 - 22 = \square$$

Rocks

Or beginning in Grade 5:

Solve the equation to find the number of rocks Evan collected last year.

$$22 + r = 34$$

What are the constants in this equation—the things we know?

What is the variable in this equation—what we do not know? How is it represented?

Or at a higher level:

Write an equation that will help you to find how many rocks Evan collected.

**35** The inequality signs ( < and > ) may be introduced as an adjunct to the focus on finding the difference. How much larger is 12 than 8? 12 > 8 means that 12 is greater than or larger than 8, and the difference is 12 – 8 or 4.

The number line can be used to help develop this concept. Attach the "less than, <" symbol to the line to show the direction of increasing value and then have students write a progressive expression of the reverse order using the "greater than, >" symbol.

$$0 < 1 < 2 < 3 < 4 < 5 < 6 < 7$$

$$\longleftarrow \boxed{7 > 6 > 5 > 4 > 3 > 2 > 1 > 0} \longrightarrow$$

In the upper grades, inequality problems that involve a known sum and difference, but unknown parts or addends, can then be solved as an extended variation of the above.

*The sum of two numbers is 27, and the difference between them is 3. If you take off the difference and put an equal amount of what is left on each side of a balance, how many will be on each side? What do you have to do to make only one side larger by the difference? What is the larger value? What is the smaller value?*

$$27 - 3 \ = 24$$
$$24 \div 2 \ = 12$$
$$12 + 3 \ = 15$$
$$12 + 15 = 27$$

**36** Beginning concepts of negative and positive integers (all the whole numbers and their opposites) may also be introduced by relating them to a number line with zero at the center. Positive values go to the right of zero and negative values to the left. We show positive and negative values by using a plus or minus sign (sometimes in parentheses, and/or as a superscript): ($^+$3) or (3). Apply this to measures of temperature as an introduction.

**Figure 40** The number line below can show the temperature on some very cold winter days. Add some numbers to both sides of the number line. The temperature on a winter day was five degrees below zero. Put a mark on the number line to show that temperature. The next day was two degrees colder. Write the symbol that shows the temperature for the next day.

The symbol for the temperature on the next day is _____

**37** Related subtraction and addition facts through 20 should be automatized before moving to multi-digit subtraction with regrouping or trading. If place value concepts and regrouping ideas are well developed for addition, the transition to subtraction with regrouping should not present a problem. Base-ten blocks and Popsicle sticks are excellent for concept development.

**38** For developing the algorithm, use a triad of connecting the concrete manipulative or real object to the words and then to the symbols and then back again. The take-away concept works best in the transition to trading or regrouping in the common algorithm. Like things have to be subtracted from like things, and if we do not have the like things, we can regroup. The transition from using concrete materials to using just the symbolic form of the subtraction algorithm is sometimes difficult because there is a tendency, with the concrete materials in front of them, for students to take away the units one by one and count the remainder instead of relying on mentally automatized combinations. This is not possible in the algorithm. In preparation for transition to the algorithm, have the students hide their manipulatives under a paper and predict the remainders before they count, and then let them check their predictions.

The baseball cards Roger bought came in packages of ten. He bought 3 packages of cards to add to the three single ones that he already had. Then he gave 16 of his 33 cards to his friend Sam for his birthday. How many cards did Roger have left? Write a vertical number sentence for this problem and use your base-ten blocks to help solve it. You will need to regroup for more ones. Before you take any of Sam's cards away, predict how many single ones will be left.

**Figure 41**

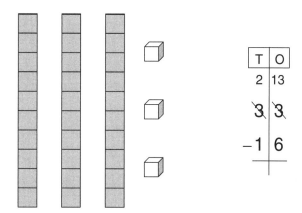

**39** One of the most challenging hurdles in learning the subtraction operation using only the rote algorithm is subtracting across zeros. Using base-ten blocks or the shoebox roll, students can see more easily that in the problem illustrated the one hundred is a source of needed ones, but it is more practical to trade first for the tens and then for the ones. Careful connections between the manipulative and the symbolic form will help.

*We don't have enough ones. Where can we get them? We don't have tens but we do have hundreds. Can we trade hundreds for ones? How many ones can we get for one hundred? It is too much trouble to count out one hundred ones, so can you think of an easier way to trade? If we trade one hundred for ten tens, how many hundreds do we have left? How many tens will we have/where can we get the ones we need? How many tens will be left? How many ones?*

*Let's write everything we just did in symbol form. Explain what each symbol means.*

**Figure 42**    Jamal had 103 pages to read in his book. He finished seven in his silent reading time. How many more pages did he have left to read?

Use your blocks to solve the problem and then describe what happens in the symbol form.

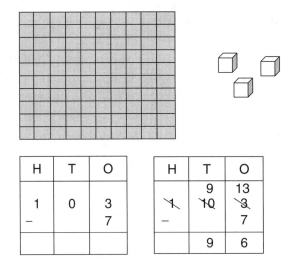

| H | T | O |
|---|---|---|
| 1 | 0 | 3 |
| – |   | 7 |
|   |   |   |

| H | T | O |
|---|---|---|
|   | 9 | 13 |
| 1 | 10 | 3 |
| – |   | 7 |
|   | 9 | 6 |

How many ones did you have to take away to find the difference?

How many did you have? How could you get more?

Why couldn't you get them from the tens? Where did you get them from? What did you do first?

How many hundreds did you have left? Then what did you do?

How many tens did you have left? Then what did you do?

Explain all your steps. Show them in symbol form.

Now subtract 7 from 1003.

**40** There are a number of transitions in the development of multiplication concepts that will occur over time as related concepts. Skip counting (see Number 9) has to progress from the rote repetition of sequence number names, through the idea of skipping numbers as we count, and on to the idea that each time we skip count we are adding another unit or group of two, three, or four—or the repeated addition of the same value. The mathematical language of "times" needs connections to "the number of times a unit value is repeated."

*What is another way to say three repeated four times? Three, three, three, and three is four times three and shown by the symbols 4 × (3). How can we describe the symbols 6 × (2) in words? How can we show this on our bead frame?* (See Figures 10 and 11.)

It may also be useful to introduce the place value concepts for multiples of ten that are described in Number 14 at the same time that beginning ideas in multiplication are approached.

**41** Pattern recognition such as doubling of the units can follow quickly and may reinforce the conceptual ideas. Start with doubling the number of times a group or unit is repeated: *Two fives are ten, how much would four fives be?*

$$2 \times (5) = 10$$
$$4 \times (5) = \square$$

Then move to doubling the size of the group: *If four threes are twelve, then how much are four sixes?*

$$4 \times (3) = 12$$
$$4 \times (6) = \square$$

Bead frames are very helpful here, but also use arrays of chips and color tiles.

Mike mowed his neighbor's lawn for a month. He got four dollars each time. He mowed three times. How many dollars did he earn for one month? Show how many *times* the four dollars are repeated on the bead frame. Tell your partner about how you got your answer. Write a number sentence for this problem.     **Figure 43**

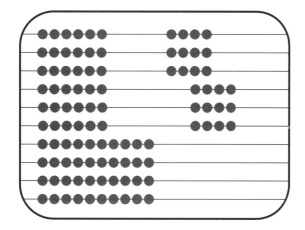

This number sentence describes how much Mike earned for the whole summer:

$6 \times (4) = \square$

Tell your partner how many times Mike mowed the lawn that summer.

Show this on your bead frame. Tell your partner how to get the answer.

Compare how much Mike earned for one month with how much he earned for the summer.

**42** When developing tables it is useful to remember that the *number of times* a value is repeatedly added is an abstract operand on the value or multiple. In the addition operation, you are combining concrete parts to form the whole, and each value can be concretely represented. In multiplication, a single concrete value is repeated a certain number of times. Consider three fours. The four is concretely represented, but there is no array of size three. Use the terms "multiple" and "multiplier" as the tables are developed. When using symbolic number sentences for multiplication some teachers also find it helpful to unitize the repeated unit or multiple by placing it in parentheses. Three fours are symbolized as $3 \times (4)$ and four threes are $4 \times (3)$. Although commutatively the totals are equal, the concept connection to what is described by these symbolic forms is different—and it will be describing a different problem.

**Figure 44**     Jill scored six points for each challenge the first time she played her video game. How many points did she score for four challenges? With practice she got even better and scored twice as much the next time she played. Show the first game score on your bead frame, then the second game score. Write a number sentence for each. What is the easiest way to get your answer for the second game?

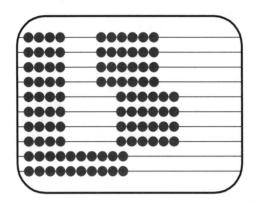

The commutative principle of multiplication is very helpful in the automatization of facts but may be a deterrent to early meaning making of the multiplication concept.

Organizing the repetitions into tables and geometric representations with color tiles can help with the recognition of patterns and automatization. Begin using the tables for pattern discoveries other than commutation, such as doubling, and then shift to commutation.

*Find the pattern. Fill in the seven missing values in the multiplication table below.*

| Column A Multiplier | Column B Multiplicand | Column C Product |
|---|---|---|
| 5 | ( 6 ) | |
| | ( 6 ) | |
| 7 | | 42 |
| 8 | | |
| | ( 6 ) | 54 |

*Describe the pattern in each of the columns of the completed table.*

**43** The commutative principle of multiplication is best discovered as students work with arrays of objects like color tiles. Using a problem like the one below, they can also regroup the same number of objects from six groups of seven to seven groups. The arrays of objects or the bead frame can also just be rotated. They can also draw arrays of objects in a computer drawing program and rotate them. The critical concept is that although the totals are the same, they represent different things.

*John has 6 packages of stickers. Each package contains 7 stickers. Which mathematical expression shows the stickers he has? What is the total for each expression? Try using your chips to explain the equal totals.*

$$7 + 7 + 7 + 7 + 7 + 7 \ = \Box$$
$$6 + 6 + 6 + 6 + 6 + 6 + 6 = \Box$$

**Figure 45**

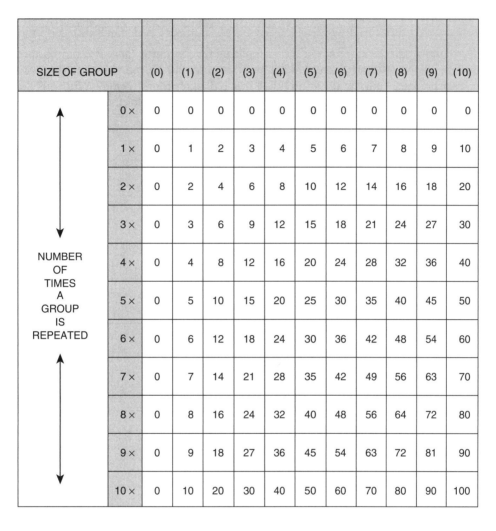

| SIZE OF GROUP | | (0) | (1) | (2) | (3) | (4) | (5) | (6) | (7) | (8) | (9) | (10) |
|---|---|---|---|---|---|---|---|---|---|---|---|---|
| | 0 × | 0 | 0 | 0 | 0 | 0 | 0 | 0 | 0 | 0 | 0 | 0 |
| | 1 × | 0 | 1 | 2 | 3 | 4 | 5 | 6 | 7 | 8 | 9 | 10 |
| | 2 × | 0 | 2 | 4 | 6 | 8 | 10 | 12 | 14 | 16 | 18 | 20 |
| | 3 × | 0 | 3 | 6 | 9 | 12 | 15 | 18 | 21 | 24 | 27 | 30 |
| NUMBER OF TIMES A | 4 × | 0 | 4 | 8 | 12 | 16 | 20 | 24 | 28 | 32 | 36 | 40 |
| GROUP IS | 5 × | 0 | 5 | 10 | 15 | 20 | 25 | 30 | 35 | 40 | 45 | 50 |
| REPEATED | 6 × | 0 | 6 | 12 | 18 | 24 | 30 | 36 | 42 | 48 | 54 | 60 |
| | 7 × | 0 | 7 | 14 | 21 | 28 | 35 | 42 | 49 | 56 | 63 | 70 |
| | 8 × | 0 | 8 | 16 | 24 | 32 | 40 | 48 | 56 | 64 | 72 | 80 |
| | 9 × | 0 | 9 | 18 | 27 | 36 | 45 | 54 | 63 | 72 | 81 | 90 |
| | 10 × | 0 | 10 | 20 | 30 | 40 | 50 | 60 | 70 | 80 | 90 | 100 |

Compare 2 × (4) and 4 × (4)

Compare 2 × (3) and 2 × (6)

How many other doubles can you find?

Why are there two rows of zeros?

Then let students discover the commutative pattern on the multiplication table. After doing the activity in Figure 45, encourage students to change the table notations so that the number of groups is on the (y) axis and the repetitions are on (x) axis and compare the tables.

**44** Multiplication can also be conceptualized as enlargement. This is different in that there are not repeated groups or multiples; instead one item is made larger. See Numbers 13 and 14 and accompanying figures for an explanation of this.

*Dan's backpack with two books weighed three pounds. He added some books that made the backpack four times heavier. How much did the backpack weigh now? Can you tell how many books he added?*

**Figure 46**

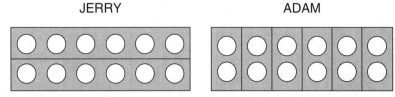

JERRY                ADAM

Jerry and Adam brought some marshmallows for the party. One of them put two marshmallows in each of six baskets and the other put six marshmallows in each of two baskets. How many marshmallows did each friend bring? Who put the marshmallows in six baskets? Finish the number sentence for this problem. What is the same about what Jerry and Adam did? What is different?

$$2 \times 6 = \square$$

$$6 \times \square = 12$$

**Figure 47**    If you know twenty, then you know plenty

| Number of times a group is repeated | 0 × | 1 × | 2 × | 3 × | 4 × | 5 × | 6 × | 7 × | 8 × | 9 × | 10 × |
|---|---|---|---|---|---|---|---|---|---|---|---|
| 0 | 0 | 0 | 0 | 0 | 0 | 0 | 0 | 0 | 0 | 0 | 0 |
| 1 | 0 | 1 | 2 | 3 | 4 | 5 | 6 | 7 | 8 | 9 | 10 |
| 2 | 0 | 2 | 4 | 6 | 8 | 10 | 12 | 14 | 16 | 18 | 20 |
| 3 | 0 | 3 | 6 | 9 | 12 | 15 | 18 | 21 | 24 | 27 | 30 |
| 4 | 0 | 4 | 8 | 12 | 16 | 20 | 24 | 28 | 32 | 36 | 40 |
| 5 | 0 | 5 | 10 | 15 | 20 | 25 | 30 | 35 | 40 | 45 | 50 |
| 6 | 0 | 6 | 12 | 18 | 24 | 30 | 36 | 42 | 48 | 54 | 60 |
| 7 | 0 | 7 | 14 | 21 | 28 | 35 | 42 | 49 | 56 | 63 | 70 |
| 8 | 0 | 8 | 16 | 24 | 32 | 40 | 48 | 56 | 64 | 72 | 80 |
| 9 | 0 | 9 | 18 | 27 | 36 | 45 | 54 | 63 | 72 | 81 | 90 |
| 10 | 0 | 10 | 20 | 30 | 40 | 50 | 60 | 70 | 80 | 90 | 100 |

Size of the group (unit)

Compare this table with the one you used before. How are they the same? How are they different? Put a circle around the number 27. What did it mean on the first table? What does it mean on this table? How can the tables help you remember the multiplication combinations? Why can we say: *If you know twenty, then you know plenty.*

**45** The pattern of a left shift of place value for multiplication in our number system is also described in preceding section Number 13. Practice with the left shift for multiples of ten should precede the following.

The generalizations that 20 × 40 is twice as much as 10 times 40 and that two tens times four tens is eight hundreds are important pattern recognitions to accompany multi-digit multiplication. They can be used to estimate problems and build number sense. Tables can help students see these patterns. Manipulatives, however, should be used to introduce the tables. Base-ten blocks are helpful with smaller values, but then grid sheets of tens or play money may be more practical.

*Gina has twenty dollars. She needs 10 times as much for her computer game. How much is 10 twenties? She needs 20 times as much for a new printer. How much is 20 times 20? She needs 50 times as much for a new computer. How much is that? Count all of these with your play money and then find the operation on the table. If 50 is 5 tens and 20 is 2 tens, what is another way to think of 50 times 20?*

**46** Multi-digit multiplication requires several conceptual transitions.

1.  The critical concept is that if each digit is repeatedly added separately and then the products are combined, the total is equivalent to repeated addition of both digits. Essentially, that adding (23) four times to get 92 is the same as adding (20) four times to get 80 and (3) four times to get 12 and then combining the partial products to get 92. This is the distributive principle of multiplication.

2.  A good way to begin is by just asking for front-end estimation and then asking for the exact amount. This will push students toward the estimation habit and better number sense. It is different from the common algorithm where we begin with the ones, but students can discover that either sequence works.

3.  Start with single-digit multipliers and double-digit multiplicands.

4.  Trading should not be a problem if the concept has been developed with addition. Use base-ten blocks or grid sheets and money at the start of concept development. Make the triad connections of manipulatives, words, and symbols.

5.  Gradually get students to combine the separate calculations into one vertical form. *A shift in thinking may be necessary for translation to the vertical form.* First of all, the convention in horizontal form is to state the operand (the number of times) first. In the vertical form the repeated unit comes first.

**Figure 48**    If you know twenty, then you know plenty

| Number of times a group is repeated | 0 × | 10 × | 20 × | 30 × | 40 × | 50 × |
|---|---|---|---|---|---|---|
| 0 | 0 | 0 | 0 | 0 | 0 | 0 |
| 10 | 0 | 100 | 200 | 300 | 400 | 500 |
| 20 | 0 | 200 | 400 | 600 | 800 | 1000 |
| 30 | 0 | 300 | 600 | 900 | 1200 | 1500 |
| 40 | 0 | 400 | 800 | 1200 | 1600 | 2000 |
| 50 | 0 | 500 | 1000 | 1500 | 2000 | 2500 |
| 60 | 0 | 600 | 1200 | 1800 | 2400 | 3000 |
| 70 | 0 | 700 | 1400 | 2100 | 2800 | 3500 |
| 80 | 0 | 800 | 1600 | 2400 | 3200 | 4000 |
| 90 | 0 | 900 | 1800 | 2700 | 3600 | 4500 |
| 100 | 0 | 1000 | 2000 | 3000 | 4000 | 5000 |
| 1000 | | | | | | |

Size of the group (unit)

Compare this table with the one you used before.

How are they the same? How are they different?

How much is 3 tens times 6 tens? How much is 4 tens times 5 tens?

Do you see a pattern? Think about larger numbers that are not on the table.

How much would 4 tens times 5 hundreds be?

$60 \times 300 = \square$

$400 \times 30 = \square$

Finish the last row of this table. Add a 200 × column.

*Shanequa had a collection of CDs. She kept them on racks. Each rack could hold 23 CDs. Round the number. About how many did each rack hold? About how many would four racks hold? Let's write that as a number sentence: 4 × 20 = 80. How many more could each rack actually hold? Exactly how many more can the four racks hold? Let's write a number sentence for that: 4 × 3 = 12. Exactly how many CDs can the four racks hold all together? Explain how we got the answer.*

**47** Regrouping of the partial products in the multiplication algorithm should reflect back to addition. Begin by showing each partial product separately and then move to consolidating them.

                     **2**

28               28

× 3   ⟶   × 3

24              84

60        (regroup 20 of the

84        24 ones into 2 tens)

**48** Before introducing double-digit multipliers, it may be helpful for students to review the concept (see Number 45) that 20 times a quantity is twice as much as 10 times that quantity and then discover that we can either make the quantity 10 times larger and then make it twice as large, or make it twice as large and then 10 times larger (the associative principle: 3 × 10 × 2 is equal to 3 × 2 × 10).

At first, use grid sheets or base-ten blocks or graphics computer programs to develop this concept. Balloons can work as well! Then shift to symbols and use the left shift with either sequence. *How can we make (37) 20 times larger? Can we make it 10 times larger? Now, how can we make it 20 times larger? Can we make it 2 times larger first?*

**49** Then allow students to discover how to combine the partial products of the two steps in the algorithm, multiplying by the digit value and shifting one place to the left for ten times—or more for larger multiples of ten.

**50** Figure 50 shows step-by-step scaffolding that may help introduce the standard algorithm. Students should work in groups to solve the problem and analyze the algorithm. Let them suggest ways to improve it or alternates. For larger multipliers (operands) and multiplicands (unit or group), the final generalizations that tens times tens are equal to hundreds, and tens times hundreds are equal to thousands should be encouraged. They are efficient and will be important for estimations of multiplication problems and as an inverse for estimation of division problems.

**Figure 49**     Marla earned 45 dollars in one week for babysitting. She babysat for the same time for each of three weeks. How much did she earn in all three weeks? Estimate your answer first, then follow the steps to do this problem.

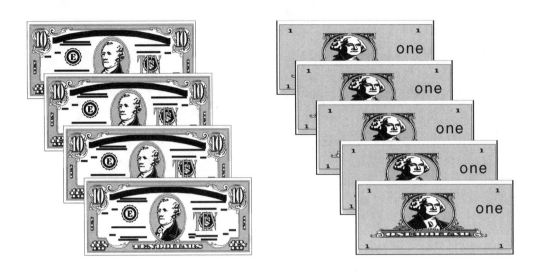

What does the picture show? How many tens did she earn for one week? How much money is that? How many ones did she earn in one week?

How many tens did she earn in three weeks? How many ones did she earn in three weeks? How much money did she earn in three weeks? How did you get that answer? Complete the number sentences that describe parts of the problem. What is inside the parentheses?

$$\square \times (4 \times 10) = \square, \qquad \square \times 40 = \square, \qquad \square \times (5 \times 1) = \square, \qquad \square \times 5 = \square$$

What do you have to do to show the whole amount she earned? Could you multiply the ones first? The number in the box that you multiplied by is the multiplier. Why is it always the same? Try an algorithm to organize your work.

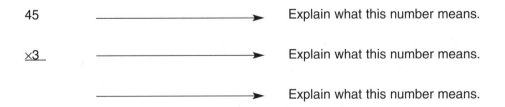

45    ⟶   Explain what this number means.

×3    ⟶   Explain what this number means.

    ⟶   Explain what this number means.

Complete the number sentence for the whole problem.

$3 \times 45 = \square$

Sean had a regular job cutting lawns. He made $35 a week. How much did he   **Figure 50**
make in the 23-week season? Show this problem in horizontal and in vertical form.
Estimate your answer; then use your play money to get the exact answer.

$$23 \times \underline{\hspace{0.8cm}} = \underline{\hspace{0.8cm}}$$

$$\begin{array}{r} 35 \\ \times \quad ? \\ \hline \end{array}$$

| | |
|---|---|
| A. How many of these for each week? | F. How many of these for each week? |
| B. How many for 3 weeks? | G. How many for 3 weeks? |
| C. How many for 20 weeks? | H. How many for 20 weeks? |
| D. How many for 23 weeks? | I. How many for 23 weeks? |
| E. How much money is that? | J. How much money is that? |
| $23 \times 5 = \underline{\hspace{1cm}}$ | $23 \times 30 = \underline{\hspace{1cm}}$ |

K. How much did Sean earn in 23 weeks?

Here is one kind of algorithm that is used for multiplication problems like Sean's.
Explain it to your group. Do you know another algorithm you can use? Can you
make this one better?

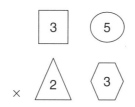

| | | | |
|---|---|---|---|
| 1 | 5 | Write the letter of the question above that this line answers. ☐ |
| 9 | 0 | Write the letter of the question above that this line answers. ☐ |
| 1 | 0 | 0 | Write the letter of the question above that this line answers. ☐ |
| 6 | 0 | 0 | Write the letter of the question above that this line answers. ☐ |
| | | Write the letter of the question above that this line answers ☐ and answer it. |

**Now try this**.

Write a number sentence for the product of the values in the hexagon and the circle.

Write a number sentence for the product of the values in the square and hexagon.

Write a number sentence for the product of the values in the triangle and the circle.

Write a number sentence for the product of the values in the triangle and the square.

**51** Cartesian multiplication requires the computation of the product of
factors, but is conceptually different from repeated addition or enlargement.

**Figure 51**   Randy had two backpacks and four caps that he wore to school. He changed the combinations often, using a different cap and different pack, but always wore a cap and carried a pack. How many different combinations of packs and caps could he get? Make a tree diagram to help you find out.

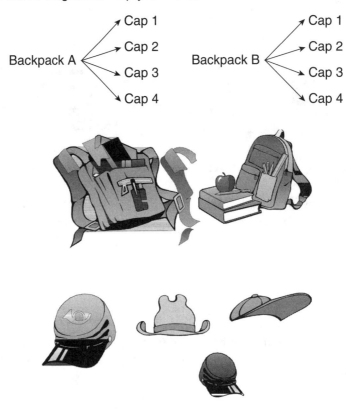

The possible number of combinations of two skirts and three blouses can be visually shown with tree diagrams and is the product of the number of skirts and blouses or $2 \times 3 = 6$ (see Numbers 195 and 196 for other combination problems).

**52** Multiplication tables can be an introduction to multiplication series and functions. Try the symbolic notation for the four table: $N = n \times (4)$, where N = each value and n is the ordinal number in a series. The value of the fifth number in the four table is $5 \times 4$ or 20. The patterns of multiplication can be observed in many ways. Make connections to the area of rectangles. Use color tiles to allow students to discover what happens when one side is increased a unit, when both sides are increased, when the sides are doubled. Examine squares and introduce the square notation.

**Illustration 3.2**

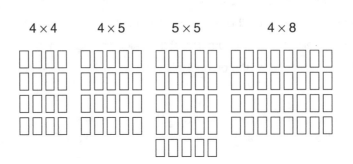

**53** Just as subtraction presents the first great hurdle for students in the early elementary grades, division presents a challenge for the upper grades. Part of the difficulty lies in the variations of the division concepts and the tendency for teachers to overlook these concepts and move too quickly to a difficult algorithm. If we think of multiplication as repeated addition, division could also be conceptualized as repeated subtraction. This does not come as easily from the experiences of children as the concept of sharing.

**54** Children do have a naturally developed understanding of the sharing process or what is termed *partition or partitive* division. Given real problems and manipulatives, they readily solve partition problems.

*We had twelve candy bars after Halloween and want to share them among three friends. How many will each friend get?*

Children will place the individual bars one by one in each of three piles or may immediately just try to equalize the piles. In a partition problem we know the whole value and we know the number of parts. What we do not know is the size of each part.

**55** In *quotition or quotitive* division (some texts refer to it as measurement division), we know the size of the group but not the number of groups. Quotition is the inverse of repeated addition and can be explained on a number line as repeated subtraction. We start with the whole group and repeatedly subtract the equal parts to discover how many there are in the whole. Quotition problems are also a good way to understand the inverse relationship between division and multiplication. Finding out how many groups of size (5) there are in 30 is *the inverse* of finding out how much six groups of (5) is equal to (Hatfield, Edwards, & Bitter, 2005).

Quotition problems are less common to the child's experience, but the standard division algorithm is traditionally taught in the frame of reference of a quotition problem (e.g., *How many 5s are there in 25?*).

Use a variety of manipulatives and the calculator to develop these concepts.

*We had twelve candy bars and gave four bars to each of our friends. How many friends got four candy bars? Enter the whole number of candy bars into your calculator. Subtract four at a time. How many times did you subtract four before you got to zero? How many fours are there in twelve? How many friends got candy bars?*

*Angelo had 62 pieces of gum for his party. The gum came in packages of five. How many whole packages did he have? Did he have any loose ones? What was the whole amount of gum?*

*What does the problem tell us? Are we trying to find out the number of parts (packages of gum) or the size of each group? Will there be more or less than ten packages? How do you know? How many pieces in ten packages? How many more pieces do we have over the ten packages? How many fives in twelve? How many whole packages do we have all together? How many loose pieces?*

Difficulties with the operation arise when we try to move students from the more familiar partition meaning of division to the quotition meanings and algorithm explanations without careful transitions. The standard algorithm and inventive procedures should be explored in connection to both kinds of problems. Students should be encouraged to *explain the differences in division problems in terms of what is given and what is sought.*

*A. Four students shared 36 pieces of candy equally. How many pieces of candy did each student get? Complete the number sentence for this problem.*

$$36 \div 4 = \square$$

*B. A different group of students also divided 36 pieces of candy equally, and each got six pieces. How many students could get six pieces of candy? Complete the number sentence for this problem.*

$$36 \div \square = 6$$

*Problems A and B are similar but different. How are they the same and how they are different? What do you know in each problem and what do you need to find out?*

**Figure 52**  Kim and her friends collected Yu-Gi-Oh cards. They decided to pool their cards and make an album. They counted 115 cards. Each page of the album held five cards. How many pages did they fill? Use your base-ten blocks to help you solve this problem. What kind of a problem is this? Write a number sentence for this problem.

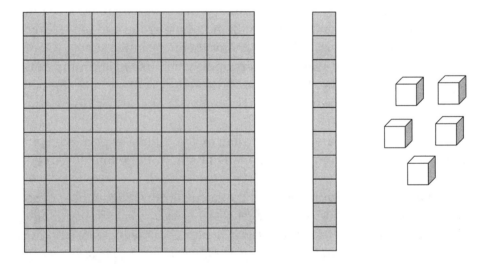

Think about this. How many groups of five were there in ten? How many in one hundred? How many would there be in one thousand? How many fours are there in twelve? How many in 120?

**56** Division as shrinkage is the opposite of multiplication as enlargement. There is neither sharing nor grouping. The operation is applied to a single object that gets smaller. A good illustration may be referral to the popular movies in which a child is enlarged or shrunken, but the number of children is unchanged. The confusing element is the way shrinkage is described. When you say that the population shrank to five times its original size or was five times smaller, the word "times" becomes confusing to children. Instead of dividing by five they may multiply. Fractional multiples may work better for shrinkage problems. Alternate the terms "5 times smaller" with "1/5 the size."

**57/58** The automatization of division facts is just as critical as the multiplication facts and should be presented as the inverse of the multiplication facts, but in the frame of reference of both quotition and partition. There should also be clarity of the fact that, like subtraction, division is not commutative when considering the whole that is divided or grouped. 12 ÷ 3 is not the same as 3 ÷ 12. However, the size of the group and the number of groups are commutative. Automatization of division facts is a precursor to the mastery of a division algorithm. Manipulatives and tables will help students recognize the patterns.

*If there are 4 sixes in 24, how many threes will there be? If we divide 32 into four parts and each part is size (8), how big will the size of each part be if we divide the 32 into 8 parts?*

*If six groups of (4) are equal to 24, how many groups of (4) are there in 24?*

*When you divide 24 into 6 groups, there are 4 in each group. How much is 6 × 4?*

*If there are six groups of (4) in 24, how many groups of (2) will there be? How many groups of (8) are in 24?*

Once the facts are automatized, estimation of quotients for multi-digit divisor problems is both possible and useful. Allow students to use a variety of approaches to the estimation process, but the inverse generalization to the one for multi-digit multiplication is very useful. If tens times hundreds are thousands (e.g., 2 tens times 3 hundreds are 6 thousands), then thousands divided by tens are hundreds and thousands divided by hundreds are tens (21,000 ÷ 70 = 300 and 21,000 ÷ 700 = 30. 21 thousands divided by 7 tens = 3 hundreds. 21 thousands divided by 7 hundreds = 3 tens.

**59** Partition division is directly related to fractions. Dividing something into four parts is like finding 1/4 of it. The connection should be made as soon as possible. It is especially useful to make the connection when expanding the meaning of fractions from parts of a single whole to parts of groups or sets of objects. Translate one form into another and finally reach the generalization that the fraction form can represent the division process. One third represents one whole divided into three parts, and two thirds is two wholes divided into three parts. See Number 69.

**60** The division algorithm should be developed within a triad of problem words, manipulatives, and symbols in reference to both partition and quotition problems. Even though we traditionally use quotition terms in teaching the algorithm, teachers may find themselves switching back and forth between the meanings. For example, partition thinking works easily for developing the regrouping or trading concepts needed for preparation within short form and two-digit operations using the algorithm. In addition to regrouping, however, use of the algorithm requires organization and careful step–by–step recording of the partial quotients, remainders, and final quotient. Try to connect this process directly to the meaning of the problem.

*We wanted to share 85 Chuckles equally among 6 children. The Chuckles came in packages of ten. How many whole packages of ten (tens) would each one get? How many extra, undivided packages of ten would there be? What will we have to do with the extra packages? How many single Chuckles (ones) would we have now? If we divide the rest of the single Chuckles among the six children, how many will each one get? How many Chuckles would they have in all?*

**Figure 53**   Here are some flowers. They were separated into three different vases. How many were put into each vase?

Write a division number sentence that describes this problem.

Write a fraction that names what part of the whole group of flowers went into each vase. Write a number sentence for the problem using this fraction.

Compare your answers.

Ten pencils were shared among 5 students. How many pencils did each student get?

What fractional part of the whole number of pencils did each student get?

How many pencils is that equal to?

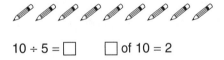

10 ÷ 5 = ☐    ☐ of 10 = 2

**61** When we get to larger numbers, however, a switch from partition to quotition seems expedient. In dividing 201 by 3 (201 ÷ 3), we think partition when we say, *"We cannot divide two hundreds into three equal parts of hundreds, and so we regroup the two hundreds into 20 tens."* Then we switch to quotition and say, *"How many threes are there in 20?"*

The estimation approach and recognition of patterns such as those in Figures 54 and 55 will help.

**62** It is easy for students to understand that zero divided into any number of parts is still going to be zero or that there are no other quantities in zero. However, dividing a number value by zero is more of an abstraction and difficult to understand. When any number is divided by zero, the quotient is

Keshawn and his three friends teamed up to earn money by making deliveries for the store.    **Figure 54**
They earned $96 dollars one day and divided it equally among themselves. How much did each one earn? Show this problem as a number sentence and as an algorithm.

$96 \div \square = ?$     $\square \overline{)96}$

Estimate your answer; then use your play money to get the exact answer.

 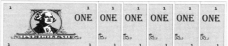

(A) How much money has to be divided?

(B) How many of the tens can each of the four friends get?

(C) How much of the whole amount of money will giving the tens use up?

(D) How many ones and tens are left?

(E) How much money is that?

(F) What do you have to do with the remaining ones?

(G) How many of the ones will each friend get?

(H) How many ones does this use up?

(I) How much money is left to divide?

Here is one kind of algorithm that is used for division problems like Keshawn's. Explain it to your group. Look at the questions in the boxes above. Use them to help explain the algorithm.

②  △4

```
  2
4 )9 6   ◄——— Write the letter of the question in the box that this line answers    _____
  8 0    ◄——— Write the letter of the question in the box that this line answers    _____
  1 6    ◄——— Write the letter of the question that this line answers               _____
  1 6    ◄——— Write the letter of the question that this line answers               _____
  0 0    ◄——— Write the letter of the question that this line answers               _____
```

Write the letter of the question that the value in the circle answers    _____

Write the letter of the question that the value in the triangle answers _____

$96 \div 4 = \square$ tens with a remainder of $\square$ tens and $\square$ ones. Then $(10 + 6) \div 4 = \square$

undefined. The problem may lie in the way we describe the division problem. From the quotitive perspective, when we ask, "How many twos are there in six?" we infer *the most* number of twos. There could, for example, be (1) group of two and (1) group of four, or (2) groups of two and (2) single ones in six, but the most number of groups of two in six is (3). There is really no limit to the number of zeros in a sum value of six and so we say that six divided by zero is undefined. Real data such as that in Figure 56 are useful.

**Figure 55**

| Size of part or number of parts | | 10 | 20 | 30 | 40 | 50 |
|---|---|---|---|---|---|---|
| Size of part or number of parts | 100 | 1000 | 2000 | 3000 | 4000 | 5000 |
| | 200 | 2000 | 4000 | 6000 | 8000 | 10000 |
| | 300 | 3000 | 6000 | 9000 | 12000 | 15000 |
| | 400 | 4000 | 8000 | 12000 | 16000 | 20000 |
| | 500 | 5000 | 10000 | 15000 | 20000 | 25000 |
| | 600 | 6000 | 12000 | 18000 | 24000 | 30000 |
| | 700 | 7000 | 14000 | 21000 | 28000 | 35000 |
| | 800 | 8000 | 16000 | 24000 | 32000 | 40000 |
| | 900 | 9000 | 18000 | 27000 | 36000 | 45000 |
| | 1000 | 10000 | 20000 | 30000 | 40000 | 50000 |
| | 2000 | 20000 | 40000 | 60000 | 80000 | 100000 |

Use this table to help estimate the following division problems:

5,976 books were placed on 30 library shelves. How many books on each shelf?

59,045 books were stacked in the library with 2000 books in each section. How many sections were filled?

For each problem, describe what you were given and what you had to find out.

Compare the two problems. How are they different? How are they the same?

Do you see any patterns?

Think about larger numbers that are not on the table. Add another row.

**Figure 56** The following table shows the number of runs (RBIs) for each baseball team that was the total for several games. For each team decide what is the greatest number of innings where there could have been two RBIs, the greatest number of innings where there could have been three runs, and the greatest number of innings where there could have been zero runs.

| Team | Total RBIs | Most possible innings with two runs | Most possible innings with three runs | Most possible innings with zero runs |
|---|---|---|---|---|
| Team A | 24 | | | |
| Team B | 36 | | | |

How did you get your answer for the greatest number of innings with two runs and three runs?

Why was it impossible to get an answer for the greatest number of innings with zero runs?

Give some possibilities for how different numbers of zero-RBI innings could be scored in one game with a score of 12 runs.

Why is any number divided by zero undefined?

**63** Once students can use and explain the standard algorithm as in Figure 54 and estimate answers with ease, it may be unnecessary to spend a great deal of time practicing multi-digit long division algorithms.

My suggestion for algorithm practice is a set of ten problems—all estimated first. The first three should then be completed without a calculator. If the answers are all correct, then the rest should be done with the calculator. If there is a mistake on the first three, then the student should correct it and do three more without the calculator. Any additional mistakes should be followed by three problems without the calculator until three problems are done correctly.

*For the division problem 24,345 ÷ 81, will the answer be closer to 3000, 300, or 30? (Think: Thousands divided by tens are hundreds, and therefore 24 thousands divided by 8 tens would be 300.) Explain your estimate. Suppose the divisor were 89; would the answer be more or less than 300? More or less than 200? Why?*

**64** Children develop beginning concepts of fractions at a relatively early age. They understand "half of it" as something less than a whole though they may not understand "one half" as the name of one part of something that has been divided into two equal parts. The next cloudy concept is the recognition that the name "one half" or any fraction name describes only the quantity in relationship to the whole, rather than a definitive quantity. In other words, *the amount of something that can be described as "half of it" depends upon the size of the whole thing.*

At the movies, Jane and Alice decided to buy and share one candy bar. What part of the candy bar would each one get? Which would you prefer: 1/2 of the one in the circle or 1/2 of the one outside of the circle? Why?

**Figure 57**

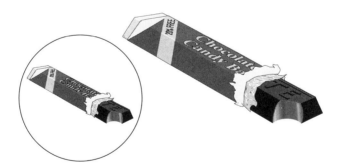

**65** Naming the bottom number of the fraction as the denominator, which tells us the number of parts the whole has been divided into, is an important adjunct to the development of this concept. As the concept is constructed, reinforce the idea that for unit fractions to be easily compared they must be parts of the same whole. 1/2 of a large pie is not the same as 1/2 of a small pie. 1/3 of a large pie is smaller than 1/2 of a large pie but may not be smaller than 1/2 of a small pie.

**66** The next important concept is that the relative quantity of one part of the same whole decreases with the number of parts. A hurdle to overcome is that an increasing denominator represents smaller relative amounts; experiences that emphasize the concept that a greater number of parts results in smaller pieces of the same whole are useful.

*These fractions show the part of 12 hours on a vacation day that some friends spent playing games on their computers. Put the fractions in order from least to greatest.*

$$\frac{1}{2} \qquad \frac{1}{4} \qquad \frac{1}{3} \qquad \frac{1}{6} \qquad \frac{1}{12}$$

*What fraction shows the most time? What fraction shows the least time? What was the most amount of hours spent out of the 12? Suppose the fraction that shows the most time was the fraction part of a 24-hour day. How many hours would that be?*

**Figure 58**

Here is the whole pie.

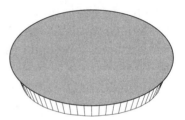

Put a circle around half the pie.

 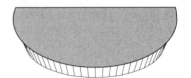

How many parts of this size would be about the same as the whole pie?

Write the fraction that describes this part.

**67** It may be a good idea to move quickly from the concept of unit fractional parts of whole things to the partition division relationship of parts of groups of things. The potato chip bags in Figure 59 allow students to make the connections between the related concepts (also see Figure 53). They can also make the connection that the numerator tells the size of the whole set and the denominator the number of parts. The actual size of the part or group depends on the size of the whole set. You have to divide the numerator by the denominator to find the size of the equal parts.

Eventually students should reach the generalization that in order to find the value of a unit fractional part of a number or set you divide the number in the whole set (the numerator) by the denominator.

Matt and his friends shared a small bag of chips. Altogether there were four people sharing. What is the fraction name for the part each friend got?

**Figure 59**

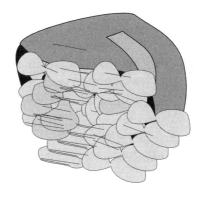

The next time the four friends were together, they bought a large size bag.

What is the fraction name for the part each friend got? Did they get the same amount each time? Explain your answer.

What would the friends have to do to know exactly how many chips were in 1/4 of the small and large size bags?

1. Use your color tiles to build 4 rectangles of 12 tiles with parts of different colors.

**Figure 60**

2. Follow the fraction color guide in the first column of the table to build your rectangles. The guide describes the parts of a whole rectangle as fractions of different colors.

| Fraction color guide | Number of tiles of each color |
|---|---|
| (1)<br>1/3 blue,<br>2/3 green | |
| (2)<br>1/2 red,<br>1/4 green,<br>1/4 yellow | |
| (3)<br>1/5 yellow,<br>4/5 red | |
| (4)<br>1/8 yellow,<br>4/8 blue,<br>3/8 red | |

**68** The transition to more-than-unit fractions for the same whole does not usually present a problem—except perhaps in the verbalization of what the numerator and denominator represent. Identification of the denominator as the number of parts the whole has been divided into should be clearly established in experiences with unit fractions. The most common way to describe the numerator is that the top number represents the number of parts of the whole we are thinking about or have. Connections to real problems are best for this concept. A good beginning for more-than-unit fractions of wholes and sets may be to strengthen the concepts developed with unit fractions by scaffolding the alternate fraction names for wholes and comparing them: 7/7 = 6/6 = 5/5 = 4/4 = 3/3 = 2/2 = 1 of the same whole. Then introduce the use of inequality signs to compare the sizes and show them on the number line. Follow this with an introduction to fractions that are more than one whole (improper fractions).

*Put these numbers in the right order and place them on the number line.*

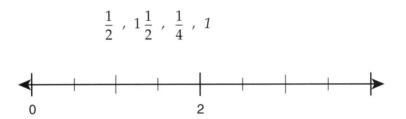

**69** The addition and subtraction operations with like fractions usually come easily with the use of manipulatives. We can add and subtract like parts. Equal denominators of the same whole or group of objects represent parts of the same relative size of that whole or like parts of the whole. They can be added or subtracted by adding or subtracting the numerators.

*I drank 1/4 of a glass of milk with my breakfast and 3/4 of a glass just after breakfast. How much of the glass of milk did I drink altogether? How much more did I drink after breakfast than I did with my breakfast?*

**70** Then move to more-than-unit fractions of a set. How did we find out what one third of twelve is? If one third of twelve is four, then how can we find out how much two thirds of twelve are?

Sometimes there may be fuzziness about the class inclusion definitions of the total set. It is easy to visualize ten computers as a whole set or group, but there is a conceptual leap to considering an aquarium with different fish as a whole group of fish and the individual kinds of fish as parts of that whole. After all, the fish are different! Examples of both kinds of wholes or sets are needed. This may also serve as an introduction to set theory. The different kinds of fish are subsets of the whole set but also can be described as fractional parts of the whole.

There may also be difficulty in translating common experiences like the pizza problem below to the fraction meaning of division. A pizza divided into eight parts for four people gives two parts to each or 2/8 or 1/4 of one whole pie. However, eight pieces of pizza divided into four parts is also 8/4 of all the pieces of pie or two whole pieces. In one case, the pie is the whole, and in the other case each piece is one of eight whole pieces.

There were ten computers in the classroom. What fraction of the whole is each computer? Two of them had DVD drives. What fraction of the whole had DVD drives? What fraction did not have DVD drives? How many did not have DVD drives?

**Figure 61**

8/10 of 10 = ☐

We also had an aquarium in the classroom. What part of our fish were guppies?

What part were angel fish?

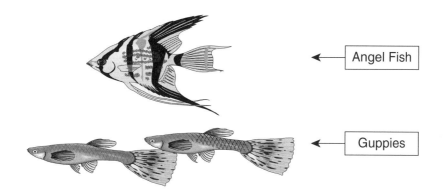

Four friends went for pizza. The pizza pie came sliced into eight pieces. How much pizza could each one get?

**Figure 62**

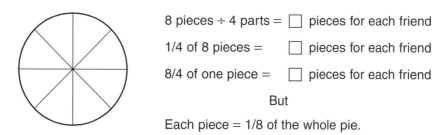

8 pieces ÷ 4 parts = ☐ pieces for each friend

1/4 of 8 pieces = ☐ pieces for each friend

8/4 of one piece = ☐ pieces for each friend

But

Each piece = 1/8 of the whole pie.

Each friend will get ☐ of the whole pie.

**71** Relating to the somewhat different concept of division as shrinkage, students should have experiences that help them develop the idea that fractions can be used to describe the relative size of single objects or groups. Refer again to the movie in which the children are shrunken or enlarged (see Number 56). A small bag of chips is half the size of a larger bag and may have half the number of chips, but conceptually there are not two parts—just one that is half-size (see Figure 59). The other half is an abstraction.

**72** The transition to an understanding of fractions as a representation of parts of a group or set where the number of parts into which the set is to be divided is more than the number of wholes is often overlooked. The first step in this transition is an understanding that even though there is more than one whole, each part is going to be less than one whole.

*We have three small pizzas to divide among the four of us. Will we each get more or less than a whole pizza? Explain your answer.*

**Figure 63**    Rhonda wanted to study a bug under her microscope. She measured it first with her centimeter ruler. It measured 2 centimeters. Her microscope had a lens that made everything four times as large. How big would it appear to be under the microscope? Then she put another insect on a slide and looked at it. The new bug appeared to be about 4 centimeters. How large was it really?

In real life, every thing Rhonda saw through her microscope was ☐ (what fraction) of what it appeared to be?

**Figure 64**    Four friends went for pizza. They bought three large unsliced pizza pies. Could each one get a whole pizza? What part of a whole pizza could each one get?

Pie #1          Pie #2          Pie #3

Each friend got ☐ of each pie. All together, it was the same as ☐ of a single pie.

Three wholes divided into four parts = ☐

How much would they each get if there were five friends?

Three wholes divided into five parts = ☐

A group of friends went for pizza. They bought three pies and each got 3/8 of a pie. How many friends were there?

A group of six friends went for pizza. They each got 5/6 of a pie. How many pies did they buy?

The next step should be the concept that each whole will have to be divided and then the parts combined.

*We can't divide the three whole pizzas evenly, so what will we have to do with them? If we divide the three pizzas into the four parts we need, how big a part of each pizza will each of us get? But we have three pizzas, so how much pizza will each of us get in all?*

Eventually this should lead to the important generalization that any fraction can represent the operation of numerator divided by the denominator.

An extension of this is that a whole number can be expressed as a fraction with a denominator of 1.

**73** The concept of simple equivalents can be easily constructed by using real materials. Fraction bars and circles are useful manipulatives to develop these concepts. I prefer the bars for equivalents because the pieces are ordered so that the equivalents are all clearly recognizable as equal parts of the same size whole that can be seen as a referent. Paper folding is also helpful. Students can actually produce equivalents as they fold equal sized paper sheets into smaller and smaller parts. Several important generalizations should come from experiences with equivalent fractions:

• First, students need to understand that the larger the number of parts into which a whole has been divided, the more parts you need for the same total amount or fraction of the whole.

• Later this generalization can be extended to the proportional relationship between the number of parts in the whole and the number of parts required. If there are twice as many parts of the same size whole, then you need twice as many of them for the same amount of whatever is being divided.

Randy and Megan each had the same chocolate bar. Randy broke hers into four pieces and ate two of them. Megan broke hers into two half pieces and ate one half. Did they eat the same or different amounts of candy? Explain your answer.    **Figure 65**

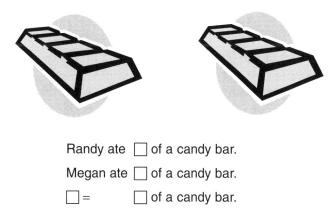

Randy ate ☐ of a candy bar.

Megan ate ☐ of a candy bar.

☐ =    ☐ of a candy bar.

One easily overcome limitation of manipulatives is that students see the whole only as a single unit. The whole also can represent a set of individual units. Empty egg cartons filled with cubes, pom-poms, or color tiles with colored threads or pipe cleaners to mark the divisions are effective. Students can see the whole as a unit—the whole-dozen carton—and at the same time the set of individual units that comprise it. One half of the whole carton is also six eggs: 6/12 of the whole carton is the same number of eggs as 1/2 of the carton or 2/4 of the carton. A combination of the bars and the cartons may be the best. Also try sets of fraction bars and papers.

**Figure 66**    Luis and his three friends went for pizza. They ordered a large pie and divided it into four equal pieces. Angelo came in with seven friends, and they ordered two large pizzas. They divided each pie into eight parts, and each of them had two pieces. Angelo bragged that he had more pizza than Luis. Was he right? Explain your answer. Suppose Angelo had shared the two pies among six friends. Would two pieces be the same as Luis's one piece? Use your fraction parts to help you think of other compare-fraction problems in the pizza store.

| ONE WHOLE LARGE PIE | | | | | | | |
|---|---|---|---|---|---|---|---|
| 1/2 | | | | 1/2 | | | |
| 1/4 | | 1/4 | | 1/4 | | 1/4 | |
| 1/8 | 1/8 | 1/8 | 1/8 | 1/8 | 1/8 | 1/8 | 1/8 |
| 1/3 | | 1/3 | | | 1/3 | | |
| 1/6 | | 1/6 | | 1/6 | | 1/6 | 1/6 |

**74** Several approaches can be used to demonstrate the patterns that lead to the generalization that the value of a fraction does not change if numerator and denominator are multiplied or divided by the same quantity. Use real problems such as the ones in Figures 66, 67, and 68. Allow the students to see the relationships in fraction bars, egg cartons, and tables of equivalent fractions.

*Jenny and Inge had equal numbers of pages in their notebooks. Jenny had hers divided into eight chapters, and Inge had hers divided into four chapters. What part of the whole was each of Jenny's chapters? What part of the whole was each of Inge's? They each counted the number of pages in two chapters of their notebooks. Which one had more pages? Whose chapters were smaller parts of the whole? How many of Jenny's chapters would be the same as two of Inge's? How many of Inge's would be the same as six of Jenny's? Jennie had her book divided into _____ as many parts of the whole as Inge, so she needed _____ as many of these parts to equal Inge's.*

**75** Then move to the symbolic algorithm for finding equivalents: that multiplying or dividing the numerator and denominator by the same *operator* forms an equivalent fraction.

*The fraction that describes two of Inge's chapters is 2/4, and the one that describes four of Jenny's Chapters is 4/8, and we found that these were equal: 2/4 = 4/8. Look at the two numerators and then look at the two denominators. Do you see a pattern? Can you find another fraction that follows the same pattern? Use your fraction bars to prove that this fraction is equal to the others.*

**Look at the A egg carton.** Find the halves. How many eggs in one half of a dozen?    **Figure 67**

$$1/2 = \text{\_\_\_\_\_ eggs.}$$

Find the twelfths. How many of these in 1/2 dozen?

$$1/2 = 6/12 = \square \text{ eggs.}$$

**Look at the B egg carton.** Find the sixths. How many eggs in 1/6 of a dozen?

$$1/6 = ?/12 \text{ (how many twelfths).}$$

$$1/6 = ?/12 = \text{\_\_\_\_\_ eggs.}$$

**Look at the C carton. Find the thirds.** How many thirds in the whole carton?

How many eggs in one third?

How many 1/12's of the whole is that?

How many eggs in 2/3 of the whole carton?  How many 1/12's is that?

$$1/3 = ?/12 = \text{\_\_\_\_\_ eggs.}$$

$$2/3 = ?/12 = \text{\_\_\_\_\_ eggs.}$$

**Look at the D carton.** How many eggs? What part of the whole is that?

$$?/12 = ?/6 = \text{\_\_\_\_\_ eggs.}$$

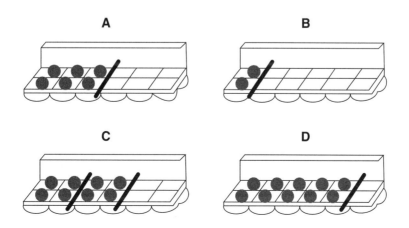

**Figure 68**    All of these fractions represent 1/3 of the whole: 1/3, 2/6, 4/12, 8/24. Look at the numerators. Do you see a pattern? Look at the denominators. Do you see a pattern? Supply the missing denominator for the next fraction in this series: 16/___.

Name at least two more fractions that are the same as 1/3.

How could you change 3/15 to an equal fraction with 5 in the denominator?

☎☎☎                                                       ÷ ? = ☎ _____

☎☎☎☎☎☎☎☎☎☎☎☎☎☎☎ ÷ ? = ☎☎☎☎☎ _____

Three parts out of 15 are the same as one part out of _____.

The concept that multiplying or dividing the numerator and denominator by the same number or factor does not change its value can be strengthened by connecting to the concept that any fraction with the same numerator and denominator is equal to 1, and therefore multiplying by such a fraction is like multiplying by 1 and does not change its value.

**76** If this has not come up previously, fractions that have values greater than 1 need to be introduced. Introduce the terms "improper fractions" and "mixed numbers" simultaneously in the context of problems. Present the commonsense practicalities of changing an improper fraction like 13/12 to the mixed number $1^{1/12}$ to simplify an answer or doing the reverse to make an operation such as finding the difference between $1^{1/12}$ and 7/12 easier; 13/12 and $1^{1/12}$ are simply different representations of the same value.

**77** I often compare fractions to actors who play different roles with different costumes and settings but underneath are always the same person. Another role for fractions is the application of the fraction form as an expression of ratio. A ratio expresses the relationship between two different values. There are alternate forms for expressing ratios. In word form, we say the ratio of new toys to old ones is one to three, or as a line expression we use a colon and write 1 : 3. The different forms should be introduced simultaneously (Lamon, 1993).

The use of the fraction notation can be confusing because we are accustomed to identifying the denominator of a fraction as the whole, and ratios can represent either a relationship between parts and the whole, "One pound of the five-pound box of chocolates is filled with nuts"; or a relationship between different parts of the whole, "The ice cream cone is two parts vanilla and three parts chocolate." Ratios can also represent both preceding relationships between groups of items, "Three out of the five girls on the team had caps on"; or, "For every three girls with caps on there were two without caps." As they are with simple fractions, analyses of ratio and proportion problems should include identification of given quantities in terms of parts and wholes.

**78** In some problems where only the parts are described, the whole may have to be computed first. Even adults frequently misinterpret this type of problem.

*For every two players with caps on, there were three without caps. If there were fifteen players, how many had no caps? The ratio of players with caps to the whole is not 2/3, it is 2/5 or 2 out of a whole of 5. Two out of every five players, or 2/5 of the 15 players, or 6 have caps on.*

There are three experienced soccer players for every two new ones on the team. **Figure 69**

What are the parts in this ratio? What is the size of the whole?

What fraction name tells us what part of a whole of five are experienced players? Suppose there were 15 players on the team. How many would be experienced? How many would be experienced on a team of 20 players?

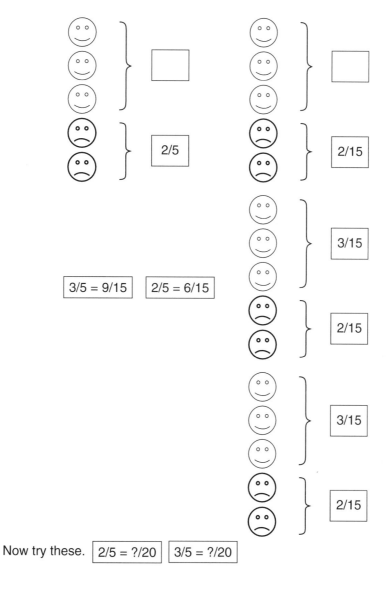

Now try these. 2/5 = ?/20   3/5 = ?/20

**79** Statements of equivalent ratios are called "proportions." The patterns of equivalent fractions or proportions can also help us compute unknown parts and wholes. Five out of ten parts is the same as one out of two parts or half the total number of parts. When the size of the denominator increases or decreases, the size of the numerator must change proportionately (by the same factor) in order for the fractions to be equivalent.

Proportions can be used to compute unknown quantities based on the equivalent relationships.

*There are three experienced soccer players for every 2 new ones on the team. There are 15 players; how many are experienced?*

Proportions can also be used to compare equal relationships.

*I have 6 video games and 1 of them is new. My friend has 12, including 2 new ones. Who has the greatest proportion of new games?*

$$\frac{1}{6} = \frac{2}{12}$$

One out of six parts is the same as two out of twelve.

Proportions can also be used to evaluate inequalities.

*I have 15 video games and 3 of them are new. My friend has 12, including 3 new games. Who has the greatest proportion of new games?*

Three out of 15 is the same as 1/5, but 3 out of 12 is equal to 1/4, which is larger. If this is introduced before students can reduce fractions to lowest terms, use manipulatives such as color tile rectangles to develop a basic concept and understanding of relative size. *When you consider an equal number of elements of a smaller and larger whole, that number of elements represents a greater proportion of the smaller whole. Three tiles out of group of six is a greater fractional part of the six than the same three tiles out of a group of twelve. The ratios are not equivalent.*

$$\frac{3}{15} < \frac{3}{12}$$

**Figure 70**    The cheese pizza pies came sliced into eight equal pieces and you got seven of them. How much of a whole cheese pizza is seven pieces? The same size pepperoni pizza came sliced into six equal pieces and you got seven of them. Did you get the same amount of pizza?

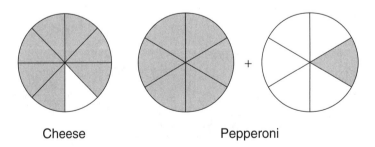

Cheese          Pepperoni

Finish this number sentence to describe your answer.    7/6 >    ☐

Which would be more: nine pieces of cheese or seven pieces of pepperoni?

Write the number sentence that describes your answer.

Mavis wanted to know how tall her house was. She couldn't get up to the roof to measure the height, but she had another idea. She took a picture of the house, and then measured the height and width of the house on the picture using a centimeter grid. Then she measured the width of the house with a tape measure and found that it was nine meters wide. How could she determine the height of the house? **Hint:** First make a scale for the picture using the given measures.

**Figure 71**

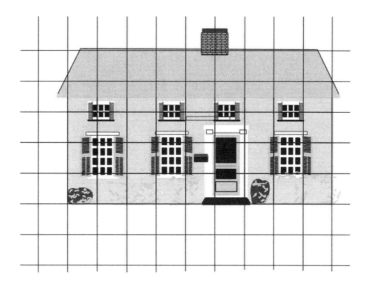

**80** Understanding of proportions is also needed in applications to the use of scale drawings and maps. They may be presented from either the shrinkage or enlargement aspect. Scaled maps represent the enlargement type. The value of the shrunken part size is given, and the true value expressed in the scale as a ratio. As an example of the first type, Figure 71 shows a scale drawing problem where the value or size of the part is compared as a ratio to a unit of measure in the scale, and the whole has to be measured in its scaled form and its actual size computed as a similar ratio.

Some ratio problems such as the one in Figure 72 have no given value for the size of either the whole or the parts—just the relative sizes. Eventually these ratio problems may be described symbolically as algebraic equations.

*My size is 1/3 of my father's size (x = 1/3y). My brother is 2 times my size (z = 2x). My brother is therefore 2/3 of my father's size (z = 2/3y), and y = 1⅓z.*

**81** Fractional inequalities should be explored in several ways in addition to finding the least common denominator.

Begin with inequalities that compare fractions to one whole:

*Is 9/8 more or less than a whole? Is 9/10 more or less than a whole? Explain why 9/8 is more than 9/10.*

After students have developed familiarity with the common equivalents of 1/2 and realize that any fraction where the denominator is twice the numerator will be equal to 1/2, inequalities can be solved by comparisons to 1/2.

*Is 5/9 smaller or larger than 8/17? 5/9 is more than 1/2, and 8/17 is less than a half (there are alternative ways to reason this), so 5/9 is more than 8/17.*

**Figure 72**

Jim's father is three times as tall as Jim.

How many of Jim's heights are in his father's?

What fraction of his father's height is Jim?

Jim's brother is twice as tall as Jim.

What fraction of Jim's father's height is his brother?

How much taller is Jim's father than his brother?

Jim's height = _____ of his father's height

Jim's brother's height = _____ × Jim's height

Jim's brother's height = _____ of his father's height

Jim's father is _____ taller than Jim's brother

**82** An understanding of multiples and factors should precede the introduction of complex operations with fractions. The concept of the associative principle of multiplication is a first step. Let students explore this with arrays of color tiles and balloon diagrams—or computer drawing programs. When they realize that enlarging a value three times and then two times results in the same outcome as multiplying it six times or the product of the separate increments, you can introduce the concept of common multiple as it relates to the principle.

*Blowing up a balloon to 2 times the original size and then making the new-size balloon 3 times bigger is the same as blowing the original up 6 times:*

$$2 \times \bigcirc \times 3 = 6 \times \bigcirc$$

The associative principle can also be illustrated with color tiles or other manipulatives that show it as applied to groups rather than a single object. Beginning, as in Figure 73, with a group value of (3) and multiplying it five times and then multiplying the product of (15) two times is the same as multiplying the original (3) two times and then the product of (6) five times, and the same as multiplying the original (3) ten or $(2 \times 5)$ times.

Build these with your color tiles.

**Figure 73**

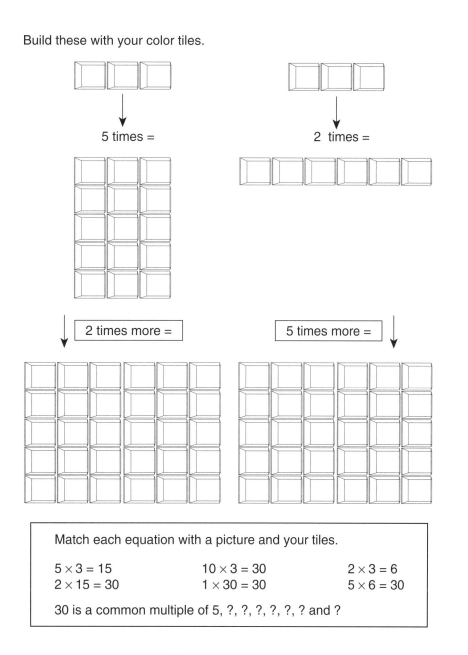

Match each equation with a picture and your tiles.

$5 \times 3 = 15$          $10 \times 3 = 30$          $2 \times 3 = 6$
$2 \times 15 = 30$          $1 \times 30 = 30$          $5 \times 6 = 30$

30 is a common multiple of 5, ?, ?, ?, ?, ?, ? and ?

**83/84** Allow students to discover other ways to explore common multiples. Let them organize the whole class into different sizes of equal groups, organize stacks of books on a shelf, or use a computer to draw copies to group, print, and share. Try rearrangements of color tiles in rectangles. The lengths and widths of each possible rectangle, measured in the number of tiles, are the factors of the multiple. Begin with common multiples such as 12, 24, 30, and 36 that have many factors. I call them "happy numbers" because they have so many different ways to have fun or be useful. They can be divided or organized in many equal ways. That is why we have 12 inches in a foot, 36 inches in a yard, 24 hours in a day with 12 of them shown on the clock, and 360 degrees in a circle. After students list all of the possible numbers of repeated units or multipliers and all the possible sizes of the unit or multiplicands that can be combined in multiplication to reach the common multiple, identify the numbers as the factors of the multiple. Doing these activities will also reinforce multiplication and division facts.

**Figure 74**

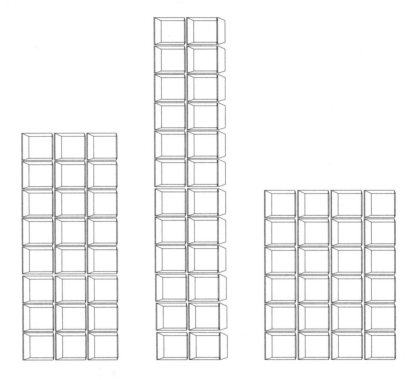

Calculate the total number of color tiles in each rectangle.

Make a list of all the different lengths and widths.

What is the common multiple of the color tile lengths and widths?

Why can we call them factors of the common multiple?

Can you build another rectangle with the same multiple?

What are all the factors of the multiple?

**85** Then use rectangles to let students discover that some multiples can have only two factors: the multiple itself and (1), and therefore form only one kind of rectangle, with one side = 1. **These are the prime numbers**. Let students discover that prime numbers above (2) cannot be even numbers, but that not all odd numbers are primes. Make lists of primes and encourage automatization of some of the smaller ones to help with reducing fractions and finding equivalents.

**86** Identify the alternative to a prime number as a composite number—a number that has more than two factors.

**87** Use the color tiles again with different multiples to discover common factors. Identify the smallest possible rectangle that is a multiple of two factors. The rectangle must be capable of being organized into equal-sized arrays of both factors. Each side of the rectangle will be a factor. The number of tiles in this rectangle is then the **least common multiple** for two factors.

**88** After the common relationships between factors and their multiples are explored with tiles, they can be organized into tables. Use the color tiles again with different multiples to discover common factors.

*There are whole groups of 12, 6, 4, 3, 2, and 1 in both (12) and (24). They are common factors of the different multiples, 12 and 24.*

*A balloon of size 12 can shrink three whole times to size 4, four whole times to size 3, or six whole times to size 2. A balloon of size 24 can shrink six whole times to size 4, two whole times to size 12, or twelve whole times to size 2.*

**89** Two and four are common factors of (8) and (12), but three is not, because there is not a whole number of threes in 8. A balloon of size (8) can shrink four whole times to size (2) or two whole times to size (4), but it cannot shrink three whole times to any whole number. It is also useful to find the **greatest common factor (GCF).**

*Use your color tiles to find all the factors of (12) and (24). Then find the factors of (8). Make a table of factors and common factors. Explain any difference.*

*For each of the multiples below find the factors and the common factors. Then circle the greatest common factor.*

| Multiple | All Factors |
| --- | --- |
| 12 | |
| 24 | |
| 8 | |
| Common factors of 12 and 24 | |
| Common factors of 8 and 12 | |
| Common factors of 8 and 24 | |

**90** Different factors can have many common multiples, but the least common multiple (LCM) is the one that is the smallest. Let students use color tiles to discover these and the generalization that, although for two prime numbers, the (LCM) is the product of the two, other LCMs can be less than the product of the factors. For example, the least common multiple for (6) and (4) is (12), not (24).

*Use your color tiles to find the least common multiples for these factors. Construct the smallest rectangle that contains whole groups of each factor.*

| Factors | Least common multiple |
| --- | --- |
| 3, 4, 2, 12 | |
| 7, 3, 1 | |
| 7, 3, 6, 21 | |

The concept of factors and common factors is critical as a basis for solving complex operations with fractions and later algebraic equations. Use the color tiles and tables as above, but factor trees can also work.

**Figure 75**

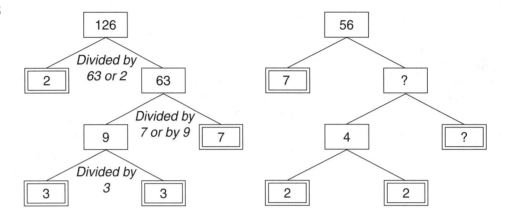

Try building a factor tree. Study the tree for (126) and then try to fill in the missing places in the (56) tree. Explain why there are no branches coming from the double line boxes. Build a tree of your own from a number you choose.

Try relating factors to measures. Use exchanges in money to make the concept real. A dime and a quarter are common factors of the dollar because you can change the dollar for only dimes or only quarters. But the dime is not a factor of the quarter because the quarter cannot be exchanged for a whole number of dimes. It is a factor of a half-dollar. Nickels and pennies are common factors of the quarter, the dime, and the half dollar.

**91** Construction of the algorithm for finding the least common denominator, and changing fractions to equivalents with common denominators so that operations can be performed, should occur in the context of solving addition and subtraction problems with manipulatives.

Fraction bars work well in developing a purpose for the common denominator and in visualizing what is happening as fractions are operated on. Use scaffolding such as that in Figures 66 and 67 (above) to review the generalization that multiplying numerator and denominator by the same operator does not change the value, and that in order to add or subtract fractions we need to find the denominators that are common multiples for the fractions we wish to operate on—preferably the least common multiple (LCM), which in the fraction is the lowest common denominator (LCD).

**92** Provide some practice with finding the LCD denominators in the algorithm form. However, it may be unnecessary to have extensive practice with these once the concepts are clear, because it is much simpler to convert the fractions to decimals by dividing the numerator by the denominator with a calculator and then performing the operation.

Maria ate 1/4 of a candy bar before lunch and 1/3 of a candy bar after lunch. How much of a whole candy bar did she eat? Use your fraction tiles to help solve this problem. Add the pieces by putting them together. Do you see an equivalent fraction that is equal to their sum? In order to add the two different fractions we had to change them into fractions that had the same denominator. How can we do that without changing the value of the fraction?

Look at the denominators of 1/3 and 1/4. Can you find their Least Common Multiple?

That will be your Least Common Denominator. Now find the numerator for that denominator that makes an equivalent for each fraction. Remember that the numerator has to be enlarged as much as the denominator because the greater the number of parts of a whole, the more parts you need for the same amount.

$$1/3 = \underline{\qquad} /12, \quad 1/4 = \underline{\qquad} /12$$

Now add them together.

$$4/12 + 3/12 = \underline{\qquad}, \text{ and therefore } 1/3 + 1/4 = \underline{\qquad}.$$

(12) is the Least Common Multiple of the numbers _____ and _____.

It is also the Least Common Denominator of the fractions _____ and _____.

**Figure 76**

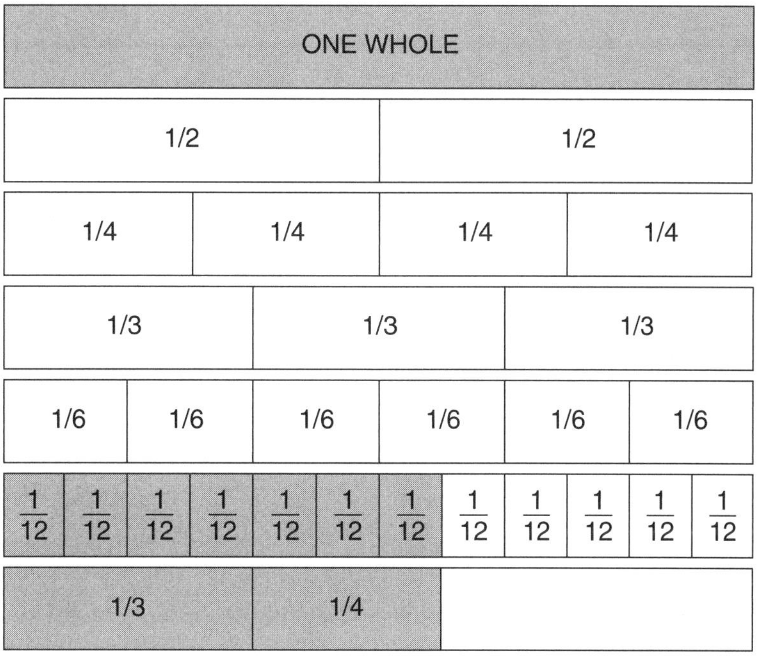

93 Practice with both the horizontal and vertical algorithm forms for addition and subtraction of unlike fractions should be attached to real problems. A critical generalization is the recognition that finding the least common denominator is a first and important step. Relating this to operations with whole numbers and the need to add and subtract like quantities helps. Use the color tiles for discovering the LCD and then allow students to suggest addition and subtraction algorithm forms, including making a note of the LCD as a reference for converting to equivalents. I suggest not shortcutting the converted full

equivalent fraction form by just recording the numerators (a traditional form) at first. This may be disjunctive to the reasoning process. Consider the following difficulty sequence transitions.

1. Present only addition problems with proper fractions and easily computed common multiples (LCDs) that do not add up to more than 1 whole.

2. Present problems that add up to more than 1 whole, develop vocabulary for *improper* fractions and *mixed numbers,* and practice changing in either direction. Compare the process to trading with whole numbers.

3. Present problems that require finding the difference between proper fractions.

4. Present problems that require finding the difference between improper fractions, but do not require regrouping or trading.

5. Present subtraction problems with fractions of all types that require regrouping.

*Steve went trick or treating on Halloween. By the end of the evening at 9:00 P.M. he had collected seven of his favorite chocolate bars. He couldn't resist eating them, however, and by 7:00 P.M. one of them was half gone. At 9:00 P.M. he had only 4¾ bars left. How much more candy had he eaten between 7:00 and 9:00 P.M.?*
*Think: Altogether Steve collected [ ] bars.*
*He ate [ ] bars before 7:00 P.M.*
*That left him with [ ] more bars of candy to eat.*
*The candy he ate between 7:00 and 9:00 is the difference between [ ] and [ ].*
*The number sentence for this is:* _____.

**94** Steve's problem is a complex multi-step problem that represents a change-unknown subtraction involving unlike fractions. The algorithm presented below by Rhonda varies from the traditional algorithm in that the equivalent fractions are shown with both numerator and denominator. The traditional algorithm, below, that shows the common denominator as a heading and the numerators as separate entries can follow. Students may suggest shortcuts and share these.
*Rhonda solved Steve's Halloween problem with this algorithm. Explain how she did it.*

$$
\begin{array}{ccccc}
A & \longrightarrow & B & \longrightarrow & C \\
6\frac{1}{2} & & 6\frac{2}{4} & & 5\frac{6}{4} \\
-4\frac{3}{4} & & -4\frac{3}{4} & & -4\frac{3}{4} \\
\hline
1\frac{3}{4} & & & &
\end{array}
$$

*What did she change to get from A to B?*
*What did she change to get from B to C?*
*How did she find the difference between 5⁶/₄ and 4¾?*

Maria ate 1/3 of a candy bar before lunch and 1/4 of a candy bar after lunch. Which was the larger piece? How much larger was that piece? Use your fraction tiles to help solve this problem. Compare the fraction pieces. Do you see a fraction that is equal to the difference between the two pieces? It has a different denominator, but the fractions we are comparing have equivalents for that denominator. In order to find the difference between two fractions with different denominators we have to change them into fractions that have the same or common denominator. What was the common denominator in this problem?

**Figure 77**

$$\frac{1}{3} = \frac{}{12} \text{ and } \frac{1}{4} = \frac{}{12},$$

$$\frac{}{12} - \frac{}{12} = \frac{}{12} \text{ and } \frac{1}{3} - \frac{1}{4} = \underline{\hspace{1cm}}$$

| 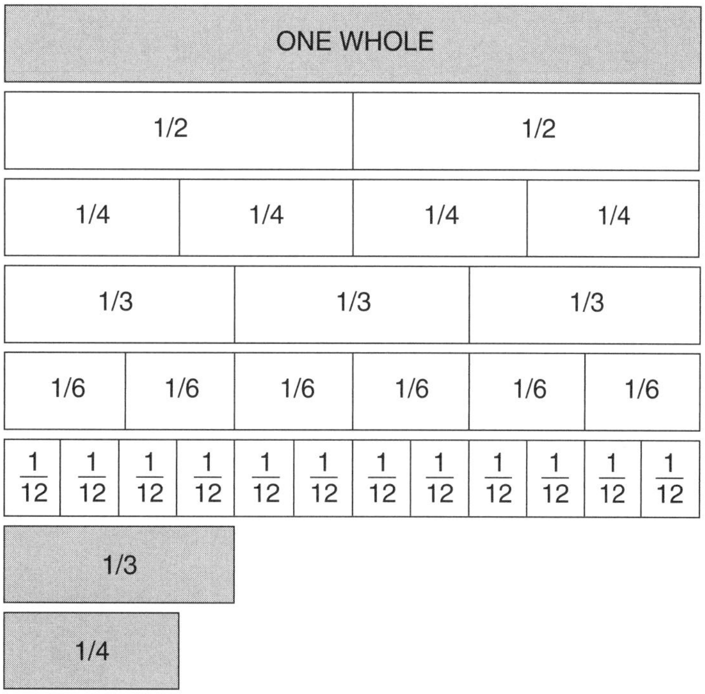 ONE WHOLE | | | | | | | | | | | |
|---|---|---|---|---|---|---|---|---|---|---|---|

| 1/2 | 1/2 |
|---|---|

| 1/4 | 1/4 | 1/4 | 1/4 |
|---|---|---|---|

| 1/3 | 1/3 | 1/3 |
|---|---|---|

| 1/6 | 1/6 | 1/6 | 1/6 | 1/6 | 1/6 |
|---|---|---|---|---|---|

| 1/12 | 1/12 | 1/12 | 1/12 | 1/12 | 1/12 | 1/12 | 1/12 | 1/12 | 1/12 | 1/12 | 1/12 |
|---|---|---|---|---|---|---|---|---|---|---|---|

| 1/3 |
|---|

| 1/4 |
|---|

**95** Multiplication of proper fractions by whole number operators should be presented as repeated addition of the same fraction. Using manipulatives and real materials, students should discover that, as in the addition of like fractions, the numerators are enlarged but the denominators remain the same. *1/3 repeated two whole times is 2/3, and 2/5 repeated three times is 6/5.*

Allow students to discover that just the numerators have to be multiplied while the denominators remain the same before moving to the horizontal and vertical algorithm.

Follow this with multiplication of mixed numbers by whole numbers—changing to improper fractions.

*The running track on which Lori ran was 1 ½ miles long. How many miles did she run in three laps? Try this problem but estimate your answer first.*

*Allan tried to solve the running track problem with an algorithm. Explain how he got from A to B, from B to C, and then to D.*

| A | | B | | C | | D |
|---|---|---|---|---|---|---|
| $3 \times 1\frac{1}{2}$ | $=$ | $3 \times \frac{3}{2}$ | $=$ | $\frac{9}{2}$ | $=$ | $4\frac{1}{2}$ |

*Did you find the same answer in a different way? Explain it to your group.*

**96** Multiplying by a fractional operator is a difficult but important concept. At the beginning students need to discover that multiplication by a fractional operator is the same as repeating the referent value less that one whole time and that therefore the product or result will have a value less than the referent. It is also the same as finding the fractional part of a value. If the operator is a unit fraction, it is the same as dividing the value by the denominator; 1/2 times 24 is the same as 1/2 of 24 and the same as dividing 24 by 2.

$$1/2 \times 24 = 1/2 \text{ of } 24 = 24 \div 2$$

*Every time the handle of a clock goes around one whole time, twelve hours pass. Two times around covers [ ] hours, but 1/2 time around is only 1/2 of the twelve or [ ] hours. Football games also play by the clock. The total playing time is one hour. How much time is used up by half time?*

**97** The next step is to consider more-than-unit fractions of whole number values. Begin to develop the algorithm for multiplication of fractions with students by generalizing back to the concept that two times 1/3 is 2/3 and thus 2/3 of a value is two times more than whatever 1/3 of that value is.

*Once you find 1/3 of a value, you just have to multiply the value by the numerator (2) in order to find 2/3 of the value.*

*For each of the following number sentences estimate whether the answer will be more or less than the value in the box.*

$$1/3 \times [4] = ?, \quad 1\frac{1}{3} \times [4] = ? = \underline{\hspace{2cm}}$$
$$5/6 \times [36] = ?, \quad 7/6 \times [36] = ?$$

*Then use the multiplication algorithm to find the answer.*

**98/99** Using the fraction tiles and referring back to the above, students can then apply their generalizations to fractional multiples of fractions. Multiplying a fraction by a proper fraction operator is like finding a fractional part of the referent fraction (multiplicand), and the resulting product is going to be less than the multiplicand fraction. Extend this with number sense analysis.

**100** When finding a unit fraction of a unit fraction, the student should be able to see from fraction tiles or fraction pattern blocks that $1/2 \times 1/3$ is going to be 1/6 (see Figure 78), and 1/3 of 1/2 is going to be the same 1/6, and then that 1/2 of 1/6 is 1/12. The generalization can them be made that this result of the operation can be obtained by multiplying the denominators of the operator and the referent value—in effect, producing a fraction with a larger denominator and smaller value.

Use your hexagon pattern blocks to discover fractional parts of fractions and multiply fractions by fractions. **Figure 78**

Look at the half of the hexagon.

Find 1/3 of the half of the hexagon.

What part of the whole hexagon is 1/3 of the half?

1/3 × 1/2 = ☐

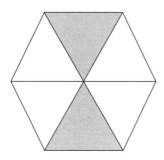 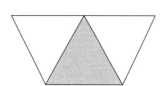

Now find 2/3 of half the hexagon.

What part of the whole hexagon is 2/3 of the half?

2/3 × 1/2 = ☐

**101** Follow this with the concept that a unit fraction of a more-than-unit fraction is going to be more than the unit fraction of the unit fraction: 1/2 of a 1/3 of a pie is less than 1/2 of 2/3 of a pie. The whole is larger so the piece will be larger. It's twice as much because the numerator is 2. Once we get the value of the unit fraction by multiplying the denominators, we simply multiply it by the numerator of the larger whole: 1/2 × 2/3 = 2/6 or 1/3.

**102** The next step is to consider more-than-unit fractions of a fraction. Referring to the hike problem below: 3 × (1/2 of 1/3) is the same as 3/2 of 1/3, and also the same as 3/2 × 1/3.

Before developing the algorithm, review the concept that in order to find a more-than-unit fraction of a whole number, we first divide by the denominator and then multiply the quotient by the numerator of the operator (3/2 of 6 is equal to 3 × 1/2 of 6, or three times greater than 1/2 × 6. Half of six, or six divided by (2), is equal to three; 3 times this quotient of (3) is equal to nine.

It follows then that if 1/2 × 1/3 = 1/6 (multiplying denominators), then 3/2 × 1/3 is three times greater or equal to 3/6 (multiplying numerators as well). These combined concepts construct the algorithm.

Prove the algorithm with fraction tiles. Prove the algorithm again with number sense operations.

*One day Lori fell when she was only halfway around the 1½ mile running track. How far had she run? She made up for it the next day by running 5½ times around the track. How far did she run that day?*

**103** The process of reducing a fraction to lowest terms has some function in making work with fractions simpler and is useful in understanding ratios. However, with calculators in everyday use, most complex fraction operations should be done by translating the fraction to a decimal. In solving a problem, the unreduced fraction is not a wrong answer unless the problem specifically says: Reduce to lowest terms. Refer back to understandings of equivalent fractions, ratios, and factors to help students generalize (see Figure 68):

1. That dividing numerator and denominator by the same factor does not change the value of a fraction

2. That dividing numerator and denominator by their greatest common factor will reduce the fraction to lowest terms

*The package of candy had 15 pieces, and Jack ate 3 of them. Ann said she had eaten 1/5 of the package, but it was the same amount. Can you prove that they ate equal amounts?*
*Write the fraction that Jack ate.*
*Write the fraction that Ann ate.*
*How can you prove that they are the same?*

*It rains in parts of Arizona on the average of about 20 days a year. We were in Arizona for 60 days and it rained on 3 of them. Was that close to average?*

1. *Express the ratio of average rainfall as a fraction.*

2. *Express the ratio of rainfall we experienced as a fraction.*

3. *How can we make the larger denominator closer to the smaller one without changing the value of the fraction?*

4. *Explain your answer and how you found it.*

**104** Before introducing the division of whole numbers and fractions by fractions it may be helpful to review the basic meaning of division and the division meaning of fractions. Fractions are related to partitive division. The numerator represents the size of the whole or the number of wholes and the denominator the number of parts into which that number is divided. If six pounds of candy were divided into seven parts, each part would be 6/7 of a pound ($6 \div 7 = 6/7$). The partition concept also works well when you are dividing a fraction by a whole number. It is easy to divide 6/7 into 6 whole parts (each part will be 1/7: $6/7 \div 6 = 1/7$), or even into 2 parts (each part will be 3/7). It is harder to grasp the concept from the quotition aspect, which is, "How many sixes are there in 6/7?" There is actually 1/7 of a 6 in 6/7. When you are dividing a whole number or fraction by a fraction, however, only the quotitive meaning applies. The partition meaning of division does not work for division by a fraction because a fraction is not a counting number. You can divide a value into two parts or one part, but you cannot divide a value into 1/2 number of parts. The quotition meaning, however, works. You can divide a value into parts that are of a size that is 1/2 of one whole. When we divide 4 by 1/2, we think: "How many parts of size 1/2 of one whole are there in 4?" From the quotitive perspective, you are simply finding out how many fraction parts of a given size there are in a given whole or part of a whole that is represented by a fraction. It is easy to understand 3 ÷ 1/2 if you think: "How many 1/2s are there in 3?" Even 5/6 ÷ 1/6 makes sense when you think: How many 1/6s are there in 5/6?

Later on this quotitive perspective can be used to explain the division-by-fractions algorithm. Once there is clarity in the concept of what is happening in the division of a value by a fraction, there is still the challenge of developing a true understanding of the algorithm for division by a fraction. Step-by-step interpretations of problems that describe real situations will help.

Reggie took the same vitamin pills each morning. The pills came in a box and each day he took two pills. One day he noticed that the box had only eight pills left and realized that he needed to know how long they would last if he continued to take two pills each day. How many days would the pills last? Reggie then decided that he would need to stretch the pills by taking one pill each day instead. How many days would they last if he only took one? How many days would they last if he took only half a pill each day? What fractional part of the normal dose would half a pill be?

**Figure 79**

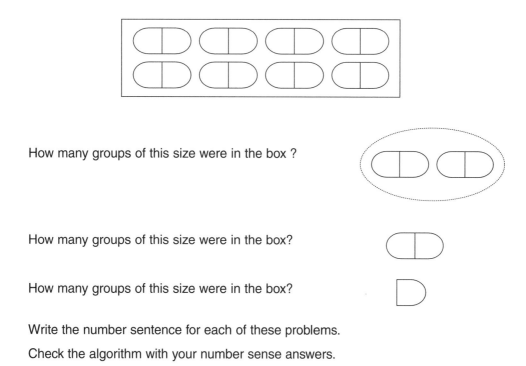

How many groups of this size were in the box ?

How many groups of this size were in the box?

How many groups of this size were in the box?

Write the number sentence for each of these problems.

Check the algorithm with your number sense answers.

**105** Division of whole values by a unit fraction divisor is frequently confused with finding a fractional part of the value and multiplication by a fraction. Start with the fractional expression of a whole. The number of unit fractions in any one whole is the same as the denominator of a fraction. One whole = 4/4. Two wholes would have twice as many units or 2 times the denominator or 8/4. The generalization here is that to find the number of unit fractions in values of more than one whole we just multiply the whole number that is the dividend by the denominator of the divisor: 6 ÷ 1/4 = 24 because there are four unit fractions of size 1/4 in one whole and 6 times as many (6 × 4) 1/4ths in six wholes.

# 106

Then proceed to whole number and mixed number dividends with more-than-unit fraction divisors. The problem 6 ÷ 2/4 means: "How many 2/4ths are there in 6?" Although there are four unit fractions (1/4ths) in one whole, there are only half as many 2/4ths. There are only half as many because 2/4 is twice as large as 1/4. There would also be only 1/3 as many 3/4ths in the same whole.

*If there are twenty-four 1/4ths in (6), then there are only twelve 2/4ths in (6) and only eight 3/4ths. In each case we found the number of more-than-unit fractions in the dividend (6) by dividing the number of unit fractions in the dividend (24) by the numerator of the divisor.*

The generalization to aim for is that dividing the number of unit fractions in a given dividend by the numerator of the divisor then tells us the number of more-than-unit fractions there are in the dividend.

This can lead to the algorithm for division by fractions. The algorithm combines the two concept steps:

- Multiply the dividend by the denominator of the divisor to find the number of unit fractions in the dividend.
- Then divide by the numerator of the divisor to find the number of more-than-unit fractions in it.

The shortcut that students should discover with help from the example below is just to invert the divisor and multiply the dividend by it.

*Jenna wanted to make some banners for the cheering squad. She went to the material store and bought five yards of material. Each banner needed 1/3 of a yard. How many banners could she make? Use your fraction tiles or a diagram to help.*

*Write a number sentence for this problem.*

*Think:*

*How many banners could she make with one yard?*

*How many 1/3 yards are there in one whole yard?*

*How many in 5 yards?*

*Jenna tried to find an algorithm to solve the material problem of dividing 5 by 1/3. First she thought about the problem as, "How many 1/3 yards are there in 5 yards?" Then she listed the steps she needed to solve the problem:*

*Explain what she did in each step:*

> A.  5 yds. ÷ 1/3 yd. = [ ] banners
> B.  1 yd. = 3 banners
> C.  5 × 3 banners = 15 banners

Then she decided that 5 ÷ 1/3 was the same as 5 × 3/1.

Do you agree?

Suppose she had 8 yards of material. How many banners could she make? Solve the problem in your head and then try Jenna's algorithm to see if it works.

Try Jenna's algorithm with $6\frac{1}{3}$ yards. You will have to change the mixed number to an improper fraction first.

$$6\tfrac{1}{3} \text{ yds.} \div 1/3 \text{ yd.} = \square$$

Suppose Jenna wanted to make double-sized banners. She would need 2/3 yd. for each. How many could she make from 6 yards of material? Try using Jenna's algorithm.

Mike and Dan were on a hike. They refilled their half-gallon jug with water at every spring and shared the water equally. How much water did they each drink before the jug was empty? How much water did each one drink by the time they filled and emptied the jug three times? Use your fraction tiles to help solve this problem.    **Figure 80**

Hint: First find out how much water each friend drank from each refill.

Mike and Dan each drank $\square$ of $\square$ 1/2 gallon of water from each refill.

That is the same as $\square$ of a gallon for each refill.

The number sentence for this problem is $3 \times (1/2 \text{ of } 1/2) = [\ \ ]$

By the end of the hike they each had consumed $3 \times \square$ of a gallon.

Think about what you did to solve the problem and think of a simple way to explain how to do it from the number sentence. There may be more than one way to do it.

Suppose the jug they shared could hold 3 quarts and each one drank 1/6 of a quart at a time. How many times could they both have a drink before the jug was empty?

The number sentence for this problem is $3 \div (2 \times 1/6) = [\ \ ]$

Think about what you did to solve the problem and think of a simple way to explain how to do it from the number sentence. There may be more than one way to do it.

Compare both problems. How are they alike and how are they different?

| ONE WHOLE | | | | | |
|---|---|---|---|---|---|
| 1/2 | | | 1/2 | | |
| 1/4 | | 1/4 | 1/4 | | 1/4 |
| 1/3 | | 1/3 | | 1/3 | |
| 1/6 | 1/6 | 1/6 | 1/6 | 1/6 | 1/6 |

**107** Construction of the meaning of decimals can begin with an understanding of the common notations for money. Children will learn these notations as alternate number names without complete constructs of what decimals are. Their cultural experience with money and intrinsic motivation to communicate about it will encourage the process. Relate the reality (money) and the manipulative representations (base-ten blocks) to each other and then to their number system place value relationships in a triad that also includes the descriptive words and the symbolic form. When using words, avoid the use of the term "point" to mark the decimal point terminus for whole numbers. Instead, use the word "and," (e.g., five and two tenths) as though it was a whole number and fraction (which it is). This forces some meaning into the words that is missing when the value is just read as digits after the decimal. Students should discover that the need for zero as a place-holder is opposite that for whole number where a zero is not needed for values larger than the largest digit value. For decimals it is not needed for values less than the smallest digit value. We do not need zeros at either end, but we need them for all the empty places in between.

**Figure 81**     Write the decimal number symbols for the amount of money each of these is worth under each picture.

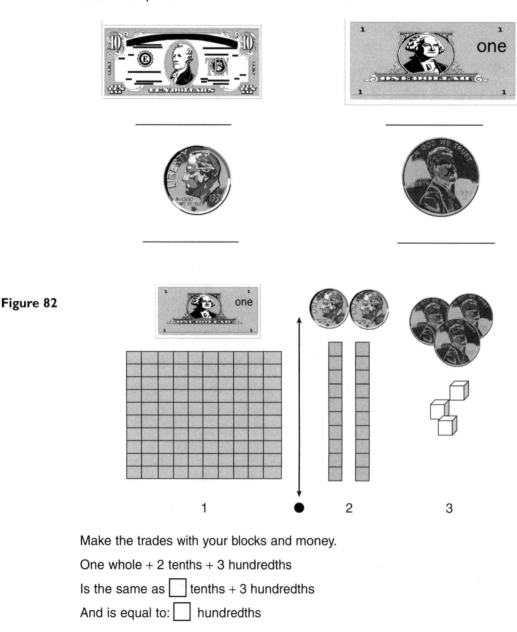

**Figure 82**

Make the trades with your blocks and money.

One whole + 2 tenths + 3 hundredths

Is the same as ⬜ tenths + 3 hundredths

And is equal to: ⬜ hundredths

**108** Decimal concepts can also be constructed with two parallel connections to prior knowledge: place value and fractions. These connections should be presented as parallel to each other in problem applications that involve decimals. Decimals are in effect a way of making fractions fit our number system— an extension of our number notation system to include values that are less than one whole—but they are therefore also fractions. They are special fractions in multiples of ten or decimal fractions. Early concepts developed for money can be expanded to develop further understanding, but base-ten blocks are also useful. Before they can be used, however, students will have to make a transition from the understanding of their application as whole number representations to decimal representations. This will need careful scaffolding. The flat that represented one hundred ones now becomes one whole or 100 hundredths. The rod or stick becomes one tenth of the whole or 10 one hundredths, and the unit cube becomes one one-hundredth of the whole.

**Figure 83**

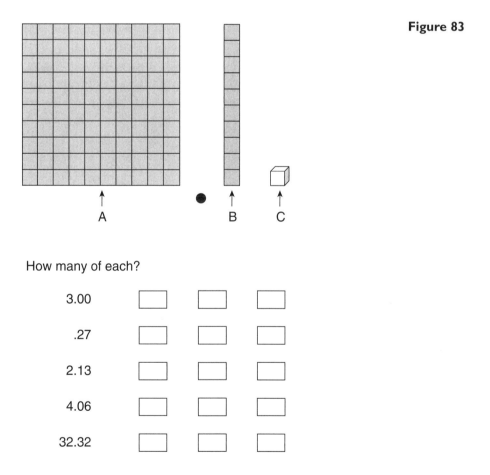

How many of each?

|  | A | B | C |
|---|---|---|---|
| 3.00 |  |  |  |
| .27 |  |  |  |
| 2.13 |  |  |  |
| 4.06 |  |  |  |
| 32.32 |  |  |  |

**109** Compare values of decimals using sequences of values in both the decimal and common fraction form.

*Use your base-ten blocks to help put the following values in order from the smallest to the largest: 1/10, .09, .2, 1/100*

Compare decimals as multiples of each other. One tenth (.1) is ten times as much as [?]. 1 whole is 100 times as large as [?].

Use a left and right shift of place value (see Number 14) to enlarge and shrink decimals by multiples of ten. Check with a calculator. If students suggest just moving the decimal point, ask them to explain why this works.

Use base-ten blocks and money to rename and trade decimals: .12 is twelve one hundredths but it is also one tenth and two one hundredths or a dime and two pennies. 1.12 is one hundred and twelve one hundredths or one dollar and twelve cents.

Use base-ten blocks and money to identify .5 as half of one whole and .05 as half of one tenth. Then round decimals to the nearest whole or tenth.

**110** Relate the rounding of decimals to the rounding of whole numbers. Five tenths or more is rounded to the next whole number. Five hundredths or more to the next highest tenth. See Numbers 16 and 17.

**111** Because decimals are an extension of our number system, addition and subtraction operations with decimals can be handled in the same way as whole number multiples of ten. Only like things can be added and subtracted, and when we have too many of one kind to fit into our system or not enough, we trade. Start with money and then use other real data that are reported in decimal form, such as rainfall amounts and batting averages. Compare decimal data by making graphs and using spreadsheet computer programs to translate data lists into graphic representations. Get data from the Internet.

*The least average yearly rainfall in the world is recorded in Arica, Chile. It is only .03 of an inch. The least annual average rainfall in the United States is recorded at Death Valley, California. It is 1.63 inches. What is the difference between the average rainfalls in these desert communities?*

*The average rainfall for the entire world is about 34 inches. How much more is that than the rainfall in Death Valley?*

*The most rainfall in the United States occurs in the Pacific Northwest where they get about 100 inches. Find the difference in average rainfall between the most and least rainy places in the United States.*

**112** Begin developing concepts related to multiplication by decimals with decimal values of wholes. The first generalization is that multiplying by a decimal fraction (as recalled from common fractions) is the same as finding a fractional part of it: .5 times a value is the same as 5/10 or 1/2 of the value. Area problems can help students visualize varying sized wholes and their decimal or common fraction equal parts. Another important generalization to recall from fractions at this time is that the size of the parts depends upon the size of the whole: .5 of 70 is not the same as .5 of 80.

Alternating between the decimal and common fraction should help students emerge with the generalization that when multiplying by a decimal, just as in multiplication by fractions, we multiply by the numerator and divide by denominator to find the fractional value.

**113** Relating the combination of fraction and decimal form to area can help to build the concepts.

Steven wanted to plant a garden. He marked off a plot that was 6 meters by **Figure 84**
8 meters. What was the area of his plot? He wanted to carefully lay out parts of
the garden and constructed a wire grid to help. He first divided it into two equal
halves. What common fraction and decimal fraction would represent half of the
plot? How much area would that be? How did you get your answer?

Steven then decided that he would like to grow vegetables in a little more than half
of his garden. He used more wire to divide his garden into 100 equal parts. The
part for vegetables is shaded on the picture below.

What decimal fraction of the whole garden plot does this represent?

Rename this decimal in common fraction form.

Can you reduce the common fraction to lower terms?

How much of the whole area would be vegetables?

Explain how you found this out.

He also wanted some herbs and decided on just .04 of the plot. Shade the part
that would be herbs. What would be the area of the herb part? Express your
answer as a decimal and as a common fraction in the lowest terms.

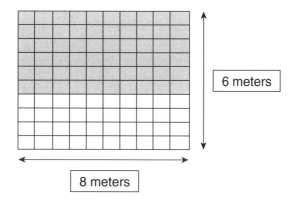

**114** Connect the multiplication of whole numbers by decimals to multiplying
by a fraction. Develop the following concepts in sequence:

- The product of any number multiplied by a decimal is going to have
  a lesser value than the original number.
- Multiplying a whole number by 1/10 or .1 results in the same value
  as dividing it by ten. If we are multiplying the whole number value
  (5) by .6, it is the same as finding 6/10 of it.
- For the fraction form we multiply the (5) by the numerator of 6 and
  divide by the denominator of 10.
- 6 times 5 = 30, but when multiplying five by six tenths (.6), (.6 × 5), the
  product is going to be less than the whole five. We have to divide
  the product of 30 by 10 (the denominator of the fraction form) to get the
  quotient of 3.
- We can use the shortcut of a right shift to do the division.
- This leads to the shortcut of just multiplying by the decimal digit and
  then using the right shift to divide the product by the place value of
  the multiplier digit, which is the denominator of the corresponding
  common fraction.

- As an example, .06 × 5 would be .30 because the digit 6 in this place represents 6/100. The product is then 30/100 or .30 in decimal form.

**115** Some generalization to prepare for multiplication by multi-digit decimals can be helpful. Compare them to whole number generalizations. One tenth × one tenth equals one hundredth (.1 × .1 = .01) because 1/10 of 1/10 is 1/100; and .6 × .3 = .18. Tenths times ones = tenths, tenths times tenths = hundredths, hundredths times tenths = thousandths: .06 × .3 = .018

**116** Once the generalization for multiplication by a decimal is in place (multiplying by the digit and dividing the product by the denominator of its place value), students can quickly progress to more than single-digit decimal multipliers. They will realize that they can proceed with the partial products and trading as though they were dealing with whole numbers. Then, for the final result, they will need to divide by the place value of the operator or multiplier (the same as the denominator of its corresponding common fraction). This can be done with a simple right shift past the decimal point. Some students will suggest the counting of decimal places for this. Teachers should get them to explain why this works.

The next step is understanding what happens when both the multiplicand and the multiplier are decimals. Revert back to the multiplication of common fractions to demonstrate that multiplying tenths times tenths will result in hundredths as the denominators are multiplied. This should lead to the realization that in the algorithm multiplying .6 × .6 will result in .36 and needs to be so recorded in the partial product. However, counting decimal places as a shortcut works here as well.

Extend the concept to: *tenths time hundredths are thousandths, and .06 × .6 is therefore .036 or 2 + 1 = 3 decimal places.*

The smallest place value in the product will be the result of multiplying the denominators of the two smallest decimal digits. Sometimes the product of the digits (numerators) will be a multiple of ten, and then because it is a decimal we reduce to lowest terms: .6 × .5 = .30, but 30/100 is the same as 3/10. *In decimal form, therefore, we ignore zeros to the right of the smallest place value that has a non-zero digit.*

*The average annual rainfall in the northwestern United States is 99.7 inches. How much rain would fall (on the average) in 3.3 years?*

1. *Round the rainfall data to the nearest whole number.*

2. *Estimate your answer in whole numbers.*

3. *Predict how many decimal places there will be in the exact answer.*

4. *Compute an exact answer using the multiplication algorithm.*

5. *Explain how the algorithm worked to get you an exact answer. Does it agree with your estimate?*

**117** Because the percentage application of decimals is in such common use in our culture, it may be wise to approach percent problems in tandem with multiplication by decimals. Finding the percent of a number and describing change in terms of percent is the everyday application of this operation—usually with the decimal rounded off to the nearest hundredth as the percent sign takes the place of the decimal point.

The development of number sense in the application of percentage concepts may be one of the most important preparations for full participation in the mathematical communications of our present culture. Spatial perceptions of objects accompanied by quantitative descriptions in both percent and common fraction form will help students achieve the necessary concepts. Students should be able to mentally visualize and estimate how large 50%, 25%, 33⅓%, 75%, and 10% of an object is. Connections to the corresponding common fractions in lowest terms for these should be computed and then automatized.

**Figure 85**

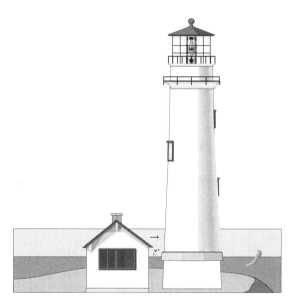

Compare the pictures of the home and the lighthouse. About what percentage of the height of the lighthouse is the height of the home? Choose from 33%, 50%, 10%, or 75%.

Draw another house that is 3/4 the size of the lighthouse. What percentage of the light house would that be?

**118** Using their previously developed fraction and decimal concepts, students should be encouraged to try alternative approaches to finding commonly used percentage values, including:

- Dividing the value by 2 (finding 1/2) for 50%.
- Dividing the value by 4 for 25% (finding 1/4) and then multiplying by 3 (finding 3/4) for 75%.
- Dividing by 3 for 33⅓% (finding 1/3).
- Right shifting one place for 10% and two places for 1%.
- Doubling the result of a one place right shift for 20%.
- Adding half of 10% to 10% to compute a 15% tip.

If the percentage is not an easy decimal to compute, changing the percentage to the decimal form and multiplying by the decimal is the algorithm form.

**Figure 86**   Evan kept a record of how much he grew each year. He showed it to his friends and said that he grew 5% each year. He always rounded his new height to the nearest inch. His friends said that he was wrong because he did not grow the same amount each year. Who was right: Evan or his friends? Explain your answer. If he continued at the same rate, would he ever grow 5 inches in one year? Predict when that would happen. Is it likely to happen? Can you find a pattern for his increase in size?

| Year | Height | Percentage Change |
|------|--------|-------------------|
| 1 | 46 in. | |
| 2 | 48 in. | 5 |
| 3 | 50 in. | 5 |
| 4 | 53 in. | 5 |
| 5 | 56 in. | 5 |
| 6 | 59 in. | 5 |
| 7 | 62 in. | 5 |
| 8 | 65 in. | 5 |
| 9 | 68 in. | 5 |
| 10 | 71 in. | 5 |
| 11 | 75 in. | 5 |

Another important functional skill in problem solving with percentages is the language distinction between 20% *off* and 20% *of* a value. Scaffolding questions to ask include:

*What part of the whole are you looking for when you take 20% off? Explain the difference between 20% of and 20% off. Twenty percent off a value is the same as what percentage of the value?*

Included in this data analysis and cultural survival skill is the realization that sequential percentage diminutions or accretions of a value are not additive. Taking 50% off of a value and then taking 20% more off the product is not the same as taking 70% off the original. The concept to connect back to is that the value of fractional parts depends upon the size of the whole. The larger the whole, the larger the value of the percentage or decimal fraction of that whole. After you shrink a value by 50%, 20% of the result is less than 20% of the original value.

This concept has other applications besides department store sales. If the crime rate goes down an even 10% a year, the actual number of crimes it goes down gets smaller each year. On the other end, if you measured your growth over a five-year period and discovered that you grew an even 10% a year, when did you grow the most?

**119** Division of decimal values by whole numbers can be explained from both a partitive and a quotitive view, like division of the corresponding fraction—just dividing the numerator and maintaining the same denominator. For example, .6 of a candy bar divided into three parts is equal to .2 of a candy bar. There are 3 parts of size .2 in .6 of a candy bar. Division of decimals by multiples of ten is a simple application of place value connected to the shrinkage concept of division. Just as we do with whole number values, we can make decimals smaller or divide them by 10, 100, and 1000 by shifting them to the left. Estimates are based on the number sense realization that we get quotients less than one whole when we divide a whole number or a decimal number by a divisor that is larger (e.g., the quotient for 1.8 ÷ 2.0 is less than one whole or .9, but 2.5 ÷ 1.2 is going to be more than one whole or about 2, because the dividend is larger than the divisor).

**120** As in the division of whole numbers, an important concept is that we can exchange decimals for their smaller size equivalents so that division is easier. The concept of trading or regrouping whole numbers for their smaller sized decimal equivalents for the purpose of dividing them can then be applied to the traditional division algorithm form. Use base-ten blocks to help develop this concept, translating the manipulative to the symbolic decimal form step by step.

*Cindy had to share her 3/10 of a package of 200 sheets of paper among five friends. She knew she could not divide 3/10 into five equal parts. How could she exchange the 3/10s into smaller parts that could be divided equally? Use your base-ten blocks to explain what she can do.*

*You just learned that .3 ÷ 5 is the same as .30 ÷ 5.*

*The quotient for .30 ÷ 5 = .06.*

*If we divide .3 into 5 equal parts, the quotient will be .06.*

*What part of the package will each friend get? Explain your answer.*

*How can Cindy find out how many sheets to give each friend?*

Division by a decimal divisor can only be considered from the quotitive aspect. The division problem, $.3\sqrt{6}$ should be interpreted as: *How many parts of size .3 are there in 6?* As preparation for the algorithm form, present the fraction form alternative 6/.3 and review the concept that multiplying numerator and denominator by the same multiplier does not change the value.

Multiplying both the divisor of .3 and the dividend of 6 by 10 allows us to eliminate a decimal divisor and not change the value of the quotient. This leads to the algorithm for division by decimal divisors: $.32\sqrt{66} = 32\sqrt{6600}$.

**121** A practical and useful application of the algorithm for the division of decimals is the conversion of any fraction to its decimal form through the process of dividing numerator by denominator. Remainders can then be regrouped to their smaller place value. The preceding requires clarity of the concept that 24/6 is the same as 24 ÷ 6. They both are equal to four wholes. Instead of converting complex fractions to varying common denominators for the purpose of operations, we can convert them to decimals, which are common denominators with easily traded and operated on multiples of ten. When this division process is applied to a common fraction where the divisor or denominator is larger than the numerator dividend (the division of a smaller number by a larger number), the sequential regrouping or trading of indivisible digits and remainders for their smaller sized decimal equivalents is required. If you divide six wholes into ten parts, the number of wholes to be divided is less than the number of parts. The result of this is that the size of each part will be less than one whole or 6/10 of one whole. When the numerator is divided by the denominator, we reach the decimal form of .6.

The calculator does this automatically. Using a calculator for the division process makes converting complex fractions to their decimal equivalents an alternative and easier way of handling complex fraction problems. Students, however, should first discover why and how this works.

*Denise got a five-dollar allowance that she wanted to spend equally over six days. What fraction of the allowance can she use each day?*

*5/6 is the same as _____ ÷ _____*

1. *How can she divide a smaller number by a larger?*

2. *As a first step, can you change the whole number 5 into an equivalent decimal with smaller units?*

3. *What are the tenths and hundredths decimal equivalents for 5 ones? 5 ones = _____ tenths, 5 = _____ hundredths.*

4. *Can you divide these equivalents by 6? Which of these might you start with as a dividend?*

5. *Trade (regroup) 5 whole ones for your equivalent smaller decimal value with your blocks and show what you do in symbolic form with the division algorithm.*

6. *If you divide the 50 tenths into six parts, the first partial quotient is: _____ tenths or (.8). This would use up _____ tenths equally divided into six parts. But we still have a remainder of _____.*

7. *Can you trade this for an equivalent decimal with a smaller place value that you can divide?*

8. *Explain how you got your final quotient.*

## 122/164 "The Measurement Magic Dozen"

Measures are the most common application in the study of numbers and operations, and should be integrated within the problems presented to develop skill in these. Because of the discrepancy in the standards, students need to learn to estimate and measure in both metrics and English (customary) standard units.

Useful estimates of conversions, such as the quart/liter/gallon, inch/cm., mile/kilometer, and meter/foot should be *automatized*, but use the calculator for the exact conversions.

There are at least 12 general concepts that cut across the various categories of measures. As teachers engage students in problem-solving opportunities to develop knowledge and skill in the more specific parameters of each separate category of measure, they should reinforce these often overlooked concepts.

1. Measures are the descriptive terms for the quantitative properties or attributes of objects and the way they move through space and time.

2. Measures allow us to communicate with each other about these properties and keep records of them.

3. Measures are important because they help us use what we know to tell us about what we do not know. For example, we can measure the area of a rectangle by measuring its length and width. We can tell how far a car will travel in an hour at the same speed if we measure the distance it travels in five minutes.

4. In order to communicate with each other about quantitative properties, we have to share or have a common meaning for the descriptive units of measure. We need consensus. If an inch is a unit of measure that we use to describe the length of an object, then we all have to agree on and know how long an inch is. If a paper clip is the unit of measure, then it has to be the same size clip all the time.

5. Most of our units of measure are standard units. Standard units or systems of units are decided upon by governments—or in primitive societies by agreements between individuals.

6. Different governments have different measures.

7. Units of measures can be grouped into larger units. The size of the grouping also has to be by consensus. Larger units (groups of smaller ones) make it easier to measure larger sizes of properties. Smaller units and parts of units allow us to measure smaller properties and be more exact.

8. When communicating about measures, larger units can be exchanged (traded) for their smaller sized units based on the agreed-upon or consensus equalities. The smaller ones can be grouped into the larger ones.

9. The equalities of the smaller and larger units are often designed to make exchanges easy. The best example of this is the metric system that, like our number system, is a base-ten system. There are similar reasons for other groups of units. The size of a foot (about the size of a king's foot) actually was agreed on before the smaller inches. But it was decided that it would be useful to divide it into twelve inches because the number twelve has so many factors, and so fractions of the foot, such as 1/4, 1/3, 1/2, 1/6, and 1/12 can easily be traded for whole numbers of inches.

10. When trading a number of smaller sized units for larger ones there will always be a fewer number of larger ones. And when trading larger ones for smaller ones there will be more of the smaller ones.

11. Measuring instruments help us make accurate measures, but it is always helpful to estimate first.

12. Measures help us make better models of the real thing.

**122** As an introduction to the study of measures, students need to be aware of some of the general purposes and the vocabulary and scope of measures as described in the "Magic Dozen." Choose grade-level appropriate items from Greg's list (and others) as an awareness-arousing beginning.

*Greg had a friend who lived in another state. They corresponded by e-mail. Greg wanted to describe himself and his home to his friend. What kinds of measures and units would he use to describe these to his friend?*

*Easy:*

1. *How tall he was*

2. *How much he weighed*

3. *How heavy his backpack was*

4. *How long his school day was*

*Harder:*

5. *How far it was to his school*

6. *How much soda pop he drank in a day*

7. *The distance he walked to school*

8. *How fast his father drove on the highway*

9. *How fast he walked to school*

10. *How fast his computer was*

11. *The size of his computer*

*Hard:*

12. *How much water there was in his swimming pool*

13. *The width of his house*

14. *How much vitamin C he took each day*

15. *How big his father's truck was*

16. *How much gold there was in his new ring*

17. *How long before they could see each other at Christmas vacation*

*Some of these were more difficult to measure, but Greg sometimes used what he knew to find out what he did not know. Greg also used some instruments. What instruments could you use to measure each of these?*

*Greg had another friend who lived in Canada. Would the measures be the same?*

The vocabulary for our English or customary standard is mainly historically related to its use, such as the size of the foot and cup, but the unit divisions have some mathematical reasoning. For example, the units in a foot and yard are multiples with many factors. The advantage of the metric system is its relationship to the place value system and the consistent vocabulary for unit subdivisions. The prefixes describe the sizes. A decimeter is one tenth of the meter, a centimeter is one hundredth, and a millimeter one thousandth. The same prefixes apply to the gram and liter.

# 123/124
Students need to practice measuring with standard instruments that already have the units embedded and the nonstandard units they decide upon themselves in a collective consensus for sharing. The need for alignment of the instrument unit edge and the measured object is a critical beginning skill. The need to avoid any gaps is also important. Later, an analysis of the precision of the instrument should also be considered.

*Brian and Ian measured their desks with blocks and with the same 12-inch ruler. Brian measured five blocks or 14 inches. Ian measured five blocks or 15 inches. What may have caused their measures with the blocks to be the same and the measures with the ruler different?*

Elena and Jose wanted to test their model cars to see which was the fastest. They built a ramp to test them with. What measures could they use to compare their cars? (Hint: There may be more than one.) What units of these measures would they use? If these were real cars, would they use the same units? Explain your answer. What else besides the cars themselves would have an effect on these measures?

**Figure 87**

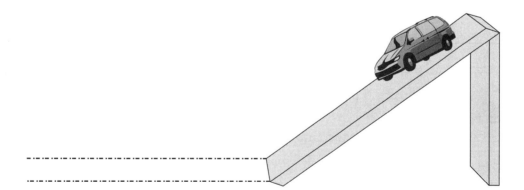

# 125
The basic concepts of conversions between units are critical. Base-ten blocks can be used here, but rulers and balances can also help. The ideas to communicate are that:

- There will always be fewer of the larger units than the small.
- To convert from the larger size unit to the smaller, you multiply by the equivalent.
- To convert measurements from the smaller size unit to the larger, you divide by the standard equivalent.

Once the concepts of fractions and rounding have been developed, measurement activities or more complex problem solving and reinforcement of operations are useful.

Read and think about the following information.

- Carrie's height is 5 ft., 2 in.
- Her brother Jason is six inches taller than Carrie.
- Their sister Lavonne is eight inches shorter than Jason.

What are the heights of Jason and Lavonne?
**Put your answers in the chart below.**

| NAME | Carrie | Jason | Lavonne |
|---|---|---|---|
| HEIGHT | 5 ft., 2 in. | | |

**126** The equivalent measures of length are relatively easy for children to learn and the instruments of measures simple and available. They are therefore a good beginning for the development of measurement concepts. Use rulers and yardsticks for hands-on experiences with both the customary and metric measures and then translate to the larger units of miles on maps. Encourage students to make observations of odometers as they are riding in cars and of signs on highways. Tables are useful to discover the patterns in the equivalent measures.

Complete the following pattern table.

| Number of Yards | Number of Feet |
|---|---|
| 3 | 9 |
| 12 | |
| 120 | |

What operation did you perform on the number of yards to determine the number of feet?

What patterns do you recognize?

**Figure 88**   Use your ruler to measure the drawing of a shark. What is the length of the drawing of the shark to the nearest quarter inch?

If the scale of the drawing was 1 inch = 1 foot, about how long would the real shark be?

**127** The understanding that standard equivalents are decided by governments and different in different countries should precede the introduction of any alternate forms. The purpose for using either the larger or smaller units for measuring and of converting one to the other should be related to the concept that larger objects are more easily measured with larger units.

*Jack measured his own desk and said it was 18 inches wide. Then he measured his teacher's desk and said it was four feet wide. Why did he use inches to describe his desk and feet to describe his teacher's desk? Could he use the same unit? Describe the desks with the same unit.*

**128** The transitions from straight-line measures to the concepts of perimeter and area require careful scaffolding and experience. The concept of perimeter as the total distance around the edge of an object or the sum of its individual sides is not difficult, but when the concept of area is introduced the two measures are sometimes confused. Students should understand that the two measures tell about different properties but are nevertheless related. Connecting the two with problems such as the ones in Figures 88 and 89 should help.

**129** Even adults sometimes have difficulty in expressing just what area is. Color tiles work very well in establishing the idea of square units as a measure of area, which is a particular space on a flat surface or the amount of square units needed to cover it. It may also be helpful to describe it as a two-dimensional measure in contrast to the one dimension of length and the three dimensions of volume. Multiplication is a shortcut for adding repeated similar groups of square units (use geoboards and grids or graph paper) Centimeter graph paper encourages the connections to actual metric units as well.

*Mandy's bedroom is 8 feet wide and 12 feet long.*

**Illustration 3.3**

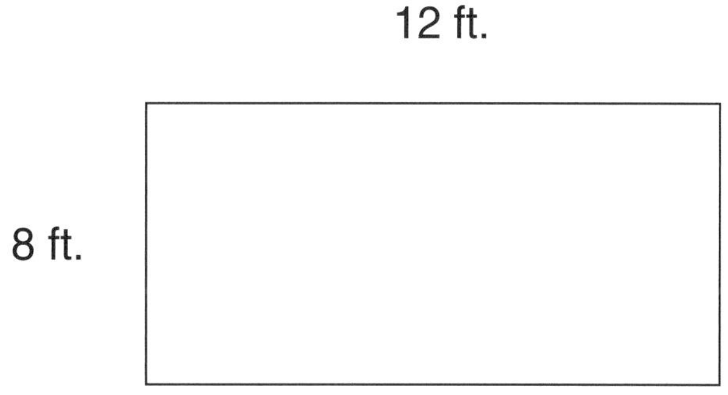

12 ft.

8 ft.

*A. What is the name given to the shape of Mandy's bedroom?*
*B. What is the perimeter of Mandy's bedroom? How did you find it?*
*C. What is the area of Mandy's bedroom? How did you find it?*

**Figure 89**    Mr. Torres wanted to plan out the new tool shed he was building, so he made a sketch on graph paper where each centimeter on the paper was equal to one meter. He wanted his shed to be six meters wide and three meters deep. How can he measure how many meters of walls he would need for his shed? What do we call that measure? How many meters of wall would he need?

He also wanted to find out how much room he would have for his tools. How could he measure this space? Can you see a unit of measure in his picture that would help him tell how large the space is? What do we call this measure? How is it different from the measure for walls? How many units of space will there be in the shed?

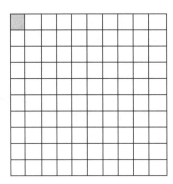

Sue is designing a flower garden. She has 115 feet of fencing to keep the animals out. A sketch of her plan is shown below.

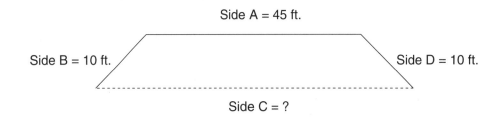

Side A = 45 ft.

Side B = 10 ft.

Side D = 10 ft.

Side C = ?

What is the greatest length Side C can be for Sue to have enough fencing?

**130** Teachers can help students develop the algorithm for finding the area of a right triangle by constructing a diagonal across a square or rectangle to discover that the area of each triangle created is equal to 1/2 the area of the rectangle (l × w).

The base of each triangle is the same as the length of the rectangle that was divided by a diagonal, and the height is the same as the width of the rectangle. The area of a triangle is therefore equal to 1/2 the length of its base TIMES the height of the triangle.

Area of a Δ = 1/2 (b × h)

They can also reverse the procedure and construct a rectangle from two duplicate right triangles. This can also be done on the computer with a simple drawing program. (Note: Any two congruent triangles can be formed into a rectangle if one of them is cut through the altitude. Students can then see that the rectangle formed has the altitude as one side and the base of the triangle as the other. This confirms the algorithm for the area of any triangle as 1/2 (b × h).

Chris wanted to find the area of a triangular piece of wood he was using to build a model plane. He traced the piece, which had a right angle, on paper and realized that if he turned the piece around he could make a square from his original tracing. Do you see a way for him to use the square to find out how large the area of the triangle was? How large was it if each side of the square was four inches? Explain how you got your answer. Prove the answer by making a diagram on centimeter grid paper.

**Figure 90**

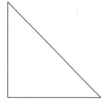 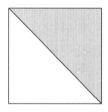 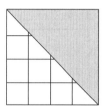

Cut two exact triangles from your centimeter paper that have a base that is 8 centimeters and a side (altitude) that is 5 centimeters. Put them together to form a rectangle. What is the area of the rectangle? Compute the area of the triangle the way you did it above and then prove your answer by counting the squares on your paper.

**131** There are several critical concepts in measures of mass and weight.

- The measures of mass and weight are used interchangeably even though they have different meanings, because our standards for mass are based on their weight on earth. However, although the mass of objects stays the same in space, the weight varies with gravity.
- We measure mass by measuring the force of gravity on the mass. The force of gravity increases with mass. We can do this by balancing an unknown mass with the standard measure. When using a balance scale, we balance the unknown quantity with a known standard weight (one decided by governments or consensus) on a fulcrum.
- These can then be used on a simple balance.

**132** A good activity for students is to use coins, metal washers, cubes, or loose sand in plastic bags and a spring scale to create and use their own nonstandard units for measures of weight, and then turn them into equivalents for the pound, ounce, gram, and kilogram.

*Jerry wanted to weigh his two history books on a balance. He had made bags of sand to use as standards. He needed one large bag and two small ones for the bigger book and three small bags for the smaller book.*

*Jerry then weighed his sand bags on a scale with measures in pounds.*
*The large bag weighed 2 pounds and the small one weighed 1/2 pound.*
*How much did each of his books weigh in customary standard measures?*

**133** The mass of an object can be determined by comparing it to standard units. The customary standards for mass or weight (use "weight" until the fourth grade) are the pound (lb.) and kilogram (kg). Smaller units are ounces and grams, respectively. A larger unit for pounds is the ton, which is equal to 2000 pounds (lbs.).

**134** We can also measure mass by seeing how much force it exerts on a spring. The standard is actually in the resilience of the spring. The greater the mass, the more the spring gives. Many commonly used scales have springs inside of them (demonstrate a simple spring scale). Students should have opportunities to measure mass/weight in both metric and English (customary) units.

**135** Students should have opportunities to weigh familiar objects and then be encouraged to estimate others. They should also be able to estimate the feel of a pound of weight as opposed to an ounce, a gram, or a kilogram, and to put objects in order based on their estimates. Checks of estimated measures with standards–based instruments should follow.

**Figure 91**     Chester wanted to know how much a clock weighed. He first measured a block with the spring scale that measured pounds. Then he put the clock and the block on a balance scale. How much does the clock weigh? Explain how you found the answer. Explain how the two instruments to measure mass and weight work. Would the clock weigh the same amount on the moon? Would the mass of the clock and block be the same on the moon?

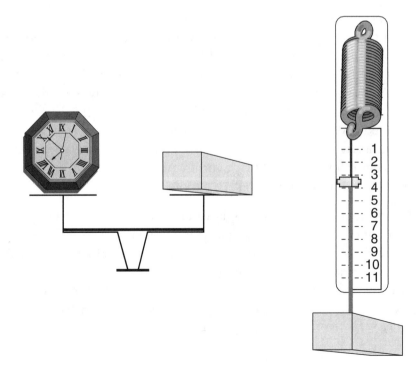

**136/137** Measures in units of mass are good applications for developing the general concepts of the "Magic Dozen" listed above. For example, it makes no sense to measure vitamin pills in pounds or truckloads of gravel in ounces. Review the concept that the larger the unit size, the fewer the number of units. Common within-standard equivalents should be automatized. For example:

1 lb. = 16 oz., 1 ton = 2000 lbs., 1 kg = 1000 gms

**138** Conversion estimates between different customary units should include that one kilogram is a little more than two lbs. (2.2 lbs.). The consequence of this is, of course, that weight measured in kilograms is a little less than half the number of pounds (.455 × lbs.).

**139/140** Although capacity and volume are related, they use different measures. Volume is applied to solid objects that have firm and measurable dimensions. Capacity is applied to liquids and small grains that assume the shape of their containers. It follows, therefore, that we measure capacity by filling a standard measure (instead of with a ruler). Students need to experience that equal amounts of liquid can look different in different containers but there is no loss of quantity when containers are changed.

Could these two containers possibly hold the same amount of liquid when they are full? Check the correct answer.     **Figure 92**

\_\_\_\_\_ Yes, because the containers are the same height.

\_\_\_\_\_ Yes, because the same amount of liquid can fit in containers of different shapes.

\_\_\_\_\_ No, because the containers are a different height.

How could you measure the exact of amount of liquid in each container to prove your answer?

**141** Children today have little experience with liquid measures. They need opportunities for discovery by using the standard measuring cup that there are 2 cups in a pint and 2 pints in a quart. They can then predict the number of cups in a quart and check their prediction. Empty milk cartons and soda bottles can illustrate the alternate use of measures in use. Sometimes students will attempt to measure liquids with a ruler. Practice with pouring liquids into different shapes of containers and comparing them will reinforce the concept of conservation and prepare students for the measurement criterion of a standard sized container for measuring capacity.

*April had a large-size quart bottle of water for the trip. Her friend had 3 pint-sized bottles and said that because she had three bottles she had more water than April. They argued about who had more. Who had the most water? How could April prove that she had more water? How can you change the larger unit of a quart into the smaller unit of pints? How would you change 12 pints into quarts?*

**142** Recipes are a good way to apply liquid measure conversions. *Cally found a recipe for making a large pot of soup, but she wanted to try a smaller quantity first. She decided to make just half of the recipe. The full recipe called for a quart of water and a half-pint of tomato juice. To make sure she was using accurate measures she changed the larger measures into smaller units.*

*What would be the next smaller unit for the water?*
*What would be the next smaller unit for the tomato juice?*
*How much water did she use for the half recipe?*
*How much tomato juice did she use for the half recipe?*

**143** The liter measure is in such common use today that the ability to estimate conversions between the customary standards becomes a high-priority skill. As we will see, the metric capacity unit has a direct relationship to the metric volume unit, and metric units are the standard in science. Relate these to their use. A quart is just a little less than a liter. A half-gallon or 2-quart milk container is slightly less than a 2-liter soda bottle. Use the calculator for other conversions.

**144** The relationship between metric capacity and volume is that one milli-liter of liquid would fit into a container that has volume of one cubic centimeter. There is no such rational relationship between capacity and volume for the English (customary) standards. There is even a difference between the dry measuring cup for small-grained flour and the liquid cup.

Students often have difficulty distinguishing between the two measures and describe volume with the capacity definition as "how much something can hold." That, of course, is not an irrational idea, but a solid object that has volume may not have the capacity to hold anything at all. Volume should be defined, in relationship to two-dimensional area, as the amount of space an object occupies in three dimensions rather than just on a surface.

**145** Three-dimensional centimeter cubes are excellent manipulatives to help students develop volume concepts. Construction of structures, such as the one in Figure 92, where the area an object occupies on the surface is constant but the volume changes with the depth or height of the object, will help develop clarity. The volume measure then just takes the area measure into one more dimension. The volume of an object is the product of its three dimensions: length, width, and height. Area is measured in square units (multiples of the product of length times width) on a two-dimensional surface. Three-dimensional volume is measured in cubic units (multiples of the product of length × width × height). Not all three-dimensional objects have repeated whole cubic units, but cubes and rectangular prisms do. The volume of a rectangular prism is equal to the area of its base times its height (or length × width × height).

**Figure E** below shows one **face** of the rectangular prism labeled **F**.          **Figure 93**

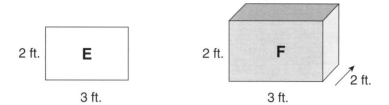

What is the area of the **face E** ?

What is the **volume** of the rectangular prism **F**?

Jim used one-centimeter cubes to build the object pictured below.

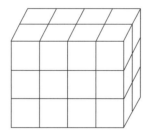

What is the volume of the object?

Equal-sized blocks were placed on a piece of graph paper that was measured into **Figure 94** equal rectangles. Which arrangements of blocks occupy the same area? Which arrangements have the same volume? If each block has a volume of 90 cubic centimeters, what is the volume of the blocks in arrangement A? If the area of each rectangle is 15 square centimeters, what is the area occupied in C? Which arrangement has the same volume as C but in a smaller area? If each 90-cc block covers one rectangle, whose area is 15 cm? Can you estimate how tall the block is?

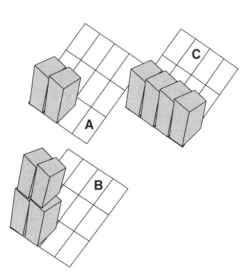

Here are some fun puzzles that students may enjoy as a little review for the preceding topics of measures.

*Choose a unit of measure for each of the following and explain your choice:*

1.  *The amount of rainfall in one day*

2.  *The size of the head of a pin*

3.  *The weight of a large truck filled with garbage*

4.  *The amount of water a plastic soda pop cover can hold*

5.  *The amount of water the pop bottle can hold*

6.  *The amount of sugar in a candy bar*

7.  *The total weight of a candy bar*

**146** The measures of money, especially because of their relationship to our number system, usually do not present a problem for students—except for the process of making change. Their difficulty with making change is probably caused by a lack of real experience, since today's cash registers automatically calculate change. Before this was the case, store clerks would count up the difference between the value of the purchase and the offered unit of money. The solution for our students is to provide simulated experiences of purchases. Class stores or computer software, even a free program on the Web, provide such opportunities. They should strengthen the vocabulary and the identification of the different coins and bills as they are related to their value.

**147** Practice with using the money and estimations of the value of items as well as putting both the items and the money in value order should provide the needed experience.

**148** Because our money system corresponds with our decimal system, problem-solving activities with money support the concept of decimals and can be an introduction as well as a major application and reinforcement for decimal operations. Begin this connection with whole dollars and then move quickly to the cent parts of the whole dollar. Connections to dimes as representative of tenths should also be included. See Numbers 107–109.

**149** A strategy I have used is to approach the challenge of giving change as "getting a fair trade." The item is traded for a unit of money that may be of greater value. The change maker must find the difference between the money offered and the value of the item.

*To find the difference we can subtract the value of the item from the money offered. However, in the action of giving change we can count up from the smallest unit value of the item to the next largest money units until we reach the value of the money offered. We begin with pennies to the fives and use a nickel to get to the tens, or we may get to them without a nickel. Dimes take us to the dollars, but if we reach a multiple of 25 we can use quarters.*

Write the **value** of each coin on the line next to it.

**Figure 95**

Penny = _____ Cent(s)

Nickel = _____ Cent(s)

Dime = _____ Cent(s)

Quarter = _____ Cent(s)

**Figure 96**

       Pennies

**+**

   Nickel

is equal to _____ cents

Add them up. Write the number sentence.

   **+**

Quarter                    Pennies

_____¢ + _____¢ = _____¢

**Figure 97**    Find the right amount of coins. Finish the table to show the number of each kind of coin you need.

Do <u>not</u> use more than <u>4</u> of one kind for each amount.

| To make this amount | Quarter | Dime | Nickel | Penny |
|---|---|---|---|---|
| 7¢ | | | 1 | 2 |
| 26¢ | | | | |
| 75¢ | | | | |
| $1.08 | | | | |

**Figure 98**    Add them up. Write the total in decimal form.

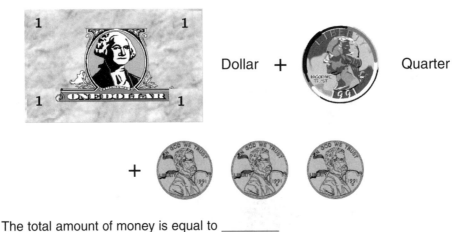

Dollar  +  Quarter

+

The total amount of money is equal to _____

**150** Operations with money are simple reinforcements and adjuncts to decimal operations. They involve renaming or regrouping up to larger units when addends total ten or more, and down to pennies (hundredths of a dollar) when you need smaller units to find the difference between two amounts. Use real money, fake money, and then calculators.

**151** Beginning concept development of the measure of time should focus on the recognition of how different times of the day associate with different activities and events, on the instruments that measure time, and on increasing perceptivity about the relationship between units and time's passage. Measures of time help us keep track of these activities and events and describe how long they take.

*What time do you get up in the morning?*
*When do you get home from school?*
*How can you tell what time it is?*
*How long did it take us to have lunch? To read that page, to play that game?*

Mr. Berry's class ran the school store. His students had to give change when the purchasers did not have the exact amount. For each purchase described below tell how you might make up the difference between the cost of the items and the money offered in exchange for them so that it would be an even trade. There may be more than one right answer, but try for the fewest number of coins.

**Figure 99**

| Money Offered in Exchange | = Cost | + Pennies | + Nickels | + Dimes | + Quarters | + Dollars |
|---|---|---|---|---|---|---|
| $1.00 | .67 | | | | | |
| $1.00 | .53 | | | | | |
| $5.00 | 1.21 | | | | | |
| $5.00 | 3.28 | | | | | |

**152** In spite of the fact that most clocks in common use today are digital, the rotary clock should be considered an important manipulative and visual for understanding our measures of time. It is also reinforces the concepts for fractional equivalents and in some of its aspects can be an introduction to the concepts of dealing with negative integers. As a consequence of the prevalence of digital clocks, the common usage of the terms "a quarter of" and "half-past" is diminishing, however, and the real-life vocabulary and experience that students used to bring to the study of the rotary clock are considerably lessened.

The actual length of a day and the number of days in a year are based on natural phenomena. The time it takes for the earth to rotate on its axis or the time it takes for the sun to return to the same place in the sky is one day. The time it takes for the earth to revolve around the sun is one year.

**152/153** Some critical concepts for understanding and telling time are:

- The division of the natural day into 24-hour parts and the hour into 60 minutes is a man-made standard. The natural day could be divided into other numbers of units that could be longer or shorter, but the numbers 24 and 60 are useful because they are common multiples of many factors and therefore easily divided into parts.

- Twelve noon is the time that the sun is most directly overhead or halfway between the east and west horizons. At twelve noon it crosses an imaginary line in the sky halfway between east and west called the meridian.
- The twenty-four hours of the day are divided at noon into twelve hours each of A.M. time and P.M. time. The beginning of the first twelve hours of any day starts twelve hours before noon at midnight, so we begin to count the 24-hour day as a new one at every midnight (students will have to make a transition from their natural perception of when *their* day begins to the standard).
- A twelve-hour rotary clock can show only a half-part of the day. It shows all the A.M. hours and then the P.M. hours. Some clocks can show all 24 hours.
- Because most of us use the 12-hour clock, we have to remember, when we try to count the time that has passed, that the clock starts over again at twelve. From 10:00 A.M to 2:00 P.M. is four hours.

**154** The actual telling of time should be simultaneously connected to both the rotary and digital clocks. The rotary clock reinforces fractional concepts. Students should be aware that

- Each whole hour can be divided into two parts (halves or 1/2 hour), four parts (1/4 hour), or 60 parts (minutes).
- There are four quarter hours in a whole hour and 60 minutes or minute parts in a whole hour. Half an hour is the same as 2 quarter hours, or 30 minutes (half of 60 minutes).
- We tell the time by naming the hour and the fractional part after it in halves or quarters or in the minutes after the hour.

**Figure 100** For each of the three digital clock times, draw clock hands that show the right time on the rotary clock. Which clock tells the time that is closest to the beginning of the school day? Which shows the time that is closest to your dinnertime? Which is the one that tells you when you should be in bed for the night? Decide which ones are A.M. and which are P.M.

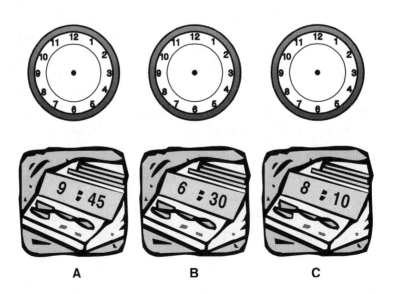

A            B            C

**155** Additional concepts related to social studies and science are:

- Because the earth is rotating, the time of day is different at different places on the earth. When it is midnight at one point on earth, the place on the completely opposite side, or 180 degrees of longitude away, is at noon.
- We have therefore divided the earth into time zones that begin in the middle of the Pacific Ocean at the International Date Line. That line reaches the new day first and the rest of the earth follows. Just as there are 24 hours in the day, there are 24 time zones.
- Because the earth rotates toward the east, we lose time when we travel to the east. The east is ahead of us. The west is behind us.
- Because the earth is tilted on its axis, the number of hours of daylight changes with the seasons. In the Northern Hemisphere the daylight hours grow shorter as we approach winter and longer as we approach summer.
- We change the clocks at different times of the year to add more daylight hours to our normal wakeful time.

The earth rotates from west to east, in the direction of the arrow. The map below shows some (but not all) of the different time zones. If it is 10:00 A.M. at point A, what time is it at point B? Can you find two places on a map of the United States where there is a three-hour time difference?    **Figure 101**

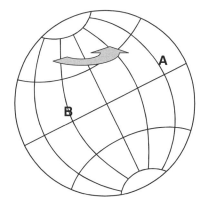

**156/157** Calculation of elapsed time does present a challenge when the time elapsed passes 12.

Manipulative clocks that allow students to move the dials as they count the hours and minutes are the most helpful. If these are not available, have students draw the clock hands on blank diagrams such as those in Figure 102.

**158/159** Beginning concepts for understanding the calendar should also focus on connecting it with life events and perceptions of where we are in the present in the calendar's terms. Naming of the days and months

**Figure 102** The class read a great story, had lunch, and then worked with their computers. They made a record of the time their clocks showed. How long did all three activites take? On the blank clock draw hands to show the time you think the clock would show after a snack break.

is a simple rote memory task, but understanding their sequence in terms of what day of the week it is today is more challenging. Again we have twelve months, so the year can be neatly organized in halves and quarters. Keeping and recording a daily calendar helps, but kinesthetic games and visual enactments that clarify the meaning of "day before" and "day after" as well as the whole week sequence will help the construction of concepts.

**160** There is nothing wrong with the verse, "Thirty days hath September, April, June, and November," and so on. It helps students to memorize an otherwise obscure pattern of the number of days in the month. Perhaps the shortness of the month of February was because calendar designers, like some of the rest of us (in the Northern Hemisphere) are happy to get rid of a month associated with winter. Students should understand that human beings do not determine the number of days in the year. It takes a fraction over 365 days for the earth to revolve around the sun. The reason for different days in different months is because, unfortunately, 365 is not evenly divisible by 12, and so calendar makers assigned different numbers of days to the 12 months, and once every four years we have a leap year to make up for the fraction over 365. The allocations of days and months in the year are man-made standards, and over time there have been other calendars. There are even alternative calendars in use today.

**161/162** Some students (and adults) have difficulty predicting the date or day of the week for days in advance—especially when the date passes the end of the month. A problem often arises in this kind of calculation: *"If today (Thursday) is the 27th, what is next Tuesday's date?* This is a two- or three-step problem. Students have to count the number of days between Thursday and Tuesday and sometimes incorrectly include Thursday in their count. They then have to count the days until the end of the month and possibly add on the new month. Use number lines and enactments such as those recommended above to help as well as real problems such as those in Figures 103 and 104.

The class wanted to have a surprise party for their teacher and needed to order a cake. They ordered the cake on Thursday, June 6, for the following Wednesday. Use the number line to find out the date of the party. Count how many days ahead the party was. What day of the week were you at when you counted one day ahead to June 7? Why don't we count the day we ordered the cake?

**Figure 103**

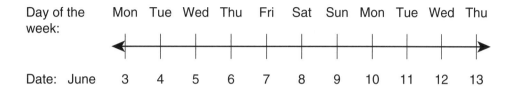

Day of the week: Mon Tue Wed Thu Fri Sat Sun Mon Tue Wed Thu

Date: June 3 4 5 6 7 8 9 10 11 12 13

Starting on the 5th of September the soccer team had practice on Tuesdays and Wednesdays, before their 10 Saturday games. The team wanted to know the dates on which they would have practice and the dates of their games. We could use a one-year calendar for this problem, but it might not work for the next year. Explain why not. Use the table below to make a game and practice schedule for the team for two different years, one beginning with a Tuesday practice and another beginning with a Wednesday practice. Put an x next to the practice dates and an xx next to the Saturday games.

**Figure 104**

Do you see any patterns that would help you make schedules in other years? If the second year is 2007, will the same pattern continue for 2008?

| Yr.1 Date | Yr.1 Day | Practice (x) Game (xx) | Yr.2 Date | Yr.2 Day | Practice (x) Game (xx) |
|---|---|---|---|---|---|
| Sept 5 | Tuesday | | Sept 5 | Wednesday | |
| | | | | | |
| | | | | | |
| | | | | | |
| | | | | | |
| | | | | | |
| | | | | | |
| | | | | | |

**163** Beginning measures of temperature should be related to perceptions of how warm or cold it is. Activities can relate a particular Fahrenheit temperature to whether or not a jacket is needed—and whether or not it will snow. Room, body, freezing, and boiling temperatures are significant benchmarks with which to become familiar. Students should also become aware of their own *normal* body temperature and how to read a thermometer. "Normal" then becomes a first look at the concept of range and average. More advanced investigations of temperature ranges can use original data retrieved over the Internet from all over the world and related to seasons and latitude. An important science-related concept in reference to the thermometer, as an instrument, is that its use depends upon the characteristic of materials to expand with increasing temperature and contract with decreasing temperature.

Problems involving differences in temperature are useful in reinforcing the subtraction operation. As skill progresses, students should also be able to measure centigrade (Celsius) temperature and be able to distinguish the important benchmarks of each standard.

**164** The customary standard in the United States is again different from most other places, but both standards use the term "degree." The temperature at which water freezes and boils are benchmarks for both the Celsius and Fahrenheit scale. An important concept to extract from the much larger range of degrees between freezing and boiling of Fahrenheit temperature (32°–212°)is that each degree Fahrenheit must be smaller than each degree Celsius (where the range is only 100. The Fahrenheit scale has smaller degree units because the range between freezing and boiling (32°–212°) is 180° wide. The Celsius range of 0°–100° between the benchmarks makes better sense, but because each degree is slightly larger, conversions between the two are difficult. Students should also become familiar with the other benchmark of average room temperature, and should be able to tell from comparing average daily ranges at different times in the same place what the season is.

*Holly kept a record of the daily temperature outside her window. At one time of the year the temperature for one week ranged from 120° to 45°. At another time of the year it ranged from 65° to 95°. Can you make a good estimate about which of the two different ranges was in the winter? When might the other range have occurred? Can you make an estimate of a range in another season?*

The zero temperature benchmark is also a good application of the need for negative numbers. A beginning of the concept of negative numbers may be applied to temperature readings (see Number 36).

**165** Beginning experiences with geometric concepts should focus on helping students perceive and communicate about the world around them from a spatial perspective. Seeing corners and sides or no corners, and describing what you see, comes before counting and measuring them.

Manipulatives such as pattern blocks, attribute blocks, tangrams, and geoboards can help students see the differences and the patterns. Just the experience of making different patterns is helpful, but teachers need to scaffold the important concepts that can be derived from them. In a triad, the manipulatives should be connected to real objects in the environment and to the pictures on paper as both two- and three-dimensional representations.

*What do we know about the shape of the Pentagon building in Washington? What is the shape of a skating rink? Why does it have that shape? Why are some places called Squares—like Washington Square? Have you ever seen an intersection that forms a triangular corner? Make a picture of it.*

Two equal sized balloons were filled with the same amount of air. One was placed **Figure 105** in ice water and the other in hot water from the tap.

Which picture, (A) or (B), describes the balloon that was placed in ice water? Which describes the balloon that was placed in the hot water?

(1) Put the approximate temperature of the ice water and the hot water on the thermometer that shows it best.

(2) Underneath the thermometer write the letter of the balloon that was put into water of that temperature.

(3) How are the thermometers and the balloon alike?

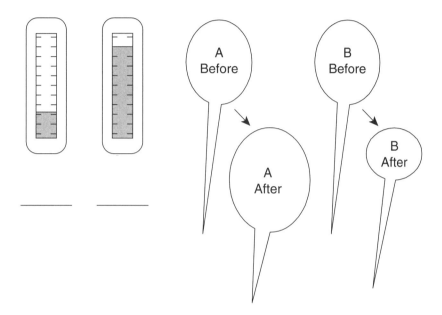

Can you find some different shapes in these buildings? Name all you can find.   **Figure 106**

For some students it may even be necessary to scaffold the connections between real objects and two-dimensional representations on paper, or they will not make the necessary connections. *Here is a block and a picture of the block. Can you make a picture of just the top of the block?*

**166** To distinguish one form from the other, let students discover the nature of the differences.

*Run your finger around the circle block. How is it different from the square? Why do wheels and spheres like the baseball roll? Why can't you put the circles together without spaces? Why do we usually use square tiles for floors? What other kinds of figures can we use so that there are no spaces? Can we use more than one kind together in a pattern?*

The concept for the above is that in order for blocks to fit together without spaces between, they must have congruent or matching straight sides. We use the term "congruent," rather than "equal," to clarify that although the measures of congruent forms are equal they may have different positions in a plane or in space. Circles cannot fit together because they have no straight sides (Schonfeld, 1986).

**Figure 107**     Mr. Taylor wanted to cover his workroom floor with tiles. He wanted them to be close together, without spaces in between. Which shapes of tile would work? Could he combine two of these to make it work? Try some other shapes to see how they fit together. What makes them work? Can you find a rule to use?

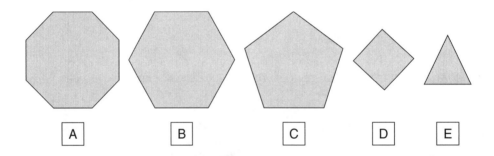

*If we join hands around the Halloween pumpkin and make a shape so that no one is closer than anyone else, what kind of shape is that? What does that tell you about the center of the circle and the outside edge of the circle? What do we call the outside edge of a circle? What property of the circle have we formed? What do we call it? How can we measure it? Make different sized circles with compasses or on your geoboard. What happens as the circle gets larger?*

**167** To discover relationships between figures, let students try to make patterns using combinations of different shapes to see how they might be related.

*Trace two copies of your triangle (or use two tangrams) and cut them out. Can you put them together to make a square?*

*Make a triangle with one straight horizontal side and one straight vertical side on your geoboard and another triangle the same size and next to it so that the third sides of both triangles (the one that is neither vertical nor horizontal) is the same line. What figure have you formed?*

*Use wooden toothpicks or pipe cleaners to make a figure with eight sides. Without changing the space inside, divide each side into two so that you have one with sixteen, smaller sides. What kind of figure did you get closer to?*

*Let's draw a big circle around the room and join hands so that we cover the circle. If we change our shape to a square so that we can still just surround the circle we drew, can we do it with the same number of people? Where is the wasted space? Why are stadiums for large numbers of people in the shape of a circle? What do we call them?*

Let students use their rulers and compasses or computer drawing programs to construct figures of squares with circles inscribed and circumscribed to discover the above and other relationships between the square and the circle, such as the fact that the diameter of circle inscribed in a square is equal to any side of the square.

Have students enlarge figures constructed with pattern blocks or use equally sized squares or color tiles to form various rectangles to discover the pattern of relationships between area and perimeter as the size of the figure increases. Students can also discover the differences between different shapes with respect to area and perimeter.

*A farmer wanted to build a pen for his rabbits. The cost of fencing was about $50 for a linear foot. What would be the least he could spend and still have a pen that had an area of at least 32 square feet? Use your color tiles to show some different shapes of pens that he could build. What shape would give him the most space for his money? How much would it cost him? Make a table record of the area and the perimeter. Look at the table and see if you can use your data to answer the following questions.*

*Why do builders like to build square houses?*

*What kind of a pen would you build for dogs?*

Robert built a larger figure using only his hexagon blocks. He compared the perimeter and area of the one hexagon with his new figure. How many times larger was the area covered by the new figure? How many times larger was the perimeter?

**Figure 108**

Explain why the answers are different.

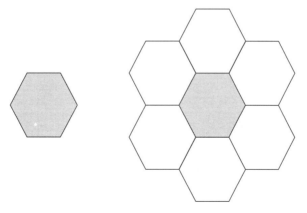

**168** To develop concepts that relate two-dimensional figures to their three-dimensional forms, which occupy space, put two-dimensional construction paper figures of squares and rectangles together to construct hollow forms of three-dimensional figures, or pile up pieces of the almost two-dimensional paper to see how the forms are related. Trace an empty circular balloon and blow it up. Then do this with the computer programs that extrude circles to form spheres and create other three-dimensional extrusions. Connect the figures to the measurement of area as it is related to volume (as explored in Numbers 144 and 145 and Figures 93 and 94).

*Solid forms are three-dimensional (3-D) objects that take up space. Solid forms have faces, edges, and corners. Different forms have different numbers of sides (edges), faces, and corners. Count the faces and count the corners of three-dimensional figures and compare them with the two- dimensional figures that are like their faces.*

**Figure 109**   Match the shape with how it might look from the top.

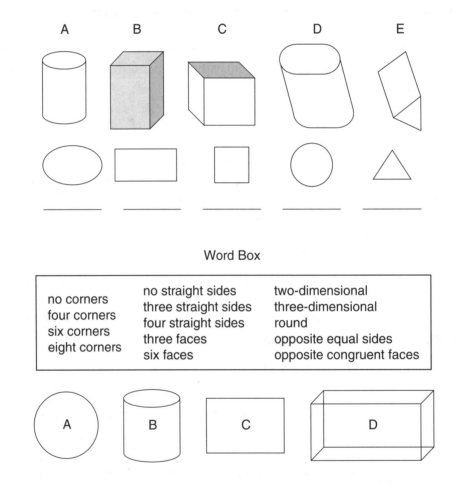

Look at the shapes labeled A, B, C, and D and decide which words in the box match each shape.

Two-dimensional pictures of three-dimensional objects complicate the fact that the three-dimensional objects have unseen parts within them. Practice with the identification of the hidden parts of figures and objects can help.

*Why are some blocks hidden when we put them together? How can we tell how many are hidden?*

Can you find the hidden blocks in this picture? How many hidden ones are there?     **Figure 110**
What is the total number of blocks?

How many would be hidden if we made this figure one block taller?

How many would be hidden if we made it one block wider?

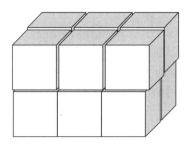

**169/170** Observations of symmetry in the environment can begin very early.

*Make a picture of the leaf we found. If you draw a line down the middle of your picture, do both sides look almost the same? How are they different?*

The observed concepts in symmetry can be strengthened by use of an ordinary mirror or, with more safety and ease, using a reflective plastic Mira, which supports itself. The geoboard is also very effective.

Connect the terms that describe symmetry to common words in the student's language, such as "bilingual" and "bilateral," "radial" and "rays" of the sun. Build the concepts with drawings and by using computer software that rotates and flips images.

Use pattern blocks and other manipulatives to put figures together to form new ones, observing the effect of symmetry on the different possibilities.

**171** The concept of radial symmetry is easily connected to bicycles and wheels. *Turn the toy car wheel or the plumber's nut around. Does it always look the same?*

You can draw lines of symmetry for three of these figures.     **Figure 111**

Find the figure that has no lines of symmetry for the figure.

Find the figure that has one line of symmetry and draw the line.

Find the figure that has two lines of symmetry and draw the lines.

Find the figure that has many lines of symmetry and draw three of them.

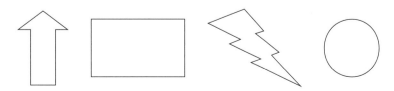

**172** Try to name different transformations with the software or diagrams, including flips and slips. Computer drawing programs that rotate and flip diagrams are excellent for these concepts. Introduce the term "congruent" as a way to distinguish the fact that a transformed figure has the same dimensions and attributes, but it has a different position in space. *Would you be the same person if you stood on your head? Would you look different?*

**Figure 112**   Jerry built two triangles on his geoboard and said that they were congruent. Alan said they were different. Can you prove who was right? Build another triangle that is congruent to one of these.

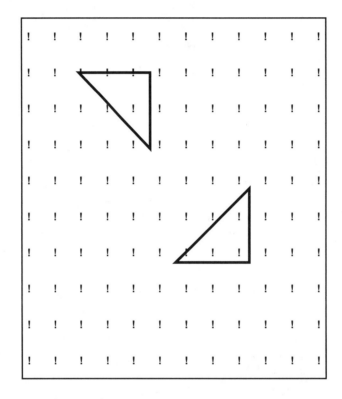

Use your geoboard or draw the figures on the picture.

Can you put these triangles together to form a larger triangle?

Can you form a square?

Can you form a parallelogram?

If there is any symmetry in the way you put the figures together, show it with a string on your geoboard or with a line on the picture.

**173** Observations of patterns in number tables will help students automatize facts and strengthen number sense. Geometric relationships to number patterns such as triangular and square patterns are also useful in solving problems. For example, seeing that an arrangement of a square number of objects such as sixteen reinforces the meaning of a square number. Students can see

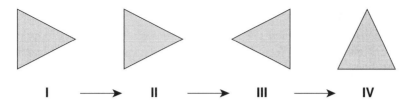

**Figure 113**

I ⟶ II ⟶ III ⟶ IV

The figures above were transformed with slides, flips, and turns.

How did the figure transform from I to II?

What was the transformation from II to III?

What was the transformation from III to IV?

Draw a flip of the figure in IV.

Why are the figures all congruent?

that the length and the width are equal, and so a number multiplied by itself is a square number. Observations of arrangements of triangular numbers of objects such as 1, 3, 6, and 10 can help to develop understanding of number patterns, but it also helps students appreciate how increases in the length of the sides of triangles affect the area. They can also compare the effects of side length increases to total area in the square and triangle.

Certain numbers can form triangles and squares of individual objects. What do you notice about the number of objects in the rows and columns of square numbers?     **Figure 114**

If the number of rows is 7, how many columns would there be for a square number? What is that square number?

➤ Square numbers: 1, 4, 9, 16, _____ , _____

How could you tell whether 225 is a square number?

Triangular numbers form different patterns.

➤ Triangular numbers: 1, 3, 6, 10, ? , ?

Can you find other triangular numbers besides those shown below?

How would this help you in planning a brick wall for a pyramid shaped structure?

**174** The mathematical concept and definitions of "line" and "point" can be easily constructed by students if they are given the opportunity to verbalize their observations. A point is location in space, and a line is what is formed when any two points are connected in a straight (the shortest) way.

*Draw a picture of houses on a street. Pick one of them as your house. Mark a point on your picture to show where your house is and another point to show your neighbor's house. How can you show me the straightest way to get from your house to your neighbor? Make five points on your paper with your crayon. How can you show that the points are connected? What do we call the connections?*

The terms "horizontal" and "vertical" are easily connected to objects in the environment. Comparison to the horizon is the best for horizontal lines. An object hanging on a string works well for the meaning of vertical for younger children. The concept of perpendicular relates two lines in an exact way: "*If you draw two horizontal lines right over each other and turn one until it is vertical you will form two lines that are perpendicular to each other. If you then keep turning the two together until one line is horizontal, the other will be vertical.*" As long as you turn them together they are perpendicular to each other and form a right angle. Perpendicular lines always form a right angle. In the beginning, relate the meaning of right angle to real examples from the environment: a building against the horizon, the corner of a book, a block on the table. Later the definition can relate a right angle of 90° to the rotation of a ray 1/2 way toward a 180° straight angle or 1/4 of a complete rotation.

**Figure 115**     Look at the picture, find the places and lines, and then match them to the letters.

Write the letter for each one you find.

Find the horizon on the picture of a skyline. _____

Find a horizontal line that follows the same direction. _____

Find a vertical line. _____

Find a place where a vertical line and horizontal line are perpendicular to each other. _____

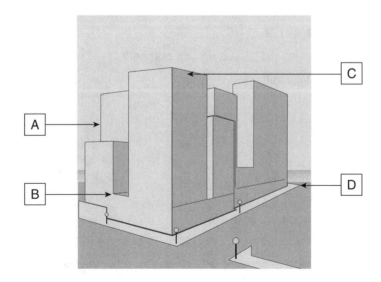

Write the letters that label:                                      **Figure 116**

    1. A ray ___

    2. A line ___

    3. A line segment ___

    4. Perpendicular lines ___

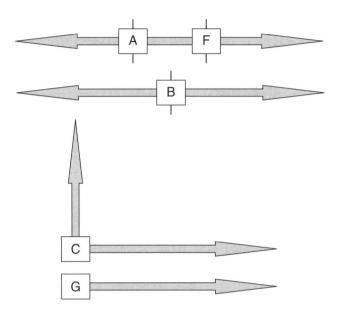

**175** Among the more difficult concepts for students in defining lines and planes is the distinction between a particular line segment and the infinite line in two directions of which it is a part, and the face of an object and the infinite plane of which it is a part. Students have to understand that the very particular language of mathematics is not the same as everyday common usage.

A helpful illustration of the definition difference might be a beam of light, which goes on infinitely until stopped by something that absorbs it. If the light is traveling in one direction from the source, like a focused flashlight beam, it is more like a ray. If there were two back-to-back flashlights focused in opposite directions, it is more like a line. The part of the ray or line from the light source to the place where it is absorbed is a line segment.

**176/177** Three points on a flat surface that are not on the same line can describe a plane. It goes on infinitely. The top of a cube is part of a plane or a plane surface. An understanding of plane is important in understanding parallel lines, because lines are parallel if they are in the same plane, go in the same direction, and never meet each other. Lines that are not parallel and in the same plane eventually meet each other (intersect), and lines in different planes meet each other frequently. Try cutting a muffin to show these relationships.

Relating parallel lines to the figure of a parallelogram, where opposite sides are parallel and opposite angles and sides are equal, is also helpful.

**Figure 117**     Jimmy thought about cutting the muffin through two different planes: ABC and DEF. What would the top of his sliced muffin look like if he cut through each of these planes? Decide between pictures 1, 2, and 3.

Plane ABC will look like picture _____

Plane DEF will look like picture _____

Cut the muffin through another plane and draw what it would look like.

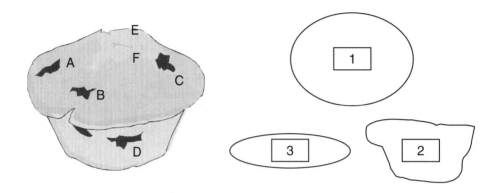

**Figure 118**     Two of the figures below are parallelograms. Which one is not a parallelogram? Explain your selection. Can you find at least two things that are true about the parallelograms that are not true about the other figure?

What is the same about all three figures?

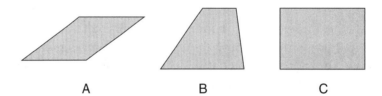

**178** Beginning concepts of what is meant by an angle and the comparative description of it as the size of opening between two lines that meet at one point can be related to real examples from the environment: the opening of a box lid, the mouth, the bend of an elbow.

*Watch the stances of the baseball batters. Compare the angles of their upper and lower arms.*

The use of appropriate vocabulary for defining angles is often neglected. Verbalizing descriptive language helps develop the concept. When two (rays) come from the same end point, they form an *angle*. The point where they meet is called the *vertex*. The rays are the sides of the angle. The larger the opening between the rays, the larger the angle.

**179/180** As described in Chapter 2, the exact measures of angles and circles should be related to each other. An important concept is the connection between the angle measure and the arc of a circle it describes—a

Find the angles in the batter's stance. List the angles A, B, C, and D in order of    **Figure 119**
their size from smallest to largest. Can you find other angles? Show them and add
them to the list in the right order. Are there any that are close to a right angle? Do
you see a straight angle? Do you see a triangle?

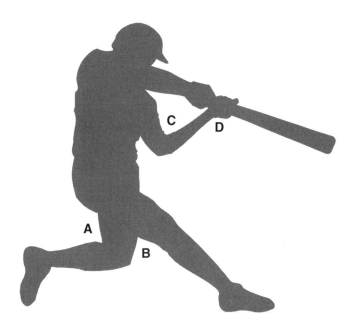

full rotation of a ray through all the angles describes a whole circle. Relate the
man-made standard of measure of the full circle as 360 units or 360 degrees to
the fact that the number 360 has many factors and can be evenly divided in
many ways: $1/2 = 180°$, $1/3 = 120°$, $1/4 = 90°$. If some confusion develops as
students see the distance between the rays of the same angle grow, let them
draw concentric circles or rotate another student at the end of a string to clarify the difference between the measure of the angle and the distance on the
circumferences.

We measure angles as the size of opening of the two rays, which as they
increase describe a circle. Since the circle has only 360 degrees, angle measures
must be less than that. The larger the number of degrees, the greater the difference between the lines (rays). The measure of an angle is the same as the part
of the circle it has described.

**181** The concept of rotating rays can be applied to specific angle measures and
special angles. If you make a duplicate of a ray and rotate the duplicate,
you form an ever increasing angle. When it reaches 180° degrees or halfway
around to form a semi-circle, the duplicate ray and the original have formed a
straight line or straight angle of 180°. If you continue to rotate the duplicate, you
have angles that measure more than 180°. Half of the rotation to 180° is 90° or a
right angle. Pencils or crayons tied on strings or safety compasses can be used to
simulate the rotation and angles. More accurate measures require the use of a
protractor. Fifth graders can be introduced to the protractor and use it to check
their angle measure estimates. This is a good opportunity to discuss the accuracy
of measures and that they are subject to human and instrument error.

**Figure 120** All of the circles in the figure below are intersected by the same angle.

For each of the circles, if the measure of the angle is 45°, how many degrees of the circle is described by the angle? If the whole circle is equal to 360°, what fractional part of every circle is 45°? How many degrees would there be in 1/2 of a circle? Draw a line to show half the circle. How would you describe an angle of 180°?

If the number of degrees in all the circles are the same, what makes circles A, B, and C different?

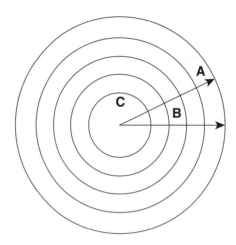

**182** Discuss the characteristics of the circle in terms of its aesthetic and mechanical advantages. Why is it better that the wheel doesn't have corners? Why do we like to see cylinder-shaped buildings? Why are targets in the form of circles? Why are flower petals arranged in circle patterns? Connect the circle to measures of its three-dimensional counterpart, the sphere; its example, the earth; and to the measures of latitude and longitude and the time zones.

**183** Let students connect the construction of a circle with compasses to the fact that all the points on the edge of the circle are the same distance from the center of the circle. The edge, which we call the circumference, is then the distance around the circle or its perimeter. The distance from the center (or compass point) is the radius of the circle. Then let students extend this through real measures to the concept that all lines that go from edge to edge through the center (the diameter of the circle) will be of equal length.

**184** The mysterious Greek letter p (pi) may be the students' first encounter with a mathematical constant. Develop the meaning of constant from easier examples such as four wheels for every car and two wheels for every bicycle. Then help students construct, by observation, the prediction that there is some *constant* relationship between the diameter and circumference of a circle.

Students can discover the constant themselves by cutting out and measuring the circumference and diameters of different circles and comparing the measures in a table. It may be a useful estimate to first inscribe a circle in a square and let them see that the diameter of the inscribed circle is equal to the side of the square. It follows, then, that if the perimeter of the square is 4 times a side, the circumference of the circle just inside it is going to be less than 4 times a side of the square or not too much less than four times the diameter of the circle. It is actually about 3.14 times the diameter, and 3.14 is the value of pi.

The diagram below shows a circle inscribed inside a square. What do you observe **Figure 121** about the diameter of the circle and the side of the square? If the perimeter of the square is equal to 4 times the length of each side, what is your best prediction about the perimeter (circumference) of the circle inside?

A. It is more than 4 times as large as the diameter (or side of the square).
B. It is two times as large as the diameter.
C. It is about three times as large as the diameter.

Cut out at least four different sized oak tag paper circles and measure the circumference of each (with a string and ruler) and then measure the diameter. Make a table and compare the diameter and circumference for each. What did you discover? How close was your prediction? What do we call the constant that describes the number of times the circumference of a circle is greater than the diameter of the circle?

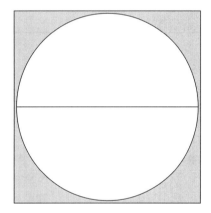

**185** The most effective way to help students to develop concepts and measurement skills for finding surface area is by providing discovery experiences that allow them to transform three-dimensional figures into the two-dimensional figures they know.

For example, they can discover by folding paper into a cube, which has equal sized faces, that there are six faces on a cube. They can then reason that the surface area of the cube is going to be 6 times the area of one face. See Figure 122 for finding the surface area of a cylinder.

**186/187** Data are the collection of measures that describe the world in quantitative terms. The value of data is in their ability to help us understand variations in our measurements and the effects of measurable phenomena on our lives, and in data's function as a basis for decision making.

The ability to collect and organize data is a critical skill in our technological and information rich society. Students are constantly surrounded by all kinds of data that may or may not have meaning for them: baseball statistics, tickets sold

**Figure 122**   Janet wanted to know the surface area of a cylinder box she was going to decorate. She took a sample box and cut it out so that it was flattened into a two-dimensional form. She had the top and bottom and then a flat piece that was the length of the height of the cylinder and the width of its circumference. How could she find the surface area of the cylinder? What would it be if the height of the cylinder were 20 inches and the diameter 3 inches?

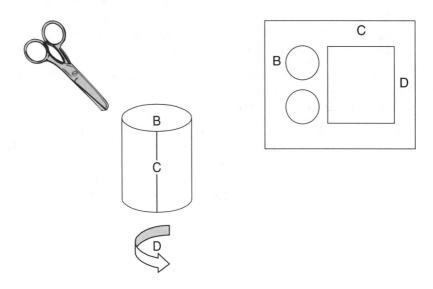

to a new movie, weather data, candy and soda sales, political polls, crime rates, and population statistics. The Internet is a source of much real data that can be retrieved and analyzed.

The usefulness of data is determined by several factors that students need to understand, which they can—even at an early age—if their attention is called to it.

There are a number of overarching concepts that bridge the construction of knowledge about the different forms of representation of data. Teachers need to address these within the context of exploring the forms. There is also a vocabulary that ranges from identification of the most and least to the more complex meanings of interval and reference line. The ability to construct and interpret tables of data is a necessary basic organizational skill.

Important concepts include the following:

- Data are only as good as the accuracy of how they are recorded.
- The accuracy of the record is dependent upon the skill and honesty of the recorder and the instrument used to measure it.

Provide students with shared experiences for collecting and recording data, such as taking the temperature of ice water as it warms and noting the differences in the records. Identify the variables—such as different students, different times, different thermometers, or different places in the room. Poll taking is a useful way to introduce the idea of experimental probability.

A toy store sells 5 Barbie dolls, 14 Spiderman figures, 9 baseballs, 11 remote control cars, and 8 airplane models. Create a tally table to show these data. **Figure 123**

| Toys | Tally | Number |
|------|-------|--------|
| Barbie dolls | | |
| Spiderman figures | | |
| Baseballs | | |
| Remote control cars | | |
| Airplane models | | |

Write two statements about the toy store data. Use the words *most* and *least*.

The students in Mrs. Murray's second grade class collected Yu-Gi-Oh cards. They decided to find out what kinds of cards were the most rare. They realized that they would have to organize their data and group them together. They each counted their cards and entered them on the following table. Which card was the most rare and which card was the most common? How did the data affect their trades? **Figure 124**

| | |
|------|------|
| Type 1 | 21 |
| Type 2 | 7 |
| Type 3 | 15 |
| Type 4 | 36 |
| Type 5 | 2 |
| Type 6 | 23 |
| Type 7 | 38 |
| Type 8 | 9 |
| Type 9 | 11 |
| Type 10 | 24 |

**188** The interpretation of data depends on their ability to show patterns clearly. Proper organization and representation helps. Tables are useful organizers. Provide students with data-recording experiences that accumulate data over time and group data on tables to show the patterns.

The kind of organization and representation of data that works best depends upon the nature of the elements of the data and the information they need to provide.

**189/190** Provide students with experiences that demonstrate the different kinds of graphs. Begin with a simple pictograph that provides an easy visual connection to the data record.

**Figure 125**    Mr. Roberts polled his class to find out what their favorite pets were. He collected the following information:

**Favorite Pets**

| Type of Pet | Number of Students |
|-------------|--------------------|
| Dog | 9 |
| Cat | 6 |
| Rabbit | 3 |
| Hamster | 4 |
| Lizard | 2 |

Use the data in the table above to create a bar graph.

A bar graph, or its simplistic form, the pictograph, shows the differences in the elements clearly but tells us less about the range and variations of individual results than a line graph or leaf-and-stem graph. A line graph tells us more clearly where most of the measures are and where the exceptions are. It also makes it easier to compare two sets of data, like the amount of rain over a six-month period that happened in the daytime compared to rain that happened at night. Some important things to consider are:

- Compare representations of grouped data where the interval is large to representations where the interval is smaller. If most people go to bed between 9 and 10, then a graph that has hourly intervals and does not show the parts of the hour between 9 and 10 doesn't tell us much. For the same reason, yearly rainfall amounts are elements that are best shown on a line graph in decimal intervals.
- The interpretation of data must consider the many other variables that may affect them.
- Provide students with poll-taking experiences to demonstrate that answers are sometimes affected by who asks the questions and how they are asked.
- When making records of plant growth, point out the need to control all the variables except the one you are measuring. If your measures are of the effect of light, then the water and temperature must be the same.
- To make sense, graphic representations must have reference lines, beginning points from which the differences in elements are measured. The reference line is usually a horizontal or vertical line on which the names of the elements or measured items are found. Another line, perpendicular to the reference line, should show equally measured intervals from the reference line to allow for accurate reading of differences. Bar graphs sometimes do not have interval lines but show the measures on top of the bar.

Mr. Edward's class was often disturbed by the loud noise of overhead planes and    **Figure 126**
so they made daily record of the planes they heard for a week. They made a list
each day and then made a graph to show the number of planes for each day.

Monday
Tuesday
Wednesday
Thursday
Friday

= One plane

What could they learn from their graph about when the noise happened?

What could have affected the correctness of their data?

How can they use the data to predict when to expect noise?

How could they find out if the pattern is always the same?

Do you have any ideas about what created the pattern?

**191** In a pie or circle graph, the whole circle is the reference, and the size of the arc that describes each part is the measure of the element. An arc of 45° is 1/8 of a whole circle, and so an element (e.g., the witch costumes in Figure 128) represented by that arc would have a measure of 1/8 of the whole (all the costumes). A pie or circle graph shows little of the range, but it allows us to see the relationship of the part to the whole. For example, it can show how many students in a class got between 90 and 100 on a test, and compare that to how many got between 50 and 60; it can then show what part the 90–100 group is of the whole class. It is useful, for example, when we want to know not only just how many students preferred the Yankee baseball team as compared to other teams, but what part of the whole class the Yankee fans represent.

Early experiences should focus on data that students can relate to, such as the number of brothers and sisters they have, the books they have read, and the games they play. A simple pictograph is a good introduction to the graphic representation of data. Children can immediately see the relationship between the item count and its representation on a line.

Later experiences should involve the collection of original data using instrumentation where appropriate and technology interfaces if possible. Students should learn how to make the necessary choices for representation and become increasingly critical in their analyses. The wide variety of representation choices in common spreadsheet programs makes evaluations of the appropriate forms a simple task. Ordinary graphing calculators now come with interactive temperature and other probes to take environmental measures. A vast amount of data can be acquired over the Internet. However, students should be able to evaluate data in reference to their own experiences with its collection and have the opportunity to use their own knowledge and creativity in its representation.

**Figure 127**    Use the graph below for the different teachers' classes at the Fourth Grade Cake Sale to make a table. What kind of a graph is it? How does it tell you how much each class made? What is the interval on the graph? Would a five-dollar interval work as well?

Use the data in the graph to complete the table. Write a heading for each column.

|  |  |
|---|---|
|  | $8.00 |
|  | $12.00 |
| Miss Sands |  |
| Mr. White |  |
|  | $13.00 |
| **Total** |  |

**192/193** Line graphs are useful representations that clearly show the distribution of elements. More than one line on the same graph can compare distributions of similar elements such as the test grades of students in two different classes or the variation in monthly rainfall in three different places. Students should develop the following concepts:

1.  The line graph has two reference lines.

2.  The horizontal reference line, which can show different elements, often shows variations of an element over time; it is called the x axis.

3.  The vertical reference line shows the intervals and is called the y axis.

4. The place where the reference lines meet is the origin. Parallel lines are drawn to both the x and y axis to separate the intervals and elements. The lines form a grid.

5. The value of each different element or the same element at a different time is a point on the grid. The points are joined to form a line.

Twenty students in Ally's class made a data list of their favorite Halloween costume. They showed their results on a pie graph. Which costume was the favorite? How many students liked that costume the best?   **Figure 128**

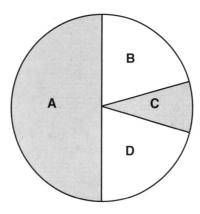

LEGEND:  A. Ghosts  B. Skeletons  C. Witches  D. Pirates

What two costumes tied for the second most liked? Which was the least favorite? From the pie graph could you tell what the favorite costume was for the whole school? Explain your answer.

The line graph below represents the number of cars sold by a dealer for the first six months of a previous year. Label the x axis and y axis of the graph. What is the size of the interval? How could he use this graph and the table to predict how many cars he might sell this year?   **Figure 129**

**Cars Sold in Previous Year**

| Month | Number of cars sold in previous year |
|---|---|
| January (1) | 90 |
| February (2) | |
| March (3) | |
| April (4) | |
| May (5) | |
| June (6) | |

**Figure 130** Below is a data map similar to those that can be retrieved off the Internet from the United States Weather Service: http://www.noaa.gov.html. What is the data element it displays? Can you think of a way to group this data that would help you see patterns? What other data might a farmer need to help him make planting decisions for the week of June 6? What other data might be useful in his planning for the year? Make one other kind of representation for this data. Get a recent map off the Internet and do the same thing.

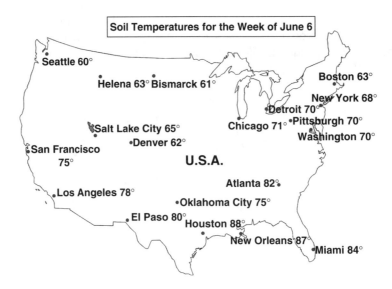

**194** We can also use horizontal and vertical reference lines and points on a grid to locate places on a map. Provide students with the experience of making grid maps of the school and locating places on it. Connect the map grids to their understanding of longitude, latitude, and time zones.

**Figure 131** The camp director gave all campers a grid map to use in finding their way around the camp. There were three points that everyone had to know about immediately. Point A was the bunkhouse, point B was the bathroom, and point C was the dining hall. There was a spruce forest in between so the campers could not go in a straight line from one point to another. Each space interval on the grid was equal to fifty feet. About how far and in what direction did they have to walk from the bunkhouse to the dining hall and from the dining hall to the bathroom?

Add some other points to the map and describe where they are.

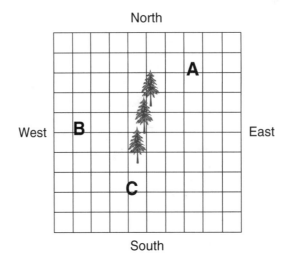

**195/196** Other kinds of graphic representations can help us organize data and understand how data are distributed. They can also show data trends. The simple line plot in Figure 132 shows how the numbers of television sets in households are distributed. There is an individual marker for each household that has that number of TVs. It shows a cluster around the numbers 2 and 3. A stem-and-leaf plot is a shortcut way of showing distributions.

The ages of people attending a party are shown in Figure 133. It easily shows that most of the people are in their 20s and the mode, or item (age) that occurs most often is 22.

Scatter plots like the one in Figure 134 can show how two different events may be coincidental or occur at the same time. In this case the relationship between power blackouts and higher wind velocities in winter storms and hurricane season is very clear, but the summer months also have a cluster of outages for different reasons. Time lines are simply number lines with intervals that show the passage of time in equal intervals and the events recorded in sequence.

Mrs. Smith's class surveyed the number of television sets the students had in their own homes. They made a line plot to show what they found. Each X stands for one TV. Why is this a good way to show how data are spread out or distributed? Around what numbers of TVs can you find clusters of the data?    **Figure 132**

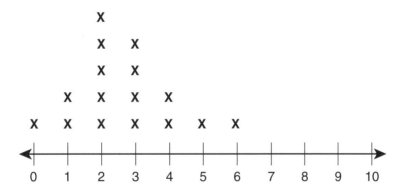

A newspaper reporter was writing an article about parties. She attended one and asked everyone how old he or she was. She then made this stem-and-leaf plot to show the ages of all the partygoers.    **Figure 133**

| 1 | 7 8 8 8 9 9 9 |
| 2 | 0 0 0 1 1 1 2 2 2 2 3 3 4 4 |
| 3 | 1 2 4 6 |
| 4 | 3 |

What was the age of the youngest person at the party? What was the age of the oldest person? What was the single partygoer age that was the most common or frequent? We call that age the mode. Which age group of partygoers was the most frequent—teens, twenties, or thirties?

**Figure 134** The local electric company kept a record of power outages over a two-year period. They recorded them by the month but also recorded the wind velocity in miles per hour (mph) at the same time. Do you notice any trends for when the outages happen? Why would there be a cluster of outages in the summer time when the wind was not blowing so hard? What may have caused the cluster in September and October?

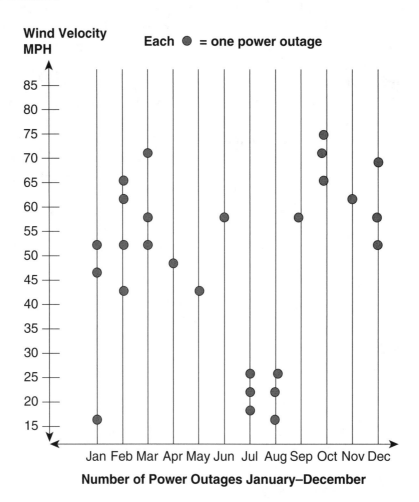

197 The variety of graphic representations allows us to share data in many ways. We need to make choices based on what we wish to communicate clearly. The ability to use and interpret the different forms of data representations is an important life skill, because it can help us make the best decisions for our own lives and those of others. Many graphs can be created using graphing calculators and computers. Use these once the concepts have been developed.

198 From the scientific, rather than religious, point of view the nature of our human existence on earth is a product of the fundamental laws of physics of our universe and chance. Some would argue, further, that even the fundamental laws of physics may be uncertain and limited to existing states—perhaps created by chance from other possibilities. The entire universe could implode, but the probability of that is as close to zero as we can get. Needless

to say, chance is a critical factor in the existence of all of us. Chance assumes that, first of all, we have no control over an event or over choice. Looking at an assortment of shirts and purposely choosing one does not involve probability for you as the chooser. There is certainty in your choice. Your choice, however, is uncertain for the storekeeper, who does not control your choice. On the other hand, if you choose something absolutely blindly, like a particular colored marble from a hat, there are other possibilities, and the ultimate outcome is uncertain. Even the very young can learn to discriminate between events that are more certain or uncertain. We are all interested in our chances, the probability of the occurrence of a desired or undesired event. We want to know the odds, and the odds depend upon the alternative possibilities. For some reason the two concepts are not always clearly connected in our school curriculum.

Probability is a measure that helps us to predict uncertain events. The probability of the occurrence of an uncertain event is dependent upon the possibility that a particular outcome can occur. If there are no possible alternative outcomes to the particular or desired outcome, then the event is a certainty and the probability is 100%. Beginning conceptual distinctions between the certainty and uncertainty of events can be developed as the result of observations in the environment itself. Discussions of examples should include comparisons such as the following: the certainty that it will be day and then night versus the uncertainty that the day will be bright and clear; the certainty that it will rain sometime in a month versus the uncertainty that it will rain on a particular day. And transferring to other mathematical concepts, there is the certainty that if you walk in a circle, you will come back to where you started.

In order to begin understanding the basic concepts of probability students need:

- To understand and appropriately use language distinctions such as likely versus unlikely and possible versus impossible
- Clarity in meanings of the terminology of "chance," "event," and "outcome"; the difference and relationship between "possibility" and "probability" are also important
- To know that uncertain outcomes and events can have different probabilities of happening; they can be more or less likely to happen
- To know that the probability of something occurring is dependent upon the possibility of it happening

**199** The likelihood (probability) of an occurrence depends upon the possibility or the number of other possible choices. If there are only two possible choices for an event happening, then the probabilities of the events are equal; it can be either one or the other. Students need to understand, however, that although the probability of an event can be mathematically computed based on the number of choices, it is still only a probability, not a certainty. There are only two possible choices for the toss of a coin, so the probability is that you will get heads 1 time out of 2 tosses, but you can get 10 heads in a row. There are over a hundred possible average temperatures for a day, and the probabilities for a particular temperature change with the seasons.

**200** The expression of probability in fraction form comes easily once the students have talked about a fraction as the number of parts out of a given whole. The numerator tells us the number of probable occurrences (or parts of the total possibilities). The number of the denominator tells us the whole number of possibilities.

*If there are six choices on a die, then what is the chance for one of them to occur? What fraction describes one part out of six parts? (1/6)*

Later, when the concepts of ratio are developed, problems involving predictions for larger values can be solved with proportions.

*If you toss the die 360 times, and the probability is 1/6, about how many times will you toss a six? (60 times) What would be the probability of tossing a six if there were two sixes on the die and no five?*

If there is only one choice for the type of an event, then the probability of that event happening is 1/1 or 1 and is a certainty. If there is no possibility of something happening, then the probability is zero. *The probability of a boy having a name is very close to 1, but the probability of his turning into a donkey is zero—except in fairy tales.*

**Figure 135**

What is the probability of spinning the number 3 on spinner A?

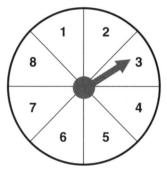

A

What is the probability of spinning the number 3 on spinner B?

What is the probability of spinning the number 5 on spinner B?

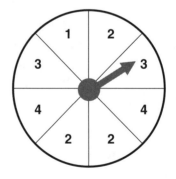

B

**201** We can predict the probability of an event based on the mathematical possibilities and experiments. Prediction of what will happen with the toss of a coin or a die is easy because there are few possibilities. When the number of possibilities is greater, however, the predictions become more complicated. For example, the probability that today will be a Saturday is one out of seven, but the probability that we will have rain, snow, clouds, or sunshine or

Shaun had two baseball bats (BA and BB) and three different catchers' mitts (ma, **Figure 136** mb, mc). He could choose from any of these to bring to the game. What is the probability that he would choose a combination of bat (BA) and mitt (mb)? Complete the tree diagram of choices to help you find the number of choices and the probability for the combination of BA/mb.

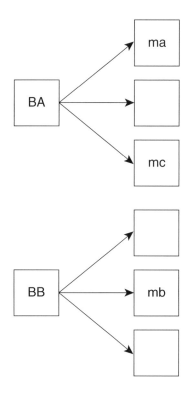

combinations of these on a Saturday depends upon the number of possible combinations and the probability of each.

The probabilities of combinations of events can also be predicted, but we must first know the number of combinations that are possible. The possible combinations for the one day, Saturday, with just the four alternative choices of rain, snow, clouds, or sunshine above are only four, but the total number of possibilities for the week are four for each day of the seven day week or 28.

**202** Sometimes we can limit the possibilities for our predictions with experiments. We can also prove our predictions with experiments and data collection. The weather bureau keeps a record of temperatures, and we can use their records for our prediction. If, based on their records, we limit the choices for June, July, and August to temperatures between 50° and 105°, we have fewer possibilities and a higher probability for 90° days. The more data we collect, the closer we will come to our mathematical prediction and proof that we were correct. If you toss a coin 1000 times, the number of heads will be close to 500.

**203** It is obvious that the first step in determining the probability of combinations of an event is the counting of all possible combinations.

The development of counting strategies should begin with the construction of sample spaces with actual placement of objects, pictures, or diagrams of all the possibilities, which can then be counted. Analysis of results can then lead to the application of algorithms such as the counting principle and factorial notation.

The number of possibilities for a particular event depends on:

- The total number of possible alternative outcomes (including the one desired).
- Whether or not the order of the selection is significant.
- The quantity selected from these alternatives or the number of choices made.
- Whether the alternatives are in a single category or in different categories.

If the *order* of selection and arrangement *does not* matter, three individually selected items (A, B, and C) from a group of A, B, and C can be arranged in only *one combination*. For any other number of events, as long as the number of choices made is equal to the total number of alternative outcomes and order does not matter, there is only *one* possible combination. You just pick them all and have them all. However, once you are more selective in the number of choices you make from the group and do not pick them all, the possibilities for your choices are greater.

*It rained on two days during one week. What are the possible kinds of combinations of days of the week that it rained?*

Because there are six other days for each of the seven you might think that there should be forty-two possibilities, but there are only half that number because the order does not count. Mon/Tues is the same combination as Tues/Mon. A tree diagram will show you the exact number of 21. Actually recording the number of possible events by filling a sample space or doing a tree diagram will demonstrate that after you pick your first day the number of possibilities for the next day diminishes by one and so on until the last one is left. For this one there is only one possibility.

In the above example, the order of the days does not matter. The days of rain are order independent. In other examples where the order does count, the number of possible combinations may be greater.

**204** When order does matter, the possibilities are called permutations. Three individually selected items (A, B, and C) can be selected (or arranged) in six different ways if the order matters: ABC, ACB, BAC, BCA, CAB, and CBA.

*There were seven different players on the team. How many different lineups at bat are possible?*

In the above case, because the order does matter, there are 210 possible lineups.

Ball games where teams play each other are good examples to use. As long as home games are not counted as different from away games, the order does not count—four teams can play each other once in six different games. But if each team has to play the other as a home team, the order counts, and there will be twelve different games.

You are going to make a sign for a school project and have a choice of 2 papers, 3 writing tools, and 3 print colors that you can use. The table below shows all the possible choices. Use the information to make a tree diagram to find the total number of possible combinations you might choose.

**Figure 137**

| Papers | Writing Tools | Colors |
|--------|---------------|--------|
| White | Pen | Blue |
| Gray | Crayon | Black |
| | Marker | Red |

**205** An important part of analyzing data sets is to look at how the data are distributed. Understanding distributions helps us make predictions and explain results. We are often interested in where the most events or outcomes are, but looking at the distributions also enables us to consider extremes or outliers less seriously. We also need to consider the range of possibilities.

Stem and leaf plots at the early levels can be used with single-variable data. They clearly show where particular values occur most of the time. Early vocabulary development includes the meaning of: "the most," "around the middle," "typical," "range," and "average." Later the terms "mean," "median," and "mode" can be related to these from the common vocabulary.

*The Girl Scout troop went trick-or-treating together. They collected 98 pieces of candy and wanted to find out what the average amount of candy collected by each scout was. They put their candy on the table, and then by moving the pieces around, separated it into evenly balanced groups. When the piles were almost even, they counted eight pieces in most groups—although two groups had nine pieces. What could they do with the two extra pieces so that they could share them evenly? What was the exact average amount of candy collected by the scouts?*

Computation of the average or mean should be put into the context of real problems. The Halloween candy problem is just one example. Let students have the manipulative experience of balancing the sizes of groups of objects as they develop the concept that what they have done is, in fact, divided the whole formed by all of the groups equally.

**206** There is sometimes confusion with the terms "median" and "mode." Nevertheless, simply lining up the data in order and finding the middle of the sequence or the place where there are an equal number of items above and below works well for the median. Just identifying the largest number of single item repeats is often enough to bring clarity to the mode. Drawing "box-and-whiskers" plots should also help. Let students discover why *outliers*, the few scores or events that are very different from most, are less significant in computations of median and mode—and have them consider the kinds of decisions where the median or mode may be better choices for looking at data.

**Figure 138**     The students collected cans on one Sunday to help clean up the park. Use the pictograph below to answer the questions.

Each ⬭ stands for 10 cans collected.

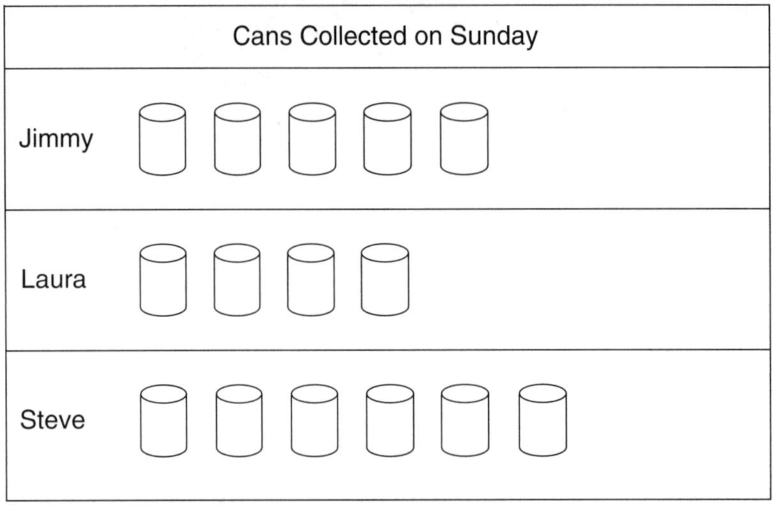

What is the total number of cans collected?

What is the range of the separate totals of cans collected by each student?

Find the mean for the number of cans each student collected.

What is the mode?

The students wanted to predict the total number of cans they could collect with five students working. How would knowing the mean for three students help?

# Resource A

# Assessing the Content Standards

**A**s previously suggested, the master list of the embedded concepts and performance indicators in Chapter 2, when combined with the explications and matching figures of developmental items in Chapter 3, can be used for assessment purposes. The following represents illustrations of how these matches of standards and items can be used to create assessments and rubrics for the purpose of group or individual analyses. Assessments can be used for a variety of purposes. In the classroom they can provide ongoing feedback to the teacher in reference to the group's or individual's attainment of knowledge. When applied beyond the single classroom, they can monitor the achievement of schools and districts, as well as analyze the differences or gaps between individual groups of students. The closing of group achievement gaps has become a major educational goal for this country, but there will always be some gaps for individual learners that teachers can expeditiously recognize and address.

## USING RUBRICS ■

Teachers can respond to individual needs or gaps in a variety of ways, but they will discover that it is most useful to first carefully identify the missing concept or lack of progress on the concept or skill. Rubrics, which verbally describe levels of attainment, can be helpful benchmarks used to assess individual needs or group gaps. The necessary language for rubrics for assessment purposes is essentially defined in the matching concepts and performance indicators in Chapter 2. Table A.1 shows how the three developmental levels and the definitions of embedded concepts and expectations can be translated into a simple

**Table A.1**   A Matching Rubric

| | | Explanation of Mastery Levels | | |
|---|---|---|---|---|
| Concept or Indicator | Level 1: Procedural Exploration | Level 2: Concept Mastery | Level 3: Procedural or Algorithmic Mastery | Level 4: Application Mastery |
| Subtraction is the process of finding the difference between two numbers | Can solve problems based on this concept using the real or concrete representative materials, but is unable to explain concept | Can solve problems and explain the concept used; may still need concrete material | Can generalize the concept and use it to solve problems without concrete material | Can generate an original problem using the concept or apply it in an unusual way |

assessment report. The exact definitions of measured concepts and expectations can be incorporated as spelled-out rubrics in the report document, or a corresponding number that refers to a separate rubric list can be used as illustrated in Table A.1. An above-standard level (Level 4) that is not delineated by grade level in Chapter 2 may also be added for assessment purposes. For more detail on assessment and the use of rubrics, see Solomon (2002, 2003).

# ■ INFORMAL AND FORMAL WRITTEN ASSESSMENTS

As the teacher implements the activities suggested in Chapter 3, the incorporated dialogue of probing questions and prompts based on pre-designed rubrics can provide ongoing informal "proximal" assessment (Solomon, 2002, 2003). Additional questions may be required, however, as missing knowledge is perceived. In a more structured or formal context, teachers can also use the rubrics to design written assessments. They can begin to develop these assessments for a grade or class by choosing those concepts and skills from Chapter 2 that are appropriate at particular time intervals. The items for the assessment instrument would then be designed or chosen to specifically measure the selected concepts and indicators. After deciding on the expected mastery level for each one, teachers can select matching items from Chapter 3 or develop similar ones. In some cases, the wording of the developmental items in Chapter 3 may have to be slightly changed for formal measurement purposes. It may be useful to organize the matches by creating a set of test specifications that might look like Table A.2.

**Table A.2**   Test Specifications

| Concept or Indicator Number | Expected Mastery Level | Item(s) |
|---|---|---|
| 17. | Level 1 | 34, 35, 36, 37 |
| 18. | Level 2 | 36, 37, 38, 39 |

## ASSESSMENT ANALYSIS ■

The assessments can provide teachers with the analytic feedback needed to guide their instruction. They may also generate feedback for students and parents. The feedback form can include a description of the individual concepts or indicators that are measured, or it can just include the number from a separately provided list that is shared among staff, parents, and students. Examples of forms and analyses are in Tables A.3 and A.4.

**Table A.3** Individual Student Feedback

| Individual Assessment of Levels—Student Name | | |
|---|---|---|
| Content/Performance Standard | Expected Level for Grade | Student's Level |
| 17. (See standard list) | Level 1 | Level 2 |
| 18. (See standard list) | Level 2 | Level 4 |

**Table A.4** Class or Grade Assessment of Achievement

| Class or Grade Assessment of Achievement | | | | | | | | |
|---|---|---|---|---|---|---|---|---|
| Content/ Performance Standard | Median expected class or grade achievement at each mastery level (in percentage of class that reaches it) | | | | Percentage of class or grade that achieved each level | | | | Item number(s) on assessment instrument(s) |
| | 1 | 2 | 3 | 4 | 1 | 2 | 3 | 4 | |
| 16. (See standard list in Chapter 2) | 98 | 75 | 60 | 10 | 100 | 85 | 70 | 15 | #34, 35, 36, 37 |
| 17. (See standard list in Chapter 2) | 80 | 50 | 40 | 5 | 53 | 37 | 20 | 0 | #36, 37, 38, 39 |

Analysis of the individual student report in Table A.3 would indicate that this student is achieving above the expected level and does not require group or individual remediation.

Group analyses are often based on comparisons with similar groups, or normed. Standardized commercial and state tests required by the federal "No Child Left Behind" legislation are normed by conducting random trial applications of the instruments. Table A.4 shows an analysis report that can be used with a teacher-made test based on individual class or school expectations. The median expectations can be determined for an individual school population by using previous grade-level tests as the norm, or they can be based on a standardized test that has been normed on a large population. The group expectation is expressed as the percentage of the group that reached the expected level.

Many states now use what are called "proficiency levels." For example, there may be four proficiency levels that range from an above-expected level to a considerably lower-than-expected level. For examples and explanations of state norming systems, see http://emsc33.nysed.gov/osa/concht/jan05/gr8ela.htmfour. These normed expectation levels can be incorporated into class and local reports (Lesh & Lamon, 1992; Linn, Baker, & Betebenner, 2002; Mathematical Sciences Education Board: National Research Council, 1993).

An analysis and response to the results in Table A.4 would include the following:

- For Concept 16 (rounding numbers one place), students in the class exceeded expectation.
- For Concept 17 (rounding numbers more than one place), even though the expectation was lower than that for 16, students did not meet it.
- This should be followed by careful analysis of the validity and reliability of item numbers 36, 37, 38, and 39.
- Individual and group score distributions should also be analyzed to make sure that a few outliers are not affecting the outcomes for a particular class.
- If the item is found to be appropriate, then teachers should analyze the materials and activities and revise them or plan additional ones for the group.
- Chapter 3 should be consulted for exemplars and scaffolds.

# References

Anderson, J. R., & Douglass, S. (2001). Tower of Hanoi: Evidence of the cost of goal retrieval. *Journal of Experimental Psychology: Learning, Memory, and Cognition, 27*(6).

Baltimore Public Schools. (1952). *Arithmetic in the elementary schools.* Baltimore, MD: Author.

Cathcart, G., & Kirkpatrick, J. (Eds.). (1979). *Organizing data and dealing with uncertainty.* Reston, VA: National Council of Teachers of Mathematics.

Chatterji, M. (2003). *Designing and using tools for educational assessment.* Boston: Allyn & Bacon.

Cobb, P. (1990). Multiple perspectives. In L. P. Steffe & T. Wood (Eds.), *Transforming children's mathematics education: International perspectives* (pp. 200–215). Hillsdale, NJ: Lawrence Erlbaum.

Cumming, J. J., & Elkins, J. (1999). Lack of automaticity in the basic addition facts as a characteristic of arithmetic learning problems and instructional needs. *Mathematical Cognition, 5*(2), 149–180.

Dillon, S. (2005, February 24). Report from states faults Bush's education initiative. *New York Times,* p. A18.

Fuson, K., & Briars, D. J. (1990). Using a base-ten blocks learning/teaching approach for first and second grade place value and multidigit addition and subtraction. *Journal for Research in Mathematics Education, 21*(3), 180–206.

Fuson, K., Wearne, D., Hiebert, J., Murray, H., Human, P., Olivier, A. L., et al. (1998). Children's conceptual structures for multi-digit numbers and methods of multi-digit addition and subtraction. *Journal for Research in Mathematics Education, 28*(2), 130–162.

Ginsburg, H. (Ed.). (1983). *The development of mathematical thinking.* New York: Academic Press.

Ginsburg, H. (1989). *Children's arithmetic: How they learn it and how you teach it.* Austin, TX: Pro-Ed.

Greenleaf, B. (1872). *New practical arithmetic.* Boston: Robert Davis.

Hatfield, M., Edwards, N., & Bitter, G. (2005). *Mathematics methods for the elementary and middle school.* Needham Heights, MA: Allyn & Bacon.

Herbst, P. G. (2002). Engaging students in proving: A double bind on the teacher. *Journal for Research in Mathematics Education, 33*(3), 4–46.

Hiebert, J., & Wearne, D. (1986). Procedures over concepts: The acquisition of decimal numbers knowledge. In J. Hiebert (Ed.), *Conceptual and procedural knowledge: The case of mathematics* (pp. 199–224). Hillsdale, NJ: Lawrence Erlbaum.

Klein, D., Braams, B. J., Braden, L., Finn, C. E., Parker, T., Quirk, W., et al. (2005). *State of the state math standards*. Retrieved January 22, 2006, from http://www.edexcel lence.net/foundation/global/index.cfm

Kramarski, B., & Mevarech, Z. R. (2003). Enhancing mathematical reasoning in the classroom: The effects of cooperative learning and metacognitive teaching. *American Educational Research Journal, 40*(1), 281–308.

Lamon, S. (1993). Ratio and proportion: Connecting content and children's thinking. *Journal for Research in Mathematics Education, 24,* 4–46.

Lamon, S. (1996). The development of unitizing: Its role in children's partitioning strategies. *Journal for Research in Mathematics Education, 27*(2), 170–193.

Lerman, S. (1996). Intersubjectivity in mathematics learning: A challenge to the radical constructivist paradigm? *Journal for Research in Mathematics Education, 27*(2), 133–150.

Lesh, R., & Lamon, S. (1992). *Assessment of authentic performance in school mathematics.* Washington, DC: AAAS Press.

Linn, R. L., Baker, D. F., & Betebenner, D. W. (2002). Accountability systems: Implications of requirements of the No Child Left Behind Act of 2001. *Educational Researcher, 31*(6), 3–16.

Mathematical Sciences Education Board: National Research Council. (1993). *Measuring up: Prototypes for mathematics assessment.* Washington, DC: National Academy Press.

Morrow, L. (1998). Whither algorithms? Mathematics educators express their views. In L. Morrow & M. J. Kenney (Eds.), *The teaching and learning of algorithms in school mathematics: National Council of Teachers of Mathematics 1998 yearbook.* Reston, VA: The Council.

National Center for Education Statistics. (2005). *The Trends in International Mathematics and Science Study (TIMSS).* Retrieved from http://nces.ed.gov/pubs2005/timss03/

National Council of Teachers of Mathematics, Commission on Standards for School Mathematics. (1989). *Curriculum and evaluation standards for school mathematics.* Reston, VA: The Council.

National Council of Teachers of Mathematics, Commission on Standards for School Mathematics. (2000). *Curriculum and evaluation standards for school mathematics.* Reston, VA: The Council.

Phillips, L. (2003). When flash cards are not enough. *Teaching Children Mathematics, 9*(6), 358–363.

Resnick, L. B. (1983). A developmental theory of number understanding. In H. Ginsburg (Ed.), *The development of mathematical thinking* (pp. 110–149). New York: Academic Press.

Riley, M. S., Greeno, J. G., & Heller, J. I. (1983). The development of children's problem solving abilities in arithmetic. In H. Ginsburg (Ed.), *The development of mathematical thinking* (pp. 115–200). New York: Academic Press.

Ross, S. (1989). Parts, wholes, and place value: A developmental view. *Arithmetic Teacher, 36(6),* 47–51.

Schonfeld, A. H. (1986). On having and using geometric knowledge. In J. Hiebert (Ed.), *Conceptual and procedural knowledge: The case of mathematics* (pp. 225–264). Hillsdale, NJ: Lawrence Erlbaum.

Solomon, P. G. (1995). *No small feat: Taking time for change.* Thousand Oaks, CA: Corwin Press.

Solomon, P. G. (2002). *The assessment bridge: Positive ways to link tests to learning, standards, and curriculum improvement.* Thousand Oaks, CA: Corwin Press.

Solomon, P. G. (2003). *The curriculum bridge: From standards to actual classroom practice* (2nd ed.). Thousand Oaks, CA: Corwin Press.

Solomon, P. G. (2005, April). *Closing the achievement gap: A systemic model.* Paper presented at the American Educational Research Association conference, Montreal, Quebec, Canada.

University of the State of New York. (1989). *Teaching math with computers: K–8.* Albany: State Education Department.

University of the State of New York. (2005). *Mathematics Standards Committee recommendations.* Albany: State Education Department. Available online at http://www.emsc.nysed.gov/3-8/mathoverview.htm

U.S. Department of Education. (2001, August 2). *Prepared remarks of U.S. Secretary of Education Rod Paige: The Nation's Report Card—Mathematics 2000.* Retrieved February 2, 2002, from http://www.ed.gov/news/pressreleases/2001/08/08022001.html

Usikin, Z. (1998). Paper and pencil algorithms in a calculator and computer age. In L. Morrow & M. J. Kenney (Eds.), *The teaching and learning of algorithms in school mathematics: National Council of Teachers of Mathematics 1998 yearbook* (pp. 7–19). Reston, VA: The Council.

# Additional Reading

Ashlock, R. (1990). *Error patterns in computation: A semi-programmed approach.* Columbus, OH: Merrill.

Baroody, A. J. (1987). *Children's mathematical thinking.* New York: Teachers College Press.

Battista, M. T., & Clements, D. H. (1996). Students' understanding of three-dimensional rectangular array of cubes. *Journal for Research in Mathematics Education, 27*(3), 258–292.

Berlinghoff, W., & Washburn, R. (1990). *The mathematics of the elementary grades.* New York: Ardsley House.

Burns, M. (1987). *A collection of math lessons: From grades 3 through 6.* White Plains, NY: Math Solutions Publications.

Carpenter, T. P. (1986). Conceptual knowledge as a foundation for procedural knowledge: Implications from research on the initial learning of arithmetic. In J. Hiebert (Ed.), *Conceptual and procedural knowledge: The case of mathematics* (pp. 113–132). Hillsdale, NJ: Lawrence Erlbaum.

Coburn, T. (1989). The role of computation in changing mathematics curriculum. In P. H. Trafton & A. P. Shulte (Eds.), *New directions for elementary mathematics: 1989 yearbook.* Reston, VA: National Council of Teachers of Mathematics.

Fendel, D., Resek, D., Alper, L., & Fraser, S. (1996). *Baker's choice: A unit of high school mathematics* (Interactive mathematics program). Berkeley, CA: Key Curriculum Press.

Fennema, E., Carpenter, T., & Lamon, S. (1991). *Integrating research on teaching and learning mathematics.* Albany: State University of New York Press.

Fey, J. (1992). *Calculators in mathematics education.* Reston, VA: National Council of Teachers of Mathematics.

Fuson, K. C. (1990). Issues in place-value and multi-digit addition and subtraction learning and teaching. *Journal of Research in Mathematics Education, 21*(4), 273–280.

Grossnickle, F., Perry, L., & Reckzeh, J. (1990). *Discovering meanings in elementary school mathematics.* Fort Worth, TX: Holt, Rinehart & Winston.

Grouws, D. A., Cooney, T. J., & Jones, D. (1988). *Perspectives on research on effective mathematics teaching.* Reston, VA: National Council of Teachers of Mathematics.

Haitians, J., & Speer, W. (1997). *Today's mathematics: Part 2: Activities and instructional ideas* (9th ed.). Upper Saddle River, NJ: Prentice Hall.

Harel, G., & Confrey, J. (1994). *Multiplicative reasoning in the learning of mathematics.* New York: State University of New York Press.

Henderson, D. (1996). *Experiencing geometry on plane and sphere.* Upper Saddle River, NJ: Prentice Hall.

Hill, H. C., Rowan, B., & Ball, D. L. (2005). Effects of teachers' mathematical knowledge for teaching on student achievement. *American Educational Research Journal, 42*(2), 371–406.

Kellough, R. (1996). *Integrating mathematics and science: For kindergarten and primary children.* Englewood Cliffs, NJ: Prentice Hall.

Kreindler, L., & Zahm, B. (1992). *Source book: Lessons to illustrate the NCTM standards.* New York: Learning Team.

Mokros, J., & Russell, S. J. (1995). Children's concepts of average and representativeness. *Journal for Research in Mathematics Education, 26*(1), 20–39.

Nesher, P. (1988). Multiplicative school word problems: Theoretical approaches and empirical findings. In J. Hiebert & M. Behr (Eds.), *Number concepts and operations in the middle grades* (pp. 19–40). Hillsdale, NJ: Lawrence Erlbaum.

Riedesel, A., Schwartz, J., & Clements, D. (1996). *Teaching elementary school mathematics.* Needham Heights, MA: Allyn & Bacon.

Reys, R., Suydam, M., & Lindquist, M. (1995). *Helping children learn mathematics.* Needham Heights, MA: Allyn & Bacon.

Silver, E. (1986). Using conceptual and procedural knowledge. In J. Hiebert (Ed.), *Conceptual and procedural knowledge: The case of mathematics* (pp. 181–198). Hillsdale, NJ: Lawrence Erlbaum.

Souviney, R. (1994). *Learning to teach mathematics* (2nd ed.). New York: Macmillan.

Sovchik, R. (1996). *Teaching mathematics to children.* New York: HarperCollins.

Troutman, A., & Lichtenberg, B. (1991). *Mathematics, a good beginning: Strategies for teaching children.* Pacific Grove, CA: Brooks/Cole.

Van de Walle, J. (1998). *Elementary and middle school mathematics: Teaching developmentally.* New York: Addison-Wesley/Longman.

VanLehn, K. (1986). Arithmetic procedures are induced from examples. In J. Hiebert (Ed.), *Conceptual and procedural knowledge: The case of mathematics* (pp. 133–179). Hillsdale, NJ: Lawrence Erlbaum.

University of the State of New York. (1989). *Suggestions for teaching mathematics using laboratory approaches: Grades 1–6: Operations.* Albany: State Education Department.

University of the State of New York. (1990). *Suggestions for teaching mathematics using laboratory approaches: Grades 1–6: Probability.* Albany: State Education Department.

Williams, W., Blythe, T., White, N., Li, J., Sternberg, R., & Gardner, H. (1996). *Practical intelligence for school.* New York: HarperCollins.

Wood, T., & Cobb, P. (1990). The contextual nature of teaching: Mathematics and reading instruction in one second grade classroom. *Elementary School Journal, 90,* 499–502.

# Index

Addition, 4, 9–11, 21, 22, 64–69, 79–88, 92
  defined, 20
  multi-digit, 22, 85
  of fractions, 30, 36, 129–131
  part/whole, 21
  repeated, 34, 95, 99
  series, 22, 88
  subtraction inverse, 21
Algebra, 6, 17, 23, 34–39,
    57–58, 85, 90–91, 95, 107
Algorithms, 8, 11. *See also* Addition; Division;
    Multiplication; Subtraction
Anderson & Douglas, 5
Angles
  defined, 54
  measuring, 55
  related to circles, 176
  rectangle, 151
  special (right, straight), 177
Area
  defined, 44
  square, rectangle, 44
  triangle, 44, 151
Assessment, xiii, xv, xvi, xvii, 10, 12–14
  analysis, 198
  embedded, 10
  expectations, 16–59
  formal, 12
  informal, 12
  resources, 197
Associative principle, 82, 124, 125
Automaticity/automatization, xv, 6, 8, 9,
    11, 12, 21, 62, 68, 81, 96, 107, 126, 143

Baltimore Public Schools, xvi
Bar graphs, 56
Base-ten blocks. *See* Manipulatives
Bead frames, 70, 95

Calendar, 50
Capacity/volume
  across system conversions,
    47, 155
  conversions, 46
  defined, 46
  estimation, 46

Cardinal principle, 17, 20, 64, 71, 79
Central tendency
  average/mean, 59
  median/mode, 59
Chatterji, 10
Circle
  circumference, 55
  constructing, 55
  defined, 52, 178
  measuring, 55
  pi, 178
  pie graphs, 57
  value of pi, 55
Cobb, 2
Combinations, 59, 191, 192
  defined, 59
  order does not matter, 192
Common multiples, 35
Communication, 5
Commutative principle/commutativity,
    21, 25, 28, 79, 89, 96, 97, 107
Composite numbers, 34
Conceptual knowledge, 1, 5
  defined, 1
Congruent
  defined, 168
Connections
  defined, 5
Consensual domain
  defined, 2
Conservation/
    number/size, 17, 64
Content branches, 15
Content standards, 2–5
  defined, 2
Coordinates, 57
Counting, 17, 62
  count all, 79
  counting each item, 67
  counting on, 20
  counting on from the first, 79
  counting on from the largest, 79
  skip-counting, 69
Cumming & Elkins, 9
Curriculum
  writing, 11

205

Data
  accuracy, 180
  analysis, 6, 56
  collection, 6
  distribution, 193
  functions of, 179
  interpretation, 181
  tables, 56
Data-based matching intervention (DBMI), 13
Decimals, 15, 19, 38–42, 77,
    138–142, 145–146
  addition and subtraction, 40, 140
  as fractions, 39, 77, 139
  conversions, 42
  division, 42, 145
  money, 39, 137
  multiplication, 41, 140–142
  ordering, 40
  place value and, 77
  place value shifts, 40
  related to area, 141
  rounding, 40
"Deliver up"/"design down," 3, 4
Developmental timing, 8
Dillon, xiii
Division, xvii, 9, 11, 15, 19, 27–31, 38–40, 42,
    69, 75, 76, 101, 104, 105, 114, 126
  algorithms, 29, 107, 136
  as repeated subtraction, 27
  as sharing, 28, 105
  as shrinkage, 28, 106, 115
  by decimals, 141
  by fractions, 134–136
  by zero, 29, 108
  facts, 107
  inverse of multiplication, 28
  long, 111
  long-form algorithm, 29
  partition, 105, 107
  problems, 109–111
  quotition, 105, 134
  related to fractions, 29
Doubling patterns, 70

Embedded assessment, 10
Embedded concepts, 2, 6, 16–59
  defined, 16
Estimation, xv, 19, 20, 22, 24, 26,
    27, 77, 78, 86, 99, 101, 107, 108
  front-end, 19
Expressions, 6

Factors, 27, 28, 33, 34, 35,
    58, 102, 124–128, 134
  common factors, 35
  factor tree, 128
  greatest common factors, 35
Feedback for students and parents, 198
Fractions, 12, 15, 26–42, 62, 107, 111–137
  addition, 130

addition and subtraction, 114
as division, 77, 116
as ratios, 32, 120
as shrinkage, 31
converted to decimals, 128
converting complex fractions
    to decimals, 145
converting to decimals, 134
division by algorithm, 136
division by and of, 38, 134, 136
division meaning, 38, 112
equal parts of wholes, 30
equivalents, 31–33, 35, 116–120
fractional parts of fractions, 37
improper, 120, 130
inequalities, 123
least (lowest) common denominator
    (LCD), 36, 128
manipulatives, 131
mixed numbers, 120
more than unit, 31, 113–114, 132–133
multiples, 132
multiplication of and by, 36, 131–132
multiplication of mixed
    numbers, 131
naming numerator and
    denominator, 30, 111
operations on like fractions, 30
reducing, 38, 122, 133
regrouping, 130
related to division, 30
subtraction of, 130
Functions, 6, 34–39
Fuson et al., 74

Geometry
  angles, 176
  definitions, 6, 174
  hidden parts, 170
  horizontal and vertical, 174
  line and point, 174
  names of shapes, 51
  plane, 175
  related to number patterns, 172
  relationships between figures, 168
  solid (3-D) objects, 52, 169
  surface area, 179
  symmetry, 171
  2-dimensional shapes, 51
Ginsburg, 9
Graphing calculators, computers, 186
Graphs
  box and whisker plots, 195
  circle/pie, 183
  forms, 181
  grid sheets, 98, 100, 101
  line, 184
  line plot, 185
  structure, 182
Greenleaf, xiv

Hatfield, Edwards, & Bitter, 105
Herbst, 4
Hiebert & Wearne, 1

Inclusivity, 7
Inequalities, 23, 30, 33, 40, 43,
    45–46, 89, 92, 114, 122, 123

Justify, 5

Key ideas, 4
Klein et al., xiv
Kramarski & Mevarich, 4

Lamon, 81, 120
Least common multiple, 127
Lerman, xvii
Lesh & Lamon, 198
Line graphs, 57
Line plots, 57
Lines/points
    defined, 53, 175
    horizontal/vertical, 53
    parallel, 175
    rays, 53
Linn, Baker, & Betebenner, xiii

Manipulatives, xvi, xvii, 5, 10, 11, 15, 21, 32,
    35, 61, 62, 69, 71, 73, 81, 85, 87, 93, 100,
    105, 107–114, 171
    attribute blocks, 166
    base-ten blocks, 68, 71, 74, 85, 87,
        93, 100, 101, 138, 139, 140, 145
    bead frames, 63
    beads and chips, 63
    centimeter cubes, 156
    color tiles, 118, 122, 125
    egg cartons, color tiles, 118
    fraction bars, 128
    fraction bars and circles, 116
    geoboards, 151, 166
    Mira, 52
    pattern blocks, 133, 166. 169
    pom-poms, 118
    shoebox roll (pom-poms), 71, 73, 87, 118
    tangrams, 166
    unifix cubes, 68
Mass/weight, x, 153–155
    conversions, 45, 154, 155
    customary/metric, 45
    different system conversions, 46
    familiar objects, 45, 154
    standard/nonstandard units, 45
    using a balance, 154
Mastery levels, 197
Mathematical communication, 4
Mathematical processes, 15
"Mean," "median," and "mode," 59, 194
Measurement, 41–43, 146–149
    area, 151
    capacity and volume, 155, 158

conversions, 43, 149
defined, 6
estimates, 43
estimation, 43
length, 43, 44, 150
magic dozen, 147
mass/weight, 151–155. *See also*
        Mass/weight
metric prefixes, 149
money, 47–48, 158
operations, 150
perimeter, 150
perimeter, area, 43
square, rectangle, 43
standard/nonstandard, 42
standards, 147, 149
temperature, 51, 165–166
time, 160
vocabulary, 42
Money, 47–48
    estimating and counting, 47
    giving change, 48, 158
    operations, 48
    place-value, 48
Morrow, 9
Multiples, 19, 25, 26, 27, 29, 32, 33–35, 37,
    40–42, 44, 46–48, 94, 97, 98, 101, 106,
    124–130, 139–140
    common, 35, 125
    least common multiple (LCM),
        35,127–130
Multiplication, xv, xvii, 2, 9, 11, 16, 19, 25–28,
    34, 36- 38, 40, 41, 44, 69, 70, 74, 76,
    94–101, 105–106, 126
    algorithm, 101
    as repeated addition, 25
    by decimals, 41, 142
    cartesian, 102
    commutative principal, 96
    decimals by decimals, 142
    facts and tables, 107
    tables and series, 104
    whole numbers and decimals, 141

National Center for Education Statistics, 1
National Conference of State
    Legislatures, xiii
National Council for Teachers
    of Mathematics (NCTM),
    xiv, xvi, xvii, 62
Negative and positive integers (signed
    numbers), 92
No Child Left Behind (NCLB), xiii
Number and spatial sense
    defined, 4
    fractional multiples, 37
Number system, 6

One-to-many correspondence, 71
One-to-one correspondence, 17

Operations
    defined, 6
    *See also* Addition; Division;
        Multiplication; Subtraction
Ordinality, 18, 71
Outliers, 195

Parallel lines
    defined, 54
Parallelogram
    defined, 54
Part/part whole, 82
Patterns
    recognition, 6, 108
Percentage, 143
    finding percent of a number, 41
    related to decimals, 41, 142
    related to fractions and automatized, 143
    sequential diminutions and accretions, 144
Performance indicators, xv, xvi, xvii, 2, 7, 10,
    11, 12, 13, 16–59
Permutations, 59, 193
    defined, 59
Phillips, 9
Piaget, xvi
Pictographs, 56
Place value, 18, 19, 40, 48, 71
Planes
    defined, 54
Prime numbers, 34, 126
Probability, 6, 58–59, 186–190
    certainty/uncertainty, 58
    chance, 186
    defined, 187
    predicting outcomes, 58
    predictions, 191
    proof of inference, 58
    related to possibility, 190
    terminology, 190
Problem solving, 10. *See also* individual topics
Procedural knowledge
    defined, 1
Proof
    defined, 4
Proportions, 33, 59, 120–123, 190
    scale drawings, 123
Proximal assessment, 198

Ratio, 30, 32, 120, 121, 123, 134, 190
Reasoning, 4, 5, 9
Regrouping (trading), 18–19, 22, 24, 26–27, 36,
    40–42, 48, 71, 74, 81, 84- 87, 92–93, 107,
    130, 142, 145–147, 160
    fractions, 36
Relationships, 6
Representation, 5
Resnick, 81

Riley, Greeno, & Heller, 10
Ross, 71
Rounding, 19, 20, 43, 77, 78
    rounding of decimals, 140
Rubrics, 197

Scaffolding, 13. *See also* Chapter 3
Schmidt, McNight, & Raizen, xiii
Schonfeld, 168
Seriation, 65
Skip counting, 18, 25, 68–70
Solomon, xiv, 3, 10, 12, 197
Sorting/classifying, 17, 65
State curriculum, xiv
Statistics, 6, 58–59, 186–190
Subitizing, 17, 67
Subtraction, 9, 11, 20–27 30, 36, 40, 48, 79–81,
    85, 88, 89–93, 105, 107
    as finding the difference, 89
    comparing wholes, 23
    defined, 20
    multi-digit, 23
    with regrouping, 23
Surface area, 55
Symmetry, 52
Systematic equalities, 19

Technology, 11
Temperature, 51, 165
    standards and benchmarks, 166
Test expectations, 2. *See also* Assessment
Test specifications, 198
Time
    A.M. and P.M., 162
    clocks, 161
    calendar, 163
    division of day, 161
    earth rotation, 49
    elapsed, 163
    rotation of earth, 163
    telling, 48
    variations, 48, 49
Time lines, 57
Trading. *See* Regrouping
Transformations, 53
Trends in International Mathematics and
    Science Study (TIMSS), xiii

University of the State of New York, xiii, 11
U.S. Department of Education, xiii
Usikin, 9, 11, 62

Verbalization, 9
Volume
    computing, 156

Zero as a place holder, 20, 73, 75

**CORWIN
PRESS**

The Corwin Press logo—a raven striding across an open book—represents the union of courage and learning. Corwin Press is committed to improving education for all learners by publishing books and other professional development resources for those serving the field of PreK–12 education. By providing practical, hands-on materials, Corwin Press continues to carry out the promise of its motto: **"Helping Educators Do Their Work Better."**